SEVEN CURRICULAR 1

An Approach to the Holistic Curriculum

Clifford Mayes

3/16/04

Bob,
Thanks for all of your kind help and wise advice over the years. Your friend,
Cliff

University Press of America,® Inc.
Dallas · Lanham · Boulder · New York · Oxford

Copyright © 2003 by
University Press of America,® Inc.
4501 Forbes Boulevard
Suite 200
Lanham, Maryland 20706
UPA Acquisitions Department (301) 459-3366

PO Box 317
Oxford
OX2 9RU, UK

Library of Congress Control Number: 2003114125
ISBN 0-7618-2720-X (paperback : alk. ppr.)

In loving memory of my dear parents

Thomas Mayes (1921-1972)
and
Barbara Mayes (1931-1998)

Contents

Acknowledgments

I would like to thank the following people for their help in bringing this work to completion. Ms. Andrea Richins very kindly and competently attended to many of the technical details in preparing the manuscript. Mrs. Bonnie Bennett and Mrs. Nelda Hess, the administrative assistants in the Department of Educational Leadership and Foundations at Brigham Young University, nurture the beautiful tone of that department with their many talents and inspiring personal examples.

Professor Vance Randall, the Chairman, has been a dear friend and mentor who unselfishly creates a departmental environment in which his faculty can thrive. Professors Buddy Richards, Scott Ferrin, Macleans Geojaja, Steven Hite, Ellen Williams, Steven Baugh, and J.D. Willardson have been exceptionally astute critics of my work over the last several years. With his high scholarly and spiritual standards, Dean Robert Patterson has greatly advanced the personal and professional progress of all of us who have been blessed to work under him, and we will miss him mightily as he leaves the McKay School of Education to move on to other endeavors. Professor Joe Matthews's masterful ability to synthesize theory and practice—so rare among educational scholars—has been a beacon to me in my work; and his wry humor, guileless heart, and undeviating friendship have seen me through more than a few rough patches. I have been the constant beneficiary of the genius of Professor Robert V. Bullough, Jr., my dissertation advisor and later colleague, to whom I owe a particularly great debt of gratitude. Gene Gillespie, a life-long friend and visionary artist, exemplifies, for all of us who love him, what it means to live and create with passion and compassion. My wonderful students in the BYU Department of Educational Leadership and Foundations have—through their humor, patience and vision—deepened and sustained me both emotionally and intellectually. Despite the assistance, patience, guidance and love of these and other good people, I am sure that this work has various shortcomings all of which I claim exclusively as my own.

I am eternally grateful for my precious son and daughter, Joshua and Elizabeth, who gladden their father's heart, as I am for the inestimable blessing of my wife, Pam. My greatest, wisest, and truest friend, Pam, although my better in virtually every respect, never hesitates to sacrifice herself to support me and help me grow. Above all, I acknowledge the gentle hand of my loving Heavenly Father in my life. Whatever in me is of any merit, I owe to Him; whatever is unworthy, I am confident He will forgive and rectify.

Introduction

In this book I offer a classification of some of the major curriculum theories and practices over the last century of American education. I have taken this "taxonomic" approach because I believe that there are various ways in which categorizations of curricula can be helpful to both the theorist and the teacher in understanding, critiquing, and making a curriculum.

First, any sound curriculum classification will give both the theorist and practitioner a broad sense of the "lay of the land." Its terms can serve as analytical lenses through which we can look in order to isolate and evaluate the theoretical assumptions and classroom consequences of various approaches to the curriculum. This permits us to celebrate as well as critique each curricular approach in a principled manner—and to decide which approach, or which combination of them, will serve us best in various educational contexts.

Second, the categories in this study are interactive, each representing what I consider to be a crucial element of human experience and potential. This allows both the theorist and teacher to honor the physical, cognitive, psychodynamic, social and spiritual purposes of education. It also makes it clear that various types of curricula which seem to stand in opposition to each other, not only can peacefully coexist but can often be mutually enriching. Thus, no category in this taxonomy inherently excludes another, no category can lay claim to being educationally necessary *and* sufficient, and all categories can potentially interact in a wide variety of combinations. But this should not be surprising, for ideally all parts of us work in concert and thereby generate limitless possibilities. In a word, my approach is *holistic.*

This is not to say that there is never any tension between the curricular categories in this study. Such a view would be unrealistic and unproductive. As William Blake said, "Without opposition, there is no progression." But where tension does exist, it should be fruitful, leading to higher syntheses and richer reconciliations in our theories and practices. Regrettably, as Macdonald observed, curricularists "are often...talking at different value levels and thus miss the whole point of each other's thinking."[1] This leads not only to talking at cross purposes, but to cross talking for no constructive purposes. Disagreement turns into politicized academic rhetoric in which oneself and one's allies wind up wearing the white hat—while all others are clothed in the rags of either fools or villains.

This is irresponsible because the educational scholar's goal should always be to help teachers and students reach their full potential, not to insist on a particular point of view or theory to the exclusion of the legitimate claims of others—as if curriculum studies were a zero-sum game. One must acknowledge and incorporate *whatever* is good, *wherever* one finds it, into theory and practice—even if it does not particularly advance one's own cause. An exclusionist approach is also wrong because it is simply naïve. No one has a monopoly on the truth—although educationists on both the far Left and far Right generally speak and act as if they did—simplistically assuming not only that all educational issues are fundamentally political but also that their politics exclusively embody the truth. No one curriculum theory or instructional practice could ever answer the multifarious needs of all learners or teachers in their endless array of contexts, capabilities, and purposes. That is why an integrative approach to curriculum is more productive than, say, a strictly postmodern, behavioral, or cognitive one. Each of these perspectives has its power and place; none presents the whole story.

Third, I believe that the present integrative approach to curriculum will be useful because various terms and perspectives I offer are new—although, to be sure, they draw on and are heavily indebted to previous classificatory approaches. At this prefatory stage in our discussion, I will give just a few brief examples of this. Whereas the few curricular taxonomies that deal with spiritual issues lump them all together into a single category (usually called "transpersonal," "transrational," or some such thing), I have divided them into two categories—"unitive spirituality," which revolves around Buddhistic forms of non-personal spirituality and their curricular expressions, and "dialectic spirituality," which centers on monotheistic, personal spirituality and its implications for the curriculum. Another example of the difference of the present approach is what I call the "Transferential Curriculum." This refers to the psychodynamics of what in both (neo)Freudian and (neo)Jungian psychology is called transference and counter-transference. These terms (which I will discuss in due course) allow us to take a fresh look at issues about the personal relationship between the student and teacher as those issues have been handled in various approaches to the curriculum. A final example is my treatment of the "Existentialist Curriculum," which, although not a new term in curriculum theory, I discuss as largely an aesthetic and potentially spiritual phenomenon.

Creative Curricular Tensions

Although one of the primary aims of this study is to propose interactive curricular categories, it would be unrealistic to take an excessively conciliatory view by saying that all curricula are equally good in all situations, that all can somehow be productively integrated in every case, or that some do not sometimes serve pernicious psychosocial purposes. What I *am* claiming is that we must be sensitive to the wide array of unique existential conditions that inform any particular educational situation before ruling out a particular approach to curriculum. In other words, to argue that certain types of curricula—let us say the academic-rationalist or the cognitive-behaviorist, to take two approaches that have fallen into disfavor in the prevailing postmodernist environment—are *inherently* oppressive is to oversimplify the variety of learners and goals as well as the complexity of contexts in which they are learning. For example, Kelly's otherwise excellent study, *The Curriculum,* falls into this trap by creating a simplistic opposition of all curricula into those that are democratically empowering in a postmodern society and those that are not.[2] But this needlessly casts us on the horns of a dilemma by creating a rigid dichotomy.

The holistic approach to curriculum theory is not new. Brown and his associates pictured curricula as four concentric, and therefore interactive, circles.[3] The first circle dealt with intrapersonal educational matters such as self-actualization, self-esteem, and motivation; the second circle, the interpersonal, dealt with relational dynamics, especially between the teacher and student in the classroom; third was the extrapersonal circle, which dealt with the student's understanding of and roles in the culture(s) of which that student was a member; finally, the authors postulated a transpersonal circle, which embraced the spiritual purposes of education. In like manner, Miller demonstrated how behavioral, subject/disciplines, social, developmental, cognitive-processes, humanistic and transpersonal curricula may often mesh.[4] Eisner, in his highly influential work *The Educational Imagination*, provided various examples of how, say, a social-relevance curriculum may be quite appropriate for one learning situation, inappropriate for another, and necessary but not sufficient for a third situation, which might also need admixtures of developmentalist and academic-rationalist approaches.[5] Despite their differences, these and other integrative curricularists posited paradigms that: 1) honor the potential value in a wide variety of approaches to curriculum, 2) allow for a principled synthesis of approaches, 3) offer criteria for judging which curricula are best suited to certain students, in certain situations, and given certain goals, and 4) provide a basis for including spiritual issues in curriculum theory.

Even a holistic anatomy of curriculum, however, which aims at being as inclusive and affirmative as possible, will undoubtedly have its own biases, excessively privileging some positions while inadequately attending to others. This is inevitable. It is impossible either to make or evaluate in a value-free manner something as psychologically, politically and philosophically complex as a curriculum—much less a theory of curriculum. An "anatomy of the curriculum" such as the present one offers an especially broad and useful approach, I believe; however, it comes informed by my own experiences, purposes, hopes and fears. Kenneth Burke often insisted that any perspective on something, no matter how useful, inevitably excludes other perspectives—that "any way of seeing is also a way of not seeing."[6] My hope is simply that my approach to curriculum will lead to more "seeing" than "not seeing"— and to "seeing" some things that were not evident before. At any rate, all one can do is take as broad and constructive view as possible, be upfront about his commitments, and leave it to the reader to sort out the rest. I will therefore inform the reader of my own beliefs and interests as they relate to this study.

I am an active member of the Church of Jesus Christ of Latter-day Saints. I am centrist politically but quite left of center regarding educational policy. In addition to being an education professor who teaches the history and theory of the American curriculum in a graduate educational leadership program, I have a small counseling practice, and my interest in psychology has informed my research into the psychospiritual aspects of both the teacher's sense of calling and the relationship between the teacher and student. Furthermore, I have a 30-year-long interest in Buddhism and meditative practices, which I have also incorporated in some of my research and practice in teacher education. In terms which will become clear in this study, then, my basic commitments and interests relate (in order of importance to me) to dialectic spirituality, unitive spirituality, phenomenology, and transferential psychodynamics. In this book, I try not to let those orientations cause me to covertly privilege some perspectives and unfairly represent others. Now that the reader knows my biases, she can judge how successful or unsuccessful I have been.

Before beginning with the first curricular landscape in Chapter 1, I would like to explain why I have used the metaphor of a landscape in the first place—along with offering a brief explanation of the terms used to characterize those landscapes.

Different Landscapes, Different Horizons

I have chosen the metaphor of the landscape because I wanted to suggest that each approach to curriculum is, in one sense, an independent territory with its own native charms, dangers, and possibilities. Each terrain poses its own set of legitimate questions and houses its own set of relevant answers. As Gadamer said, every question implies and allows certain universes of discourse and not others.[7] Every question generates certain intellectual territory, projects certain theoretical horizons, and launches certain practical journeys. Simply by virtue of posing certain questions in certain forms, a person is already operating from a set of assumptions about: 1) what questions are important—indeed, what questions are even *possible*, 2) what kind of evidence will count as germane and what sorts of procedures will be considered valid in analyzing that evidence, 3) what sorts of answers are permissible in that they advance the agendas of a *particular* community of discourse, and 4) what uses the researcher intends for her research to be put. In brief, a "question" already contains one's basic commitments and practical goals—albeit in interrogative form. Each landscape is uniquely "terra-formed," then, by the shaping force of certain curricular questions. That is one reason for speaking of curricular landscapes.

Nevertheless (and this is the next reason for using the image of the landscape), I also want to stress in the use of the landscape metaphor that just as territories as political entities can overlap and interact in shifting configurations and contested territory, so can different curriculum orientations overlap and interact in their histories, purposes, and procedures. In political geography, boundaries are often indistinct and negotiable. Inhabitants visit and carry on important transactions with each other, and in this way shape and are shaped by other cultures.

Even the vantage points and horizons that each landscape offers can shift, depending upon the current weather pattern, the sophistication of the observer, and the scope allowed by one's tools of observation. Hence, just as the metaphor of the landscape suggests that each realm of curriculum is distinct, it also suggests that realms are always in some degree of flux, and that they can interact in endlessly creative ways.

The Seven Landscapes

The first landscape is the home of what I have called *the organismic curriculum.* This curriculum deals with issues relating to the student as a biological organism—a developing creature. Second is *the transferential curriculum.* Typically built upon (neo)Freudian foundations, second-landscape curricula are concerned with the psychodynamics of the relationship between the student and the teacher, especially as that relationship reflects parental issues that the student projects onto the teacher as an authority figure. Third is what I have called *the concrete-affiliative* landscape. On this landscape, curricula focus upon the student in her physically and culturally immediate contexts, generally in an attempt to form her primary racial, ethnic, socio-economic, political and even religious identities and allegiances. *The interpretive-procedural* curriculum on the fourth landscape concerns itself with the emergence and maturation of hypothetico-deductive capacities and the search for propositional truth. Cognitive activity on this landscape is also characterized by "metacognition"—or thinking about thinking.

As we enter the fifth landscape, we will see the curriculum take a distinctly Existentialist turn with *the phenomenological curriculum.* In the Existentialist pedagogies, the emphasis is on helping the student *experience* herself as a morally free and unique agent whose purpose is to authentically, independently and courageously decide and act upon her "life-project" as she defines it in terms that are most consistent with who she, in particular, discovers herself to be. It is the curriculum that attends to Schiller's dictum that "We must become who we are!" For reasons that will become clear later on, I have identified this type of curriculum as "proto-spiritual." Residing on the sixth landscape is *the unitive-spiritual curriculum.* Generally relying upon Buddhist philosophy and geared toward holistic psychosocial purposes, this is the curriculum of choice in most theories that characterize themselves as spiritually oriented. Meditative practices, eclectic spirituality, and ecological politics are at the core of this type of education. The last curriculum is what I have dubbed *the dialectic-spiritual curriculum.* Although much less common in educational discourse, this type of curriculum stems from a monotheistic perspective. To suggest some possible contours, horizons, and borders for this type of curriculum (which is, in a sense, still "geologically" forming), I have turned primarily to such theologians as Kierkegaard, Buber, Niebuhr, and Tillich, as well as to the person who, in my opinion, was the greatest curriculum theorist of the 20th century, Duane Huebner—now at Yale Divinity School. I have also explicitly drawn on principles of my own faith.

The reader who has studied developmental psychology may have already noticed that some of my terms are loosely related to certain developmental theories. For instance, the "organismic" landscape is clearly tied to Piaget's sensori-motor phase, just as the "concrete-affiliative" landscape bears some resemblance to the upper reaches of his concrete operations stage and Kohlberg's conventional moral reasoning. The "interpretive-procedural" landscape contains some elements of Piaget's formal operations and also draws upon Kohlberg's post-conventional moral reasoning. Although he did not use the term "Existentialist curriculum," Maslow was quite explicit that this is exactly the kind of curriculum that he considered most consistent with the culminating developmental stage of "self-actualization" in his hierarchy-of-needs model, so there is a parallel between the Existentialist curriculum and Maslow's self-actualization phase. Maslow's later statements regarding the psychological need for a sense of cosmic connectedness (or "religion with a little 'r'," as he put it) also laid the groundwork for transpersonal psychology and education, which have defined the unitive spiritual landscape. Here I have particularly drawn from later transpersonal developmental theorists, especially Ken Wilber, to whom I am deeply indebted for his groundbreaking research.

Developmentalism and Curriculum Theory

Now, since I have promised to disclose my commitments, I must also emphasize that, in many ways, I consider the seventh, dialectic-spiritual landscape to be the highest rung on a seven-step philosophical, educational, and developmental ladder. In that sense, I *am* presenting a *normative* theory of education. But then again, *any* vision of education—by virtue of the fact that it *is* a vision—is necessarily normative because we all operate from of a set of ultimately unprovable assumptions and imperatives (or, at least, unprovable in this realm of being) which direct our thoughts and deeds. What are such life-determining assumptions and imperatives if not an ethical "system"—whether formal or informal? This is simply to underscore the point that each individual has an internal system of commitments which Polanyi has called the person's "fiduciary framework."[8] In this light, we can better understand Tillich's insistence that there is no such thing as an atheist, for everyone has some *concern* which defines his existence in *ultimate* terms, and that ultimate concern is really nothing less than that person's "god." In the last analysis, it is not really a matter of *whether* one worships but rather of *what* one worships.

Having stated my fondness for developmental theories, however, I also want to make it quite clear that I do not always see the developmental categories in this taxonomy merely in developmental terms, nor do I think that developmental theories are without their unique set of problems. Why?

First, each curriculum landscape serves a crucial, indeed indispensable, role as an element of human experience and functioning; and in that sense, no stage is more important than any other. One may, for instance, have a "sound" spiritual view and commitment on the sixth and seven landscapes but be so reckless physically, so unconcerned socially, and so inauthentic existentially that it undermines one's personality and makes one's professed spirituality quite legitimately suspect in the eyes of others. Or, one may be engaged affiliatively in working for the valid claims of one's own racial or ethnic group—but be doing so without any particular sense of responsibility to the larger social body, with very little awareness of one's own psyche, and with no broader sense of the historical, moral, or religious facets of one's cultural work. Examples of the need for synergy among the categories could be greatly multiplied.

The second reason that I do not consider my terms to be simply developmental is that development is a tricky concept. There are just too many cultural, historical, socioeconomic, psychological, and biological differences in how people "unfold" in all their many settings and needs for us to speak of a single "correct" model of development. Insisting upon a particular paradigm of development too easily becomes a tool for psychosocial control. Besides, even when we are justified in using a certain developmental model in some situations because the model is theoretically strong, empirically credible, and practically useful, we still find that development is rarely linear or unitary. People often skip stages, move from one stage to another in certain respects but not in others, revisit stages, combine stages with endless inventiveness and variety, and generally unfold in such a complex series of permutations and recursions that it is futile to attempt to identify a single, universal, invariant path from point A to point B, and from there to C and D.

Having stated those qualifications about developmental theories, however, I want to stress again my basic commitment to the developmental approach because of my conviction that some developmental models do portray fairly general dynamics of fairly general aspects of human development in theoretically, clinically, and educationally useful ways—so long, that is, as those models are used with a generous portion of caution, cultural sensitivity and humor. In forming my categories, then, I devised certain developmental terms because: 1) I felt they were roughly accurate and thus provided a credible model for a developmentally appropriate approach to curriculum and instruction, and 2) they seemed powerful as classificatory tools.

Although I believe I present a fair and representative selection of curricular work on each landscape, I am presenting just that—a selection, not a catalogue of all the curricularists and their work. This has been a conscious decision on my part not to overburden the reader by unnecessarily multiplying examples. In some cases, I have probably left out a theorist who may be important simply because I do not know that person's work. I have tried, however, to review the field and present well chosen instances of significant approaches to curriculum as accurately as I can and as completely as is practical.

One more word about the examples which I give in each chapter. I often examine, in a particular chapter, an aspect of a curriculum theory or a passage from a curriculum document because the analytic lens provided by that chapter offers insight into that aspect or passage. Yet, that same theory or document (and sometimes even the very same aspect or passage) may also be significant in other ways that are outside of that chapter's scope, and thus that same example may appear in another chapter. For instance, when in Chapter 1 I examine the historically important 1918 report of the National Education Association, *Cardinal Principles of Secondary Education,* I do so in order to demonstrate how that document attended to *organismic* issues—the sensori-motor domain of learning—in the public school classroom with an urgency that had not really appeared in American educational reform documents until that point. However, I do not mean to imply that the NEA's document was simply an *organismic* approach to education. It was other things as well—as I discuss later, particularly in Chapters 3 and 4. In short, I have frequently chosen examples in a particular chapter in order to accomplish two goals: first, to demonstrate—in a broader sense—the interpretive scope of the theoretical category that informs that chapter; and second, to cast light—in a narrower sense—on a particular curricular theory or practice because of the intrinsic interest of that theory or practice. In those few instances when I think a theory or document can be adequately explained simply by means of the approach offered by the chapter in which it appears, I say so. Mostly, however, each of the curricula examined in this book ramifies in many complex fashions on various landscapes. It is the genius of holistic theory that it recognizes and builds upon this fact.

The reader will note that each chapter ends with a set of questions and suggestions designed to stimulate discussion and research. Additionally, to orient the reader, I have prefaced each chapter with a brief outline of the major themes that it contains.

In order to avoid sexist pronoun usage, I have employed the female pronouns as the general ones in Chapters 1, 3, 5 and 7, and the male pronouns in chapters 2, 4, 6, and the conclusion. I believe this is fair and avoids the frequent stylistic dilemmas caused by the rhetorically unwieldy "he or she" and "he/she."

Notes: Introduction

1. J. Macdonald, *Theory as a Prayerful Act: The Collected Essays of James P. Macdonald* (New York: Peter Lang, 1995), 101.
2. A. Kelly, *The Curriculum: Theory and Practice*, 4th edition (Thousand Oaks, California: Sage Publications, 1999).
3. G. Brown, M. Phillips and S. Shapiro, *Getting It All Together: Confluent Education* (Bloomington, Indiana: Phi Delta Kappa, 1976).
4. J. Miller, *The Educational Spectrum: Orientations to Curriculum* (New York: Longman, 1983).
5. E. Eisner, *The Educational Imagination: On the Design and Evaluation of School Programs* (New York: Macmillan, 1985).
6. Burke, K. (1989). *On Symbols and Society*. J. Gusfield, ed., Chicago: University of Chicago Press.
7. H. Gadamer, *Dialogue and Dialectic: Eight Hermeneutical Studies on Plato* (New Haven: Yale University Press, 1980).
8. Polanyi, M. (1962). *Towards a Post-Critical Philosophy*. Chicago: University of Chicago Press.

1

THE ORGANISMIC LANDSCAPE

Pivotal Themes in Chapter 1

* Comenius, Pestalozzi, and Froebel and their insistence in the 17th through 19th centuries on the educational importance of recognizing and nurturing the child's physical nature and needs.

* The central importance of the child as a physical being in certain Progressive educational visions in the early 20th century. A few of the examples of this are the American adoption of the Kindergarten idea, the Project Method, attention to the physical dimensions of teaching and learning in the NEA's 1918 document, *Cardinal Principles of Secondary Education.* Other examples are the advent during the early Progressive movement of physical education and sports programs, lunches, school health services, health and sex education, and more ergonomically appropriate architecture and furniture in the public schools.

* The recent emphasis (especially in the holistic education literature) on the need to attend to the child's physical self in order to achieve a pedagogy that is politically, culturally, and spiritually liberating for the *whole person.*

* The importance of the physical domain in phenomenological approaches to teaching, teacher reflectivity, and curriculum theory.

* Behaviorist curricula as essentially organismic. The uses and misuses of behaviorism in education.

The Organismic Politics of Classroom Experience

Although there is some controversy in current developmental literature over the degree to which a newborn is able to differentiate between itself and its physical environment, most developmental theorists agree that it has at most but very little ability to do so.[1,2] Rather, the child believes the surrounding world to be more or less a literal extension of itself. Soon, however, the infant begins to register the fact that the physical world that it perceives is not necessarily coextensive with itself. This marks the onset of the awareness that there is a fundamental distance separating self and other.[3] If for some reason the infant fails to (literally) "grasp" this fact—or is substantially delayed in doing so—the groundwork has been laid for potential psychoses in later development, for a feature of many psychoses is "adualism"—the inability to fully recognize oneself as a distinct entity embedded in a discrete physical body.[4] The result is a *dis*-embodiment of consciousness which, unanchored, is apt to get lost in a free-floating and all-engulfing sense of either omnipotence or exposure. Despite the scrutiny and challenges that developmental psychology has experienced in the last 20 years or so—especially in terms of cultural variability in developmental patterns and schedules—it is still clear enough that the complex construction of the ego almost always takes place initially upon somatic foundations, what Wilber has called the "hatching of the physical self."[5]

Well before modern developmental theory, some curricularists intuitively understood the physical dimensions of teaching and learning at what Piaget called the sensori-motor level and in what I shall call the organismic domain. Thus, between the 17th and 19th centuries, Comenius, Pestalozzi, and Froebel made the student's engagement with the physical world an integral part of their pedagogies. Their recognition that education needed to include the physical domain helped distinguish their theory and practice from many of the pedagogies that had preceded them.[6] What Plato recognized in his vision of education—that the physical development of all children was the basis of more advanced learning—was again acknowledged and elaborated by Comenius, Pestalozzi, and Froebel.

Comenius's insisted in his 17th-century classic, *Opera Didactica Omnia,* that the education of the child should unfold in a developmental fashion that paralleled general evolutionary patterns that were readily observable in nature. This was the basis of his multi-sensory approach. "The sense of hearing should always be conjoined with that of sight, and the tongue should be trained in combination with the hand. The subjects that are taught should not merely be taught orally, and thus appeal to the ear alone, but should be pictorially illustrated and thus develop the imagination by the help of the eye."[7]

The focus on physicality grew even sharper 150 years later in the work of Pestallozi, who felt that the child learned best when there was sensory engagement with objects—which he therefore called "object lessons." If the child was to learn in meaningful and lasting ways, she needed to begin with *realia,* which would then serve as the cornerstones of cognitive and affective elaboration in subsequent instruction. In addition, Froebel, in his focus on sensory data gained by physical engagement with objects, prefigured Piaget's idea of the sensori-motor stage. The father of the kindergarten movement, Froebel "was enthusiastic about Pestalozzi but not uncritical." Froebel's main disagreement with Pestalozzi was that Pestalozzian pedagogy was not integrative— was not, as we now say, "holistic." In its mechanical approach to decontextualized physical tasks, said Froebel, Pestallozi ignored the fact that the cosmos is an

> organized unity, a unity in which any given thing is a whole in itself yet a part of a larger whole. The distinctive aspect of this relationship is not simply that of inclusiveness. It is rather that every individual thing exists *only* in its higher unity; the finger exists *only* in the hand and in that higher unity has a special function.... Pedagogically, this sort of theory has the effect of leading the pupil on and on from one perch of significance to another more inclusive one. Furthermore, the individual pupil's significance swells as he is related to ever higher and more inclusive entities.[8]

Froebel assumed that the physical domain was rich with metaphysical import; neither could the metaphysical be apprehended apart from its physical embodiments. This interaction was especially important to Froebel because of his belief, common at the time, that "ontogeny recapitulates phylogeny," which means that the stages of an individual's development mirror the stages of the species' development. He claimed that very young children would see, think and act from those primarily physical—even animalistic—levels of consciousness which were supposed to have characterized our earliest evolution as a species.

Froebel provided many of the pedagogical tools and much of the philosophical scaffolding of Robert Owens's "infant schools" in the utopian community of New Lanark in Scotland in 1816. These schools stressed the importance of "an examination of actual objects, and encouragement of questions. Answers were always to be rational, instruction to emphasize the examination of actual objects, and the schedule to include plenty of exercise, music, and dance."[9] "Having become intrigued with the infant schools developing in the British Isles, educators from the United States made pilgrimages across the seas to observe the phenomenon in action."[10]

It did not take long for these devotees to begin establishing their own schools back home. In 1827, Joanna Bethune, following Owens's lead, founded the Infant School Society of New York for children between 18 months and six years old. Soon thereafter, infant schools were established in both New England and the South in such cities as Boston, Worcester, and Salem, Massachusetts; Hartford and New Haven, Connecticut; Providence, Rhode Island; and Charleston, South Carolina.[11] So popular did infant schools become in some areas that it is estimated, for example, that by 1840 "40% of all three-year-olds in Massachusetts were enrolled in either an infant school or regular private or public school."[12]

This early 19th-century focus on the organismic realm in the total education of the child influenced certain of the more liberal Progressive pedagogies in the late 19th and early 20th centuries. Herein also lie the roots of the kindergarten movement in the United States, which would finally come to fruition in the closing decades of the 1800s under the guidance of William Torrey Harris and Francis W. Parker.[13] Indeed, a key difference between many of the Progressive "pedio-centric" (or "child-centered") pedagogies and the more conservative "scholio-centric" (or "school-centered") instructional approaches that had preceded them was precisely this attunement to the physical dimensions and goals of teaching and learning—especially with very young children but with adolescents and even adults as well. For "the map is not a substitute for personal experience," proclaimed Dewey in his 1902 classic, *The Child and the Curriculum*. "The logically formulated material of a science or branch of learning, of a study, is no substitute for the having of individual experiences. The mathematical formula for a falling body does not take the place of personal contact and immediate individual experience with the falling thing."[14]

"Logical formulation," then, was not enough to optimize teaching and learning. What was equally necessary was that the teacher be allowed to teach and the child to learn in ways that were psychologically rich and relevant. This would happen only if pedagogy accommodated the fact that the child's psychological experience was grounded in organismic soil. Dewey was not claiming, of course (as were the early behaviorists who were breaking onto the scene at about the same time), that psychological reality and the nuances of inner experience could be fully explained (or conveniently ignored!) by a purely materialistic philosophy. He *was* insisting that experience grew out of the functioning of the whole person as she literally manipulated and acutely examined her surrounding life-world. If our pedagogy was to be psychologically potent, it simply could not ignore the organismic aspects of the child's inner and outer realities.

Although attending to this domain required the teacher to be more physically involved in what she was teaching, more innovative in how she taught it, and more global in how she assessed the child, Dewey promised that the extra effort would pay ample educational dividends, for the result would be a curriculum that that was not only *logically* valid but also *psychologically* vital. "The problem of the teacher is a different one" from that of the scientist or scholar, insisted Dewey.

> As a teacher he is not concerned with adding new facts to the science he teaches; in propounding new hypotheses or in verifying them. He is concerned with the subject-matter of the science as representing a given stage and phase of [the student's] experience. His problem is that of inducing a vital and personal experiencing. Hence what concerns him, as a teacher, are the ways in which that subject may become a part of experience; what there is in the child's present that may be usable with reference to it; how such elements are to be used; [and to] determine the medium in which the child must be placed in order that his growth may be properly directed. He is concerned, not with the subject-matter as such, but with the subject-matter as a related factor in a total growing and experiencing. *Thus to see it is to psychologize it.*[15]

Perhaps I can be forgiven a personal example of this. I never did particularly well in science in elementary or secondary school, but one of my most memorable lessons was a 6th-grade demonstration of the speed of sound. Mr. Mascari had been teaching us about how the speed of sound was much slower than the speed of light. Here was another boring and irrelevant fact for me to remember, and one which was not only uninteresting but downright counterintuitive! How could light be faster than sound? When you turned on the T.V., didn't the picture and the sound reach you at the same time? Mr. Mascari took the class to the baseball field. With a track-and-field starting gun, he stood at home plate. We all stood in center field. He had given one of the girls in the class a stopwatch and told her to start the watch when she saw the plume of smoke come out of the barrel of the gun and stop it when she actually heard the shot. I'll never forget seeing the plume of smoke issue from the muzzle but not hearing the loud rap of the gun until a heartbeat later. A whole world of teaching happened in that brief second between heartbeats. Light *was* faster than sound! I knew it because I had *experienced* it—with my ears, eyes, and even nose because of the acrid smell of the smoke. When we later calculated the speed of sound by using the data we had collected on the baseball field, it was simply logical confirmation of what was already psychologically real for me. For to *see* and *hear* the speed of sound lagging behind the speed of light had indeed allowed me to *psychologize* that fact, and thus to *appropriate* it as something real, proximate, and personal.

Probably without knowing it, Mr. Mascari had admirably met every one of Dewey's criteria for psychologically fruitful teaching on the organismic landscape. He had "induc[ed] a vital and personal experiencing" by drawing on what was in "the child's present...in order that his growth may be properly directed."[16] Mr. Mascari was able to accomplish this because he was concerned "not with the subject matter as such, but with the subject-matter as a related factor in a total growing and experiencing."[17] Thus, forty years later, those ten minutes on my elementary school playground are as vivid and vital for me as the day they happened whereas I can scarcely remember the top story this morning on CNN. Was Mr. Mascari aware, I wonder, of David Hawkins's Elementary Science Study (ESS) in the early 1960s, which appeared at about the same time as I was receiving my memorable lesson on the baseball field?

David Hawkins, the director of the ESS, believed that children should learn science by doing science, not by being told about science. Hawkins was responsive to progressive methods.... The curriculum developed at ESS consisted of a series of units which used concrete materials—both everyday objects and special equipment—to demonstrate the process of scientific thinking.... The ESS units were intended to be used by individual students, in no special order, and to encourage what British infant school proponents called "messing about."[18]

Cremin, in listing Progressivism's most enduring accomplishments, suggests that many of them resided in the organismic domain: 1) more focus on doing, less on reciting; 2) more attractive texts and other media; and 3) architectural changes in the school itself, including assembly rooms, gyms, labs, fields, kitchens, cafeterias, playgrounds, infirmaries, and better lighting and ventilation.[19] One of the major objectives of the Progressive Education Association in 1918 was to encourage schools to become responsive to their students' physical needs—both immediate and developmental. If Cremin is right in his analysis of the legacy of Progressivism, then it is in the organismic realm that a good deal of that inheritance lies; for American education did, by and large, respond to the plea in *The Cardinal Principles of Secondary Education,* the highly influential document produced by the NEA in 1918, that attention to the physical dimensions of schools and schooling be given at all levels—not merely the primary years.

It is in the organismic realm of the "extra-curriculum" that we can also place the growth of the health-related courses and services in the American public schools throughout the 20th century. Even physical education classes, however (perhaps the most obvious example of the organismic curriculum), have not been without their problems ideologically, psychologically and physically. For instance, with the advent of the First World War, some Americans began to feel that physical education classes should serve a vital national interest by keeping young men fit, perpetually poised for combat.[20] Other policy makers believed that organized sports in the schools would draw boys back into the classrooms (where girls were outperforming them) by promising the boys the after-school athletic field on which they could gain glory and repair their scholastically injured egos.[21]

Furthermore, it is not clear that physical education as traditionally conducted contributes nearly as much as it could to the total psychophysical functioning of the child. Reviewing the literature on holistic physical education, Miller reports that

> even physical education programs which are aimed at developing the body can contribute to a lack of integration. Masters and Houston believed that physical exercises should concentrate on building up a person's body image or the ability to connect the body to our consciousness. Unfortunately, many physical education programs focus only on either building up the muscles or the cardiovascular system or both.... In contrast, Masters and Houston offer a program in psychophysical awareness.... The exercises focus on different parts of the body but most of the exercises include an imagery component to help connect mind and body.... Problems can arise because the body can get the wrong message from the nervous system. Feldenkrais, however, argues that the body can be reeducated.[22]

Other health-related extracurricular initiatives in the first half of the 20th century were even more problematic. For example, in 1946 Congressman Flannagan, a Democratic representative from Virginia, wrote Public Law 396—a piece of legislation which, in the minds of some, was evidence of creeping socialism. Flannagan proposed that the federal government should match the states in money spent on free lunches for needy children. The proposal, eventually codified as the *National School Lunch Act*, stirred some of the most contentious debates of that legislative session. This debate was resurrected during the conservative revolution in the 1990s, in which Speaker Gingrich and others vociferously called for scaling down and even eliminating free lunches in the public schools.

A further conservative critique of liberal approaches to organismic extracurricular issues concerns the increasing role of social workers in public schools—a phenomenon which, in one form or another, has existed at least since Stanton Colt's first settlement house in the U.S. in 1886 in New York City. The settlement house was an early welfare institution—based on London's Toynbee Hall in 1884, the first settlement house in the world—that aimed at improving living conditions in urban areas. Jane Addams's settlement houses, beginning with her famous Hull House in Chicago in 1889, attempted to address the combined physical, social, and educational needs of the inner-city poor, especially immigrants. President Franklin D. Roosevelt's New Deal is ideologically related to this movement, which many educational historians feel gained special momentum in U.S. public schools in the 1940s.[23,24,25] Regarding a broad range of issues from truancy to homosexuality, from substance abuse to sex education, many conservatives contend that liberal policy makers have attempted to both socialize and medicalize these issues—stripping them of their ethical complexity in order to render them in the dispassionate yet simplistically "scientistic" terms of the behavioral sciences. As Sedlak puts it, conservatives tend to feel that in dealing with organismic (extra)curricular issues, liberals have "substituted a medical, psychiatric model for the prevailing moral model."[26]

Clearly, the inclusion and articulation of organismic curricular and extra-curricular items was, and continues to be, an occasion for highly politicized rhetoric from both the Right and the Left—with the Right typically casting a jaundiced eye at these elements in the curriculum and the Left typically promoting them.[27]

Organismic Curricula and the Physiology of Freedom
The Brazilian Critical theorist Paolo Freire, one of the most radical educationists of the 20th century, often insisted that a merely intellectual understanding of an unjust situation is rarely enough by itself to cause an oppressed person to cast off her shackles.[28] As most therapists know, for a client to simply *understand* her dysfunction rarely cures it. There are even ways in which a complex understanding of one's neuroses can make matters worse. Rather, the psychic blockages must be lived with and worked through at the most basic somatic levels before they begin to dissolve. It is for this reason that the body-based therapies such as Rolfing and Hakomi therapy arose in the first place. Fay's suggestions for creating a critical social science that is profoundly liberating apply equally well to any pedagogy that strives to liberate.

> Critical social science assumes that people's activities can be understood in terms of the false consciousness which they possess about themselves and their society, and it furthermore assumes that it is by changing this false consciousness that a social scientific theory can be an instrument of social transformation. But what if oppression is much more physical than this? What if, that is, oppression leaves its traces not just in people's minds, but in their muscles and skeletons as well? If this were to be the case...then a quite different approach to understanding op-

pressive regimes, and a quite different conception of therapy to undermine these regimes, would be required.[29]

Giddens has also argued that sociology can be liberating only if it honors those psychic/somatic therapies that are a defining feature of what he calls "late modernity."[30] The approaches of which Fay speaks rest squarely on organismic foundations, and can be found in certain liberatory educational statements as well—especially in the holistic work of Schutz in "Education and the Body,"[31] Hendrick and Fadiman in their vision of a "Curriculum for Feeling and Being,"[32] and Saredello and Sanders in their guide to "Care of the Senses: A Neglected Dimension of Education".

> One essential task for educators is to recognize that the senses, and therefore perceptions and experiences, are disrupted and will continue to be disrupted by the stimulated world of technology, science, and economic pursuit. Balance in and of the senses, and the subsequent freedom of thought and actions, can be consciously sought and taught, but it cannot occur naturally. As more people live in areas of high population and as technical devices of every sort intervene in our sensory contact with the world, we will need to become trained in the art of living in our senses....[33]

As I have written elsewhere,[34] the Existentialist and transpersonal psychologies also offer many techniques and exercises that teachers such as Whitmore[35] have shown us how to employ in the classroom to "bring students to their senses." In this manner, teachers can learn how to access and harness the enormous creative potential of what Gardner has termed the kinesthetic and naturalistic intelligences.[36]

It is largely this scrupulous nurturance of the child's organismic growth that distinguishes such alternative schools as the Waldorf schools from traditional education. Even in dealing with such abstractions as numbers, the Waldorf educator takes an organismic and psychologically rich approach to introducing children to the world of math.

> First graders live in a world of imaginative pictures; they have a natural feeling for the archetypes implicit in the world of numbers.... The number one, for instance, represents more than a digit. It can be thought of as the largest number, for it contains all other numbers within it. The number two, in contrast, denotes duality, contrast, oppo-

sites. The children in first grade might encounter some of these dualities in stories which contrast a bright, sunny day and dark, gloomy night, or a mighty king and the queen who rules with him. With the number three comes a dynamic quality, with four a quality of stability and form. There are four seasons, four directions, four elements.... A student who has gone through this process will never again consider a number simply as an abstraction or merely as a mark upon a page.[37]

In Waldorf schooling, the fastest growing independent school movement in the world today, knitting, dancing, painting, modeling clay, and caring for animals on the school farm also make knowledge tangible in ways that rarely happen at traditional schools.[38]

Yet one does not need to enter the rather rarefied atmosphere of private holistic education in order to find and implement more organismically sound approaches to physical education. Even in the public schools it should be possible to attend to Foshay's seven dimensions of physical education.

Seven aspects of the physical self should be sought out if one intends to find opportunities to increase students' awareness of their physical selves: 1. Physical growth—changes in the body that accompany increasing age; 2. health—prevention of physical disorders; 3. body image—awareness of the bodily organs and functions, awareness of one's appearance; 4. movement—including sports and dance; 5. body language—nonverbal expressiveness; 6. metaphors deriving from primarily physical experience; 7. image schemata, including path, cycle, blockage, and so forth.[39]

Macdonald has captured the significance of the organismic realm in his discussion of "disembodied intellect" versus "sensori-motor presence."

In everyday life communication in its cultural context is a complete organismic response involving facial gesture, bodily posture, emotional mood, tacit understanding, and personal organic needs. The activity of school in contradistinction focuses almost entirely upon formal structures of communication, primarily language. Thus, the curriculum goals are essentially divorced from the concrete biology of the student.... This divorcement of the verbal from affect and psychomotor activity...helps teach students to distrust their own values, emotions, and bodies as basic aspects of life and to this extent diminishes the full meaning of being alive.[40]

Finally, the sensori-physical domain is integral not only to the student's psychosocial growth but to her spiritual growth as well. We believe in my faith community that every human being "is spirit, the elements are eternal, and spirit and element, inseparably connected, receive a fullness of joy."[41] Spirit and body being inseparable, there is no such thing as disembodied liberation—whether that liberation is psychological, political, or spiritual.

First Landscape Roots of the Phenomenological Turn in Curriculum Studies

If Merleau-Ponty is right that all we can know about ourselves is rooted in our status as "body-subjects," then there are unavoidable ties between the phenomenological aspects of education and the student's body. What is phenomenology? Pinar noted that the phenomenological investigator, whether curricularist or philosopher,

> questions how phenomena—"the things themselves"— present themselves in the lived experience of the individual, especially as they present themselves in lived time.... The term consciousness speaks to the multiple ways in which objects, events, and other human beings are presented via the distinctly human process of perceiving, judging, believing, remembering, and imagining. Phenomenologically understood, consciousness is characterized by intentionality: it is always *of* something which, when apprehended, relates to the act of consciousness involved as the meaning of that act.[42]

Although the phenomenological approach goes beyond the world of sensation, it is rooted in it. Insofar as the curricularist or teacher want to help the student experience herself as *Dasein*[43]—as the "Being There" of the whole person—then they must help her experience "the horizon of perceptions and understandings" that make up her "situation."[44] I will have much more to say on this topic when we examine the phenomenological curriculum in Chapter 5.

The Behaviorist Curriculum

The organismic domain is also the foundation of a very different theoretical orientation from that already discussed—namely, behaviorist psychology and learning theory, expressed with particularly chilling economy in Skinner's *The Technology of Teaching*.[45] In radical contrast to the organismic pedagogies discussed above, which stress inner enrichment, classical behaviorist learning theory at best ignores the student's inner life and at worst denies its existence. What is more, along with his predecessors Thorndike, Bobbitt, and Charters, Skinner has been roundly (and justly) criticized over the last several decades for the psychologically and politically oppressive danger inherent in his mechanistic approach to teaching and learning. Treating the student as merely an organism to be shaped by positive and negative reinforcements violently strips the student of her basic human dignity and ignores the teacher's desire to existentially nurture the student. Claiming to be politically neutral, the strict behaviorist pedagogies, stemming from a robotic view of the individual, are in fact inherently prone to be misused by corporate entities and agendas whose totalitarian purposes are served all too well by manipulative approaches to the student.

From Kant to Buber, ethicists have claimed that the essence of immorality is to treat another person as an object—as an "It" instead of a "Thou."[46] It follows that moral discourse can occur only when two people honor and explore each other's complexity and uniqueness. This is equally true, and in many cases especially true, in the relationship between the teacher and student. Yet Skinner sees the objectification of the student as the core of any truly "scientific" and "modern" pedagogy. Bemoaning the backwardness of educators who still use and care about such messy phenomena as "learning," "discriminating," "generalizing," and "abstracting," Skinner wrote that

> when we teach a child to press a button by reinforcing his response with candy, it adds nothing to say that he responds because he "knows" that pressing the button will produce candy. When we teach him to press a red button but not a green, it adds nothing to say that he now "discriminates" or "tells the difference between" red and green. When we teach him to press a red button and then notice that he will press an orange button as well, it adds nothing to say that he has "generalized" from one color to another. When we bring the response under the control of a single property of

stimuli, it adds nothing to say that the child has formed an "abstraction."[47]

There is very little distance between this philosophy of education and the ideology of the totalitarian state, as we sense in the rhetoric of control that typifies Skinner's view of the child as merely one type of organism among others.

> There are certain questions which have to be answered in turning to the study of any new organism. What behavior is to be set up? What reinforcers are at hand? What responses are available in embarking upon a program of progressive approximation which will lead to the final form of the behavior? How can reinforcements be most efficiently scheduled to maintain the behavior in strength?[48]

Does all of this imply that all behavioral curricula are always politically and ethically repugnant? Is behaviorism simply an educational atrocity which, as various postmodern and critical theorists have claimed, we must completely avoid in either our theory or practice? Not necessarily.

It is much rarer today than it was, say, forty years ago for a behaviorally oriented psychologist or instructional theorist to take a classically behaviorist view of learning. Instead, there has been a healthy melding of the behaviorist and cognitivist approaches into what is called cognitive-behaviorism in current psychotherapy.[49] The synthesis of these two approaches has yielded impressive results regarding anxiety and depression disorders, for which cognitive-behaviorism is now the treatment of choice. As Brandt and Tyler have noted, what in current educational parlance and practice is called "behaviorism" is really "cognitive behaviorism."

> To some persons the word "behavior" carries the meaning of an observable act, like the movement of the fingers in typing. To them, behavioral objectives refer only to overt behavior. Others use the term "behavior" to emphasize the active nature of the learner. They want to emphasize that learners are not passive receptacles but living, reasoning persons. In this sense, behavior refers to all kinds of human reactions.[50]

In short, when behaviorist approaches do not make the error of taking an exclusively organismic approach to learning but also include other sorts of functioning and analysis that occur on other curricular landscapes, then they still have great potential value. As I have already suggested, and as we will see throughout this study, it is always disastrous when theory and practice on a curriculum landscape attempt to deny the validity of other landscapes. When this happens, the proponents and inhabitants of that landscape attempt to colonize the other landscapes under the banner of special philosophical and pedagogical privilege. This is called a "category error." However, when theory and practice on a given landscape are open to interacting with theory and practice on other landscapes, then many salutary consequences can result. The overlapping of the first curricular landscape and the fourth, as in cognitive behaviorism, is just one instance of this combinatory power.

This particular fusion of the cognitive and behavioral—which Ornstein and Hunkins[51] call the behavioral-rational curriculum and Eisner and Vallance[52] call the behavioral-aims curriculum—has proven sufficiently effective that it continues to dominate the practical world of curriculum design and delivery, for it is

> the oldest and still the major approach to curriculum. As a means-ends approach it is logical and prescriptive. It relies on technical and scientific principles, and includes models, plans, and step-by-step strategies for formulating curriculum. Goals and objectives are specified, content and activities are sequenced, and learning outcomes are evaluated in relation to the goals and objectives. This curriculum approach, which has been applied to all subjects for more than two-thirds of this century, constitutes the frame of reference against which other approaches to curriculum are compared.[53]

The sheer practicality of such curricula for the teacher in her everyday classroom life is evidenced by the durability and relevance of Tyler's famous formulation of his four basic curricular questions: "What educational purposes should the school seek to attain? What educational experiences can be provided that are likely to attain these purposes? How can these educational experiences be organized effectively? How can we determine whether these purposes are being attained?"[54]

Even though it has become unpopular to say so in much of curriculum theorizing, I believe that there are some instances in which a more or less classical form of behaviorism *does* serve important purposes. A good example is the role that positive reinforcement schedules can play in special education settings, where the functional control of disruptive or self-destructive behavior is often a precondition for any further learning—and often for simply getting through the day! Even Jere Brophy's richly cognitivist text *Motivating Students to Learn* has many instances of the judicious use of behaviorist principles in order to define learning strategies and educational goals.[55] And many would argue that a modified and cognitively enriched behaviorism has been productive in such reading approaches as DISTAR, SQ3R, and Continuous Progress.[56]

As long as behaviorism avoids the arrogance of Thorndike's disturbingly counterintuitive assertion that "whatever exists, exists in some amount and can be measured"—then it can perform vital and varied educational functions in combination with other curricular orientations.

Conclusion

In this chapter I have examined some of the historical roots and political controversies surrounding the organismic curriculum. We saw that many of Progressivism's most salient characteristics and goals grew out of organismic educational issues involving both the curriculum and extra-curriculum. We noted a few of the political storms that swirled, and continue to swirl, on the plains of the organismic curriculum.

The organismic landscape houses multifarious—and, in some instances, contradictory—approaches to curriculum, which range from behaviorism to holistic education. Each of these approaches has its unique value and applicability so long as it does not attempt to negate the legitimate claims of other types of educational theory and practice. Any pedagogy that lays claim to being psychologically, politically, or spiritually liberating must authentically honor and skillfully address the concrete realities that make up the first curricular landscape.

Topics for Discussion

1. The chapter contains a personal example of the importance of the physical domain in a 6th-grade science class. Can you remember a moment, or series of moments from your elementary or secondary school, when the physical "texture" of the environment in which the experience occurred—as well, perhaps, as the physical means that were used to convey a lesson—had a lasting influence on you?

2. Nel Noddings and Maxine Greene (among other feminist educational scholars) have claimed that an education which does not attend to the physical domain but focuses only on cognitive excellence is an example of an oppressive patriarchal discourse because it is tends to deal mostly with abstract principles, system-building, and all in the service of personal and political control—not with nurturance and relationship, which they claim is more characteristic of women. What is your opinion?

3. In this chapter the claim was made that there are some legitimate assumptions and purposes of behaviorist education. It is arguable, however, that any educational theory or approach which sees the student as an organism responding to a stimulus, and which then aims at conditioning her into a "desirable" behavior, is by definition attempting to turn the student into an object and is thus inherently immoral. Do you agree with this latter position? Or do you share the view that there are some valid, if limited, uses of behaviorist principles in certain teaching situations?

Topics for Research

1. Examine the rise of healthcare and social service delivery in the public schools, especially from the early 20th century until now, focusing on the political controversies that have attended each step in the growth of this key, and contentious, element of the extra-curriculum in the public schools.

2. B.F. Skinner's 1956 work *The Technology of Teaching* claims to present an educational approach that is effective, economical, and morally and politically neutral. Analyze that book closely to see if this is, in

fact, the case. Or is there evidence within the text itself of hidden political agendas, cultural assumptions, and epistemological biases?

3. What are some of the major controversies that have surrounded sex education in the last 40 years or so? Have they changed very much since the appearance and growth of AIDS on the scene, and, if so, how? What are the ethical and political assumptions of conservative and liberal stances on AIDS education?

Notes: Chapter 1

1. J. Wade, *Changes of Mind: A Holonomic Theory of the Evolution of Consciousness* (Albany, New York: State University of New York Press, 2001).
2. M. Washburne, *Transpersonal Psychology in Psychoanalytic Perspective* (Albany, New York: State University of New York Press, 1994).
3. H. Kohut, *The Search for the Self: Selected Writings of Heinz Kohut, 1950-1978.* (Madison, Conn.: International Universities Press, 1978).
4. J. Gebser, *The Ever-Present Origin.* Athens (Ohio: Ohio University Press), 1985.
5. K. Wilber, *A Brief History of Everything* (Boston: Shambhala, 1996), 162.
6. H. Broudy and J. Palmer. *Exemplars of Teaching Method* (Chicago: Rand McNally & Company, 1965).
7. J. Comenius as quoted in Broudy & Palmer, 102.
8. Broudy and Palmer, 120.
9. Carl Kaestle, *Pillars of the Republic: Common Schools and American Society, 1760-1860* (New York: Hill and Wang, 1983), 47.
10 K. Ridd, An unpublished manuscript, Department of Educational Leadership and Foundations, Provo, Utah: Brigham Young University, 2000), 2.
11. Kaestle.
12. D. Ravitch and M. Vinovskis, eds., *Learning from the Past: What History Teaches Us about School Reform* (Baltimore, Maryland: The Johns Hopkins University Press), 245.
13. L. Cremin, *The Transformation of the School: Progressivism in American Education, 1876-1957* (New York: Vintage Press, 1964).
14. J. Dewey as quoted in G. Willis, W. Schubert, R. Bullough, Jr., C. Kridel and J. Holton. *The American Curriculum: A Documentary History* (London: Praeger, 1994), 126.
15. Ibid., 127, emphasis added.
16. Ibid, 15.
17. Ibid.
18. D. Ravitch, *The Troubled Crusade: American Education, 1945-1980* (New York: Basic Books, 1983), 243-244.

19. Cremin, 20.
20. L. Cremin, *American Education: The Metropolitan Experience: 1876-1980* (New York: Harper and Row, 1988).
21. V. Bissell-Brown, "Fear of Feminization: Los Angeles High Schools in the Progressive Era," *Feminist Studies* 16 (1990), 493-518.
22. J. Miller, *The Holistic Curriculum* (Toronto, Ontario: The Ontario Institute for Studies in Education, 1988): 90-91.
23. J. Dryfoos, *Full-Service Schools: A Revolution in Health and Social Services for Children, Youth, and Families* (San Francisco: Jossey-Bass, 1994).
24. Cremin, *"American."*
25. M. Sedlak, "Attitudes, Choices, and Behavior: School Delivery of Health and Social Services," in *Learning from the Past: What History Teaches Us about School Reform,* eds. D. Ravitch and M. Vinovskis (Baltimore, Maryland: The Johns Hopkins University Press, 1995), 57-94.
26. Ibid., 86.
27. J. Spring, *The Intersection of Cultures: Multicultural Education in the United States and the Global Economy* (New York: McGraw Hill, 2000).
28. P. Freire, *Pedagogy and Freedom: Ethics, Democracy, and Civic Courage* (New York: Rowman and Littlefield, 2001).
29. B. Fay, *Critical Social Science: Liberation and its Limits* (Ithaca, New York: Cornell University Press, 1987), 146.
30. A. Giddens, *The Consequences of Modernity* (Stanford: Stanford University Press, 1990.
31. W. Schutz, "Education and the Body" in *Transpersonal Education: A Curriculum for Feeling and Being,* eds. G. Hendricks and J. Fadiman. (Englewood Cliffs, New Jersey: Prentice Hall (1976), 104-110.
32. G. Hendrick and J. Fadiman, eds., *Transpersonal Education: A Curriculum for Feeling and Being* (Englewood Cliffs, New Jersey: Prentice-Hall).
33. R. Sardello and C. Sanders, "Care of the Senses: A Neglected Dimension of Education" in *Education, Information and Transformation: Essays on Learning and Thinking,* ed. Jeffrey Kane (Columbus, Ohio: Merrill/Prentice Hall, 1999), 226-227.
34. C. Mayes, "The Use of Contemplative Practices in Teacher Education." *Encounter: Education for Meaning and Social Justice* 11(3) (1998): 17-31.
35. D. Whitmore, *Psychosynthesis in Education: A Guide to the Joy of Learning* (Rochester, Vermont: Destiny Books, 1986).
36. J. Gardner, "Are there Additional Intelligences? The Case for Naturalist, Spiritual, and Existential Intelligences," in *Education, Information, and Transformation: Essays on Learning and Thinking,* ed. Jeffrey Kane (Columbus, Ohio: Merrill, 1999), 111-131.

37. R. Trostli, "Educating as an Art: The Waldorf Approach," in *New Directions in Education: Selections from Holistic Education Review*, ed. Ron Miller (Brandon, Vermont: Holistic Education Press, 1991), 343-344.
38. J. Miller.
39. A. Foshay, *The Curriculum: Purpose, Substance, Practice* (New York: Teachers College Press, 2000), 45.
40. J. Macdonald, *Theory as a Prayerful Act: The Collected Essays of James P. Macdonald* (New York: Peter Lang, 1995), 124.
41. *The Doctrine and Covenants of the Church of Jesus Christ of Latter-day Saints* (Salt Lake City, Utah: The Church of Jesus Christ of Latter-day Saints), 93: 33.
42. W. Pinar, W. Reynolds, P. Slattery and P. Taubman, eds. *Understanding Curriculum: An Introduction to the Study of Historical and Contemporary Curriculum Discourses* (New York: Peter Lang, 2000), 405-406.
43. M. Heidegger, *Being and Time* (New York: Harper and Row, 1964).
44. Pinar et al., 412
45. B. F. Skinner, *The Technology of Teaching* (Englewood Cliffs, New Jersey: Prentice Hall, 1968).
46. M. Buber, *I and Thou* (New York: Vintage, 1965).
47. Skinner, 120.
48. Ibid., 19
49. G. Wilson, "Behavior Therapy," in *Current Psychotherapies: Basics and Beyond,* eds. R. Corsini and D. Wedding (Itasca, Illinois: F.E. Peacock, 1995), 229-261.
50. A. Brandt and R. Tyler, "Goals and Objectives," in *Contemporary Issues in Curriculum,* eds. A. Ornstein and L. Behar-Hornstein (Boston: Allyn and Bacon, 1999), 22.
51. A. Ornstein and F. Hunkins, *Curriculum: Foundations, Principles, and Issues* (Boston: Allyn and Bacon, 1988).
52. E. Eisner and E. Vallance, *Conflicting Conceptions of Curriculum* (Berkeley, California: McCutchan Publishing Corporation, 1974).
53. Ornstein and Hunkins, 2.
54. R. Tyler as quoted in Eisner and Vallance, 11.
55. J. Brophy, *Motivating Students to Learn* (Boston: McGraw-Hill, 1994).

2

THE TRANSFERENTIAL
LANDSCAPE

Pivotal Themes in Chapter 2

* The rise of psychoanalytical approaches to curriculum and instruction during the early Progressive period and their present state.

* The teacher as therapist. The psychotherapeutic idea of transference and counter-transference as applied to teacher/student relationships. The increasing number of psychologically distressed students.

* Joyce Dryfoos' idea of the Full Service School as a place to respond to a wide range of physical, psychological, and social needs of students—particularly students from lower socioeconomic areas.

* The application of archetypal (Jungian and neo-Jungian) psychology to curriculum and instruction.

* Nel Noddings's ideal of the teacher as nurturer.

Early Theories of Transference and Counter-transference

In order to understand the transferential curriculum, it is necessary to look first at object-relations psychology. Object relations refers to the nature of a person's earliest relationships with the first "objects" of his attention and affection. Typically, of course, these initial objects are the mother and, to a lesser degree, the father, siblings, and other caregivers. The assumption in object-relations psychology is that the roots of how the person sees and interacts with others in the world as an adult reside in the soil of his earliest object relations.[1] This brings us to the pivotal psychodynamic fact of what has been dubbed "the transference."

Greenson has summarized the classical view of the transference as

> the experiencing of feelings, drives, attitudes, fantasies, and defenses toward a person in the present which are inappropriate to that person and are a repetition, a displacement of reactions originating in regard to significant persons of early childhood. I emphasize that for a reaction to be considered transference it must have two characteristics: it must be a repetition of the past and it must be inappropriate to the present.[2]

As Freud put it in a line that has become a classic in the psychoanalytical literature, the transference is "a new edition of an old problem." Freudian, neo-Freudian, Jungian, neo-Jungian and Transpersonal theorists and therapists take somewhat different views of the origins and operations of the transference. The classical Freudian model of the transference is, however, still the one that is the most highly regarded and widely employed. Particularly in this model of the transference, the "significant persons of early childhood" are the mother and father, and the "person in the present" is the analyst. Hence, a male patient's relationship to the female or male analyst will reflect the nature of the patient's relationship to his own mother and father in the specific Oedipal dynamics which psychically (mis)shaped him in the "family romance triangle." Similar passions and processes are at play for the female patient except that they ostensibly originate in her "Electra" desire for psychophysical union with her father instead of the male's Oedipal impulse for psycho-physical union with his mother.

Whatever the differences in theory and practice regarding transference, most theorists and therapists share the belief that it involves the symbolic displacement of primary emotions about some significant figure in the analysand's early object relations onto someone in the present. Many depth psychotherapists believe that the transference causes crucial subconscious material to surface which they and their analysands can use to understand psychological issues with unique clarity. Moreover, the transference can be either positive or negative. In other words, the analysand will project either positive or negative emotions onto the analyst depending upon the patient's original feelings toward the figure in his past whom the analyst symbolizes.[3]

In the early years of psychoanalytic theory at the turn of the 20th century, Freud insisted that all transferences "invariably go back to erotic sources."[4] Toward the end of his career, however, Freud seemed to be expanding the idea of the libido (or *Eros*) to include not only sexual energy but all energy that strives to affirm life against the countervailing subconscious impulse towards dissolution and decay—the death impulse, in short—which Freud called *Thanatos*. Later Freudian cultural theorists, like the Marxist Herbert Marcuse, even argued that industrial capitalism was the economic expression of *Thanatos* whereas it was the liberating ideology of socialism that alone could honor and unfetter both the individual's and the culture's libido.[5] However, it was Carl Jung and his followers who first saw that the transference might involve the transmission of supra-sexual energy onto a significant person in the present.

Archetypal Dimensions of the Transference

Jung agreed with Freud that there was often an "undeniable" sexual element in the transference; however, according to Jung, that element "is not always the only one and not always the essential one."[6] Jung expanded the Freudian notion of transference by demonstrating that the patient may project "psychic contents" onto the analyst which are deep and powerful but which are not necessarily (or not primarily) sexual. According to Jung, transference could also occur at the archetypal level. What are archetypes?

In their most basic "form," archetypes can be pictured as innate clusters or nodes of psychic energy which are at the very core of the psyche. They are thus primordial psychic lenses through which we experience and interpret reality at the most fundamental levels. A good example is the archetype of the trickster, who, through his playful (and sometimes dangerous) pranks, turns our socially constructed definitions of normalcy and reality on their head. According to Jung, we are all born with a predisposition to occasionally see (and sometimes even be) this character in our personal and social experiences. The fact that this predisposition exists in everyone explains why this archetypal energy shows up so frequently in dreams, myths and fairytales across time and cultures. Yet, *how* this archetypal energy will manifest itself in dreams, myths, and fairytales varies from person to person, time to time, and place to place, depending upon one's individual and cultural circumstances.

To continue with the example of the trickster archetype: cultural anthropologists and comparative literary critics have discovered that it typically appears in Native American culture as a wolf; in Celtic lore, trickster are often homunculi; Shakespeare's drama is filled with tricksters, such as Lear's fool, whose apparently absurd antics are really meant to jolt Lear into awareness. In American pop culture, it has often been the comedian who plays the trickster, using scathing and even scandalous humor to jolt society out of its collective stupor and thereby awaken it to its inadequacies and injustices. Groucho Marx, Charlie Chaplin, Mae West, Lenny Bruce, Gilda Radner, Lily Tomlin, Robin Williams and many others have played the fool *for* us, and played tricks *on* us, to force us to go beyond the easy half truths of our social conventions.

Because they are shared and "objective" (in the sense that we are all born with them), archetypes exist in what Jung called the "collective unconscious." Jung never denied the existence of the personal subconscious that had been shaped by each individual's unique history. It was here that he felt Freudian psychology still had great explanatory and therapeutic power. But Jung insisted that the *personal* subconscious is simply a small boat on the vast psychic sea of the *collective* unconscious. Archetypes can also be pictured metaphorically as

> the invisible potential existence of the crystalline structure in a saturated solution. [Archetypes] first take on a specific form when they emerge into consciousness in the shape of images; it is therefore necessary to differentiate between the unapprehendable archetype—the unconscious, preexistent disposition—and the archetypal images. [Archetypes] are human nature in the universal sense. Myths and fairy tales are also characterized by this universal validity which differentiates them from ordinary dreams.[7]

By the Jungian view, psychospiritual health is a dynamic balance between ego and archetype—between the reality function of our quotidian consciousness as it daily negotiates our shared social world, and the archetypal function which lends depth, universality and thus a sense of spirituality to our experience.[8] Achieving this balance allows one to live and work in ways that are practical yet invested with psychospiritual intensity. Without the reality function intact, the individual is overwhelmed (or "possessed" as Jungians say) by archetypal energy and images. Yet, without steady infusions of archetypal energy, the ego lives in a flat and colorless world of facts and figures that are devoid of any sense of universality or mystery. Reconciling the two is the key to psychological and moral well being.

We are now in a position to see how transference can be either personal, archetypal, or both, for

> just as the analysand projects *personal subconscious* contents onto the analyst, so the analysand also may project his *[archetypal]* contents onto her. Some Jungians even maintain that "archetypal transference" is a feature of any therapeutic situation (Kirsch, 1995; Knox, 1998). If this is true, then at the center of every personal "complex" is a transpersonal, archetypal core, whose power radiates from the depths of the collective unconscious and permeates the individual's unique identity and issues.[9]

And as if transferential issues were not thorny enough, they can get even sharper. For just as the analysand may transfer personal and archetypal contents onto the analyst, so the analyst may engage in a reverse process of *counter-transference*. In counter-transference, the analyst—because of her own unmet needs and unresolved neuroses—succumbs to the powerful influence of the analysand's projections by internalizing and acting out on them. A typical example is the male patient who projects onto a female analyst both the need for maternal nurturance (which he perhaps never got from his emotionally distant biological mother) as well as his desire to return to the cosmic womb of the archetypal "Great Mother."[10] So seductive are these personal and archetypal projections onto the female analyst that she may fall under their sway and act out on them in ways that are inappropriate, exhausting, and even unethical.[11] The web pages of most state boards of psychology update everyday the growing lists of therapists whose licenses have been revoked because of transferential energies run amok in the form of sexual involvement with patients. The delicate balancing act for the analyst in any transference is to use the images that are transferred onto her as information about the analysand and his issues, not as an occasion for inappropriately identifying with them.[12]

Armed with this basic understanding of personal and archetypal transference and counter-transference, we are now in a better position to understand how these topics are addressed in transferential models of teaching.

The Transferential Curriculum

Most American curricularists who have dealt with these complex issues have been concerned with personal transference from the student toward the teacher. Certainly, this issue was central to the psychoanalytic wing of Progressive education. Focusing on the oedipal conflict in the male child and the Electra complex in the female child, these educational scholars and practitioners argued that the classroom was a place where the student would display and project his libidinal passions regarding his parent(s) onto the teacher. This classroom dilemma stemmed, they claimed, from the child's *emotional fusion* with the opposite-sex parent which that child would now reenact with the teacher. Psychoanalytic Progressivism was interested in how teachers could help the student *de-fuse* (i.e., undo the primitive identification of consciousness with its earliest relational "object") in a healthy way. Obviously, this cast the teacher somewhat in the role of a psychotherapist.

As we saw in the previous chapter, it is precisely this attempt of some educational theorists and practitioners to extend their influence into the child's biological and psychic life that angers many conservative educationists, policymakers, and ordinary citizens.[13] Yet, given the increasing emotional distress of various students by the time they enter the schools, it is difficult to see how teachers and administrators can simply turn a blind eye to these issues. People such as Joyce Dryfoos even argue that public schools must be "full-service" sites of psychological and social agencies—especially schools in socioeconomically troubled areas.[14]

Transference in the classroom possesses an intensity that may equal and even eclipse that of the consulting room. That the classroom may be a theater for personal and archetypal dramas should not surprise us. We all tend to project our needs, fears and expectations onto others in those "attachments of daily life" that make up our everyday world.[15] And we all do so especially when it comes to authority figures like teachers, who stimulate complex and passionate transferences because we see these figures as particularly potent—and thus "attractive," using this term, as do the psychotherapist Spiegelman and the physicist Mansfeld, in its almost literal electromagnetic sense.[16,17]

Applying psychoanalytic terms to its pedagogy, the therapeutic wing of Progressive pedagogy said that the child would "transfer" his psychosexually charged parental *imago* onto the teacher. The teacher could help the child resolve the primal "family romance" at home by helping him negotiate it at school. This would be possible because, as Isador H. Coriat, an early president of the American Psycho-Analytic Association, proclaimed, "in school, the teacher becomes a substitute for the father or mother of the child and in the emotional tie which exists between teacher and pupil, the earlier parent-child relationship is re-lived and re-animated."[18] Speaking of how teachers are transferential objects, the great Freudian psychiatrist of adolescence August Aichhorn wrote in the middle of the 20th century:

> we know that with a normal child the transference takes place of itself through the kindly efforts of the responsible adult. The teacher in his attitude repeats the situations long familiar to the child, and thereby evokes a parental relationship. He does not maintain this relationship at the same level, but continually deepens it as long as he is the parental substitute. [With a neurotic child] with symptoms of delinquency…, the tendency to transfer his attitude toward his parents to the person in authority is immediately noticeable.[19]

Because the teacher may be so instrumental in helping the child work through these delicate psychosexual dynamics of fusion and separation, Aichhorn thought it imperative that every teacher understand the transference,[20] a point which I have echoed in some of my other work.[21,22] During the Progressive period, some experimental schools dedicated themselves to the appropriate nurturance of the child as he formed his psychosexual identity. Most notable of these was Margaret Naumburg's Children's School—later called the Walden School—and its arts-based curriculum, designed to help the child experience, express, and resolve some of the object-relations problems that defined his earliest interpersonal world. Curriculum, by this view, was primarily a form of therapy.

> In searching for a curriculum that would really nurture independence of thought and spirit, the faculty—at least half of whom had undergone analysis at the urging of Miss

Naumburg—tended to emphasize the arts, arguing that artistic creations serve to bring into conscious life the buried
material of the child's emotional problems.[23]

The primary mission of the teacher at the Children's School was to
relate to the child in a developmentally appropriate way that satisfied
the child's needs for nurturance while at the same time fostering his
growth and autonomy. This is very similar to Nell Noddings's idea of
teaching as care, which in many respects is a transferential, object-
relations pedagogy. Drawing on feminist psychological theory,[24,25]
Noddings's approach to teaching asserts a female propensity for caring.
"In almost all cultures, women seem to develop the capacity to care
more often and more deeply than men.... [T]he hope of moral educators is that both sexes can learn to care." Noddings ultimately elevates
this psychodynamic impulse to the status of a moral imperative for rational dialogue, as we shall see in Chapter 5. Nevertheless, at this point,
it is well to emphasize that Noddings's approach has many psychological as well as organismic roots. This is clear when she claims that

> boys should have care-giving experience. Boys, like girls,
> should attend to the needs of guests, care for smaller chil-
> dren, perform housekeeping chores, and the like. The sup-
> position, from a care perspective, is that the closer we are
> to the intimate physical needs of life, the more likely we are
> to understand its fragility and to feel the pangs of the inner
> "I must"—that stirring of the heart that moves us to re-
> spond to one another.[26]

In sum, where the organismic curriculum is rooted in biology, the
transferential curriculum stems from the personal subconscious and
collective unconscious. For better or worse, the teacher is probably the
object of the student's desires and antipathies regarding his own parents
a good deal more often than that teacher is generally aware of. If the
child comes from a dysfunctional setting (and increasing numbers of
them do), it is all too likely that those hopes and fears may play out in
the classroom in ways that may be difficult, even draining, for both the
student and teacher.[27] The 10-year-old boy who has been beaten into
submission by an authoritarian father may be unresponsive to a male
teacher. Yet the same boy, perhaps also enmeshed in an oedipal relation
with a troubled mother and overly attuned to her psychosexual needs,
may be painfully aware of his female teacher's slightest emotional

shifts and respond to them with a sensitivity which, although initially flattering to the teacher, increasingly disturbs and puzzles her. These different attitudes in the boy may have little to do with the two actual teachers but much to do with the transference. Although teacher education programs do not presently do so, they should consider including discussion of such matters in their curricula, for it is a very rare prospective teacher in a college of education who ever hears a word about the transference and its potential classroom appearances. Teachers who are ignorant of these issues—both in themselves and in their students—run the risk of teaching in ways that are dull or dysfunctional.

We could, for instance, help teachers understand that when a student challenges them in an inappropriate way that seems to go quite beyond the academic point being discussed in class, this might be the result of transference—an emotional assault by the student much less than a conceptual gambit. Teachers also need to know in more than simply a vaguely intuitive way that, especially in adolescent students, "resistance to instruction" can be a healthy sign of the increasing need of children at this developmental stage to sever the ties with the oedipal mother (in a Freudian sense) or the archetypal Devouring Mother (in a Jungian sense) in order to achieve psychospiritual independence. Jung specifically recognized the existence of archetypal transference onto the teacher, calling it "perfectly natural."[28] But by "natural" he clearly did not mean that it is always pleasant and wholesome but simply an inevitable consequence of the asymmetrical power relationship between student and teacher, which resembles the intimacy and power asymmetry between the analyst and analysand.[29]

In previous work I have attempted to illustrate the dynamics and benefits of reflecting upon one's teaching from the archetypal perspective. For instance, I have used archetypal reflectivity to try to make sense out of certain individual and group processes in my own classes. I have probed how and why my students project the archetypes of the trickster, the wise old man, the shadow, the senex, the redeemer, the priest, and the devil onto me as well as probing my own countertransferential responses.[30] I have also discussed what I consider to be the four major archetypes that emerge in the teacher reflectivity literature dealing with the teacher's spiritual sense of calling. Those archetypes are: (1) the teacher as philosopher, (2) the teacher as "federal prophet," (3) the teacher as Zen master, counselor, and mother, and (4) the teacher as priest. I have also examined how possession by an archetype—specifically the archetype of the Great Mother—can lure a fe-

male teacher (and sometimes even a male one) down a perilous path
into professional, emotional, and ethical quicksand.[31]

The Corporate Capitalist Curriculum
and the Crisis of Relationship in the American Classroom

With the growing obsession on higher standardized test scores in
the service of corporate profitability, there is decreasing attention being
given to the experiential and moral needs and capacities of teachers and
students. Instead of being allowed to resolve basic physical and emotional issues at a natural pace, children are increasingly forced to acquire information and cognitive skills at a breakneck speed that runs
roughshod over healthy developmental rhythms. Instead of engaging in
those relational activities that are the most fertile ground for the blos-
soming of the child's early physical, emotional, imaginative and verbal
potentials, he must devote growing numbers of hours, even in the earliest grades, to memorization and acquiring skills that will allow him to
"test well." This collective national fixation upon high scores on norm-
referenced tests is particularly damaging when it comes to the very
young, resulting in what some public health officials are calling "the
new morbidity" among children.

> In the United States...the number of children with a diag-
> nosis of attention deficit disorder (ADD)...combined with
> hyperactivity is growing rapidly. The drug Ritalin is often
> being prescribed for such children. Statistics vary but range
> from 1 million to 1.5 million children in the United States
> now receiving Ritalin.... Whereas some children genuinely
> need help because of constitutional problems in the nervous
> system, many others appear to need help primarily because
> they cannot accommodate to current educational prac-
> tices.[32]

This excessive use of Ritalin and similar drugs in our schools today—those chemicals that constitute a *pharmaceutical extra-
curriculum of control*—is a consequence of our political economy.
Pressured by the demands of corporate capitalism (and whether those
demands are expressed in the rhetoric of neo-liberal educational "reform" or neo-conservative "reform" hardly matters), schools are com-
pelled to treat students as "human capital" to "develop." The consequence is a sad picture of our children in the classroom, depleted and
dispirited from learning skills and performing tasks that are physically

constraining, psychologically irrelevant, and ethically vacuous. And when a child who cannot dance to this frenetic corporate tune begins to act out his resistance in any fashion, he is drugged into submission. Indeed, it has very recently become *illegal* for a child in a British classroom to refuse to take such drugs when they have been prescribed for him—as if the classroom were a state psychiatric ward. The only way to stop these practices and the lifelong damage that will follow in their wake is to attend to the organismic and transferential needs of our children—as indeed most teachers want to do, and continue to do, despite the fact that doing so constantly puts them under the institutional gun.

The Therapeutic Classroom

Therapeutic Progressivism's emphasis on the emotional nurturance of the child continues to underlie many approaches to curriculum.[33] Despite the positive—and in our increasingly troubled society, crucial—aspects of this approach, the object-relations curriculum runs the risk of trapping the student and teacher in an unhealthy transference. I have argued in this chapter that in the preparation of teachers and educational leaders we need to discuss this aspect of classroom interaction. This will help us to become even more effective in identifying and addressing the many complex emotional and moral questions about how best to relate to children in the classroom.

This is a matter of considerable importance considering the fact that so many people become teachers precisely because of the need to enter into relationship with their students but ultimately burnout because those relationships become too emotionally depleting.[34] It is clear that the transferential landscape uniquely provides the theoretical and practical metals that we need to mine in order to construct curricula that are interpersonally rich, emotionally appropriate, and professionally sustaining—and that do not fall under the sway of military-industrial agendas that serve to depersonalize the classroom.

Topics for Discussion

1. In addition to performing their more traditional roles, should public schools become, as Dryfoos maintains, Full Service Schools, where a wide range of physical, psychological and social services are offered not only to the student but also to parents to a much greater extent than they presently are—especially in low-income urban and rural areas?

Some would argue that this would simply be tantamount to "exporting" even more social problems to beleaguered, under-funded schools and teachers than they already have. Others believe this reform would undermine the influence of the family by shifting responsibility for the psychosocial development of the child to the schools to an even greater extent than presently exists. Some accuse the plan of being a disingenuous attempt to introduce socialism through the educational back door. Conversely, others assert that, at least since the days of Jane Addams and her Settlement Houses in Chicago in the late 19th century, this far-reaching vision of education has not only existed but has represented the noblest example of American educational activism in addressing social problems. Still others claim that, regardless of the historical and philosophical arguments for or against Full Service Schools, they are simply a practical necessity to meet the needs of children who live in difficult economic, familial, and cultural circumstances, arguing that without such measures these children will add to the already swelling numbers of the growing American underclass. Where do you stand on this issue?

2. It was suggested in Chapter 2 that every teacher should know at least the rudiments of the transference and counter-transference in order to deal with instances of these processes in his classroom. Would such knowledge actually be useful to the teacher, or would it instead inappropriately draw the teacher into a therapeutic role which he is not really fit to fill? Given the greater life experience and teaching experience of many prospective school administrators as compared with many prospective teachers, might it be better to examine these psychodynamic topics only with graduate education students? With both graduate and undergraduate students, but differently with each group? With neither group? Why?

3. The curricula of the Walden Schools as well as Rudolf Steiner's Waldorf Schools emphasize art to help students explore and resolve psychospiritual issues. Are such curricula appropriate, or even possible, in the public schools given the different types and degrees of political and parental pressures as well as legal and institutional constraints on public schools? Can such curricula be adapted to public schools? If so, how? And even if they can, does access to such curricula tend to be limited to wealthier students and thus ultimately serve (as Marxian

educational scholars claim) as just another form of political and cultural reproduction through educational means?

Topics for Research

1. Analyze Dryfoos' book *Full Service Schools* in terms of its suitability to troubled areas in your city and/or state.

2. What has been the progress of the Full Service School agenda since the appearance of Dryfoos's book in 1994?

3. Review the literature on Noddings's idea of teaching as care. What are some of the major advantages and disadvantages of this view of teaching as discussed in this literature?

Notes: Chapter 2

1. H. Kohut, *The Search for the Self: Selected Writings of Heinz Kohut, 1950-1978* (Madison, Conn.: International Universities Press, 1978).
2. R. Greenson, "The Working Alliance and the Transference Neurosis," in *Essential Papers on Transference,* ed. A. Esman (New York: New York University Press, 1990), 151.
3. S. Freud, "The Dynamics of Transference," in *Essential Papers on Transference,* ed. A. Esman (New York: New York University Press, 1990), 32.
4. Freud, 31.
5. H. Marcuse, *Eros and Civilization: A Philosophical Inquiry into Freud* (New York: Vintage, 1962).
6. C. Jung, *Memories, Dreams, Reflections* (New York: Vintage, 1965), 9.
7. E. Jung and M.-L. von Franz, *The Grail Legend* (Boston: Sigo Press, 1986), 36-37.
8. E. Edinger, *Ego and Archetype: Individuation and the Religious Function of the Psyche* (Baltimore: Penguin Press, 1973).
9. C. Mayes, "Personal and Archetypal Transference and Counter-transference in the Classroom," *Encounter: Education for Meaning and Social Justice* 15(1) (2002): 36.
10. E. Neumann, *The Origins and History of Consciousness, vol. 1* (New York: Harper & Brothers, 1954).
11. M. Woodman, "Transference and Countertransference in Analysis Dealing with Eating Disorders," in *Transference/Countertransference,* eds. N. Schwartz-Salant and M. Stein (Wilmette, Illinois: Chiron Publications, 1995), 53-66.

12. B. Woolstein, "The Pluralism of Perspectives on Countertransference," in *Essential Papers on Counter-Transference,* ed. B. Wolstein (New York: New York University Press, 1988): 339-354.

13. M. Sedlak, "Attitudes, Choices, and Behavior: School Delivery of Health and Social Services," in *Learning from the Past: What History Teaches us about School Reform,* eds. D. Ravitch and M. Vinovskis (Baltimore, Maryland: The Johns Hopkins University Press, 1995): 57-94.

14. J. Dryfoos, *Full-Service Schools: A Revolution in Health and Social Services for Children, Youth, and Families* (San Francisco: Jossey-Bass, 1994).

15. L. Stone, "The Transference-Countertransference Complex," in *Essential Papers on Counter-Transference,* ed. B. Wolstein (New York: New York University Press, 1988), 273.

16. M. Spiegelman, *Psychotherapy as a Mutual Process* (Tempe, Arizona: New Falcon Publications, 1996).

17. M. Cohen, "Countertransference and Anxiety," ed. B. Wolstein, *Essential Papers on Counter-Transference* (New York: New York University Press, 1988), 70.

18. I. Coriat as quoted in L. Cremin, *The Transformation of the School: Progressivism in American Education, 1876-1957* (New York: Vintage Press, 1964), 210.

19. A. Aichhorn, "The Transference." In *Essential Papers on Transference,* ed. A. Esman (New York: New York University Press, 1990), 97.

20. Ibid., 98, 106.

21. C. Mayes, "The Use of Contemplative Practices in Teacher Education," *Encounter: Education for Meaning and Social Justice* 11(3) (1998): 17-31.

22. Mayes, "Personal and Archetypal," 2002.

23. L. Cremin, *The Transformation of the School: Progressivism in American Education, 1876-1957* (New York: Vintage Press, 1964), 213.

24. M. Belenky, B. Clinchy, N. Goldberger and J. Tarule, *Women's Way of Knowing* (New York: Guilford Press, 1986).

25. N. Chodorow, *The Reproduction of Mothering: Psychoanalysis and the Sociology of Gender* (Berkeley, University of California Press, 1978).

26. N. Noddings, "Care and Moral Education," in *Critical Conversations in the Philosophy of Education,* ed. W. Kohli (New York: Routledge, 1995), 143.

27. R. Bullough, Jr., *Uncertain Lives: Children of Hope, Teachers of Promise* (New York: Teachers College, Columbia University, 2001).

28. C. Jung, *The Psychology of the Transference* (Princeton, New Jersey: Princeton University Press, 1992), 8, fn. 16.

29. B. Wolstein, ed., *Essential Papers on Counter-Transference* (New York: New York University Press, 1988), 64-83.

30. C. Mayes, "Reflecting on the Archetypes of Teaching," *Teaching Education* 10(2) (1999): 3-16.

31. C. Mayes, "The Teacher as an Archetype of Spirit," *Journal of Curriculum Studies,* 34(6) (2002): 699-718.
32. J. Almon, "From Cognitive Learning to Creative Thinking," in *Education, Information, and Transformation: Essays on Learning and Thinking,* ed. J. Kane (Columbus, Ohio: Merrill, 1999), 254.
33. D. Whitmore, *Psychosynthesis in Education: A Guide to the Joy of Learning* (Rochester, Vermont: Destiny Books, 1986).
34. M. Huberman, M. Gronauer and J. Marti, *The Lives of Teachers* (New York: Teachers College Press, 1989).

3

THE CONCRETE-AFFILIATIVE LANDSCAPE

Pivotal Themes in Chapter 3

* The Concrete-Affiliative curriculum as concerned with the development of the ability to understand *concrete* operational rules and primary *affiliative* (i.e., social) roles.

* Recent theories about how students' concepts change, or resist change, in the course of instruction.

* Theories that focus exclusively on individual perception and cognition in fixed developmental terms. The social constructivist challenge to Piaget with its insistence that all knowledge is mediated by the various social contexts in which the individual exists.

* Vygotsky's General Genetic Law of Cultural Development. Language as the primary affiliative mediator of knowledge. The Sapir-Whorf Hypothesis that our linguistic systems largely determine how we see and interpret the world. Halliday's and Bernstein's Systemic linguistics and its pedagogical applications. Culturally sensitive pedagogies as essentially affiliative. The affiliative vision of the classroom

culture as a "community of learners." Vygotsky's Zone of Proximal Development.

* The roots of multiculturalism in the affiliative curriculum. The various racial, ethnic, socioeconomic, gendered, and volitional (i.e., Jocks, Preps, Goths) subcultures of students at a school site, and how these subcultures form an "affiliative extracurriculum" that can subvert the official curriculum of the school. Reference-group theory.

* The affiliative values curriculum: its uses and limitations.

* Concrete-Affiliative psychological dysfunctions, their educational manifestations, and how to address them pedagogically. Script pathologies (negative internal "scripts" about herself that the student consciously and unconsciously has). Helping students learn how to "re-script."

* Concrete-Affiliative issues as central to the more conservative wing of Progressivism in the early 20th century. William Torrey Harris and his Durkeheimian/Hegelian vision of education in the service of the state. The ideological roots of certain tensions within Progressivism.

"Rules and Roles"

The issues of the affiliative landscape roughly correspond to those of the upper reaches of Piaget's concrete-operational developmental stage and the lower reaches of his formal-operational stage. In concrete operations (such as striation, sequencing, and conservation, as Piaget called them) the focus is on rules governing the basic operations of the physical world. Early formal operations deal (among other things) with the dawning awareness of the rules governing the social world. On the concrete-affiliative landscape, then, the developmental task is to understand basic physical *rules* and rudimentary social *roles*. Wilber thus calls this developmental terrain the "rules/roles" landscape.[1]

On this landscape a person begins to define herself as (for instance) a student at a particular school, or as a member of a particular religious organization, club, or racial or socioeconomic group. Traditional developmental theory has identified early adolescence as the time when this type of self-concept starts to take on recognizable form. Not surprisingly, then, it is also then that a child's peers typically begin to assume increased significance in her life—greater than that of the teacher or classroom in most cases, and greater even than the family in some.[2] Indeed, one of the most important educational implications of affiliative dynamics (particularly during the adolescent years) is that if the norms of the child's primary social "reference groups" run counter to the official curriculum of her classroom, those norms may well become a subcultural "shadow curriculum" that can undermine the official curriculum.[3]

Landscape Three Curriculum and Instruction in Conceptual Change Theory

Much of the research in the growing field of conceptual change theory deals with how children form, test, and change concepts about the physical operation of the world—often quite "unscientifically"! Let us look at how the rules/roles perspective sheds light on conceptual change.

In its examination of so called "primitive universals" (or inborn ways that people tend to filter and process the raw data of their space-time worlds), conceptual change theory lends some support to Piagetian psychology, which posits the existence of "cognitive primitives" and their subsequent development in each individual in a strictly sequenced evolution. Nussbaum in his research regarding children's ideas and images of "the earth as a cosmic body" noted that there do indeed seem to be *a priori* epistemological structures that are: 1) "naïve," 2) more or less constant over cultures, 3) ultimately situated in the individual, and 4) central to how children interpret their physical world.[4] Moreover, children, using these structures, can resist and reinterpret more "mature" scientific concepts. A child who hears that the world is round and that *that* is why a boat can sail around it may interpret this information to mean that the earth is still flat, but that it is now a circular disk, the boat going around the disk by following a river around its circumference. In both children and adults, such "central commitments," as Posner and his associates call them,[5] make up one's "conceptual ecology" regarding the world of time and space.[6] Not only do these cognitive primitives span cultures, according to some researchers, but they also seem to cut across time. In his historical review of theories of motion, McCloskey found a "close correspondence between the medieval impetus theory and the naive theory held by [his] subjects...."[7] If "ontogeny recapitulates phylogeny" (that is, if individual development mirrors the

general evolution of the species) even weakly, perhaps it does so because cognitive primitives, latent in the individual psyche, can emerge
and develop only in the context of a larger historical unfolding. In general, however, early conceptual change theory in the 1980s tended to
view learning mostly as an individual phenomenon divorced from social contexts.

An example of this is Bereiter's attempt to solve the conundrum of
"the learning paradox": How can we learn something that we don't already know? For if we did not already know about it at some level, at
least to some degree, how would we have any basis at all upon which
even to construct a first question about it?[8] In handling this problem,
Bereiter does not look at interpersonal processes that might be involved
but focuses upon individual cognition. Winn, too, looks at metacognition (or thinking about thinking) as an individual act performed by the
"metacognitively able student," presumably in isolation.[9] This "interpretive individualism" does not preclude group activity in the classroom, but it does make it secondary and merely optional. This "individual constructivism" (as I call it) has been roundly criticized by the
"social constructivists," who offer an alternate explanation of how a
person understands the rules and enacts the roles of her world. The social constructivist view elegantly unites the concrete and affiliative
realms by asserting that *children learn about their physical world in the
context of their larger identity-formation as social beings.*

Beginning with a very different set of epistemological assumptions
from those of Piaget, Vygotsky, a Marxist, claimed that it simply
makes no sense to speak of a student, or anyone for that matter, in isolation—apart from the collective.[10] For what we call "consciousness" is
no more (and no less!) than a specific node of awareness which has
been produced, and is constantly being reshaped, by a certain interplay
of social forces. We *are* our constantly shifting, always relative *position* in the social systems that, literally, make up our lives. *Even such
apparently straightforward knowledge as that of basic physical entities
and processes is socially mediated,* according to the social constructivists. Hence, there are no *a priori* cognitive absolutes that unfold in the
individual in an invariable sequence, as Piaget claimed. Curricularists
who operate on these assumptions are, insisted Vygotsky, merely the
dupes of a capitalist ideology that would be all too well served by a de-
nial of the social basis of reality and a reification of "individualistic"
consciousness. Consciousness is situational from start to finish. It is
awareness *of* a situation. It is also awareness produced *by* a situation.

Not only that, but *being* in a situation also has performative dimensions, for, as Leont'ev insisted, *to be* in a situation is necessarily *to have* and *do* some kind of role or task in it. We only exist in terms of our *social work*—an unmistakably Marxist tenet, of course, which reflects the Soviet origin of Vygotskyan social constructivism.

Over the past 20 years or so, curriculum theory has worked out many of the educational implications of social constructivism. A good example of this is the work of Brown and his associates in a study entitled "Situated Cognition and the Culture of Learning." As they put it, "situations might be said to co-produce knowledge through activity."[11] According to hard social constructivism, such pioneering conceptual change theorists as Hewson[12] were wrong in looking at the child's awareness of its physical world as evidence of primitive absolutes— i.e., "generalized knowledge"—from which increasingly complex concrete and formal operations would evolve as a developmental inevitability. Instead, we need to look at all knowledge as situation-specific competency and make our curricula hinge on the reality of interpersonal dynamics, for if a child learns anything, she will learn it in social contexts—or not at all.

In fact, ask the social constructivists, does not memory itself, one of the most important functions of cognition, amount to just this—the recollection of specific *situations?* Thinking is situational at its very core, for at the very core of thinking is memory, and memory is of *things* in *social contexts.* As Vygotsky wrote,

> if you ask a child to tell you what a snail is, he will say that it is little, it slithers and it sticks out its foot; if you ask him to tell you what a grandmother is, he is likely to reply, "She has a soft lap." In both cases, the child gives a very clear summary of the impressions which the topic has made upon him and which he recollects. The content of the thinking act in the child when defining such concepts is determined not so much by the logical structures of the concept itself as by the child's concrete recollections. It is syncretic in character and reflects the fact that the child's thinking depends first of all on his memory.[13]

How does this mediating process take place? To answer this question, it will be necessary to look at what Vygotsky termed the General Genetic Law of Cultural Development. After that we will turn to some recent developments in sociolinguistics which operate on the assumption that the primary origins and functions of language are social. An infant sees a pretty object that he wants. He grasps in its direction. His mother sees this and gets the object for him. A simple situation, to be sure, but one which for Vygotsky is a treasure chest of implications. For when "the mother comes to the child's aid and realizes his movement indicates something," observed Vygotsky,

> the situation changes fundamentally. Pointing becomes a gesture for others. The child's unsuccessful attempt engenders a reaction not from the object he seeks but *from another person.* Consequently, the primary meaning of that unsuccessful grasping movement is established by others.... At this juncture there occurs a change in the movement's function: From an object-oriented movement it becomes a movement aimed at another person, a means of establishing relations.... Its meaning and functions are created first by an objective situation and then by people who surround the child.[14]

Vygotsky summarized the process thus:

> 1) an operation that initially represents an external activity is reconstructed and begins to occur internally.... 2) An interpersonal process is transformed into an intrapersonal one.... 3) The transformation of an interpersonal process into an intrapersonal one is the result of a long series of developmental events."[15]

This is the General Genetic Law of Cultural Development. Perhaps the most intriguing item in Vygotsky's list is the second one, where an interpersonal event becomes an internal event. To understand what this means, try to think a thought without talking to yourself internally. The reason you cannot do this, said Vygotsky, is because our thoughts *are* our language. And our language is precisely the written and spoken symbols that we use *to interact with each other.* Thus, when you think, you are engaging in an internal dialogue between yourself and your imagined auditor. Or better, you *are* that dialogue between the internal speaker and auditor. You *are* a social process.

Despite Vygotsky's insistence upon the social essence of self, thought, and speech (ultimately the same things in a sense), it would be wrong to conclude that Vygotsky claimed that the individual's internal experience of a situation is merely an introjected photocopy of an external social situation. There is indeed an "isomorphism" between the external and internal realms.[16] However, what is most interesting to Vygotsky, and to the social constructivist in general, is how, through a series of transformations of consciousness, the individual makes the situation cognitively and existentially her own.[17] "We shall," said Vygotsky, "place this transition from a social influence outside the individual to a social influence within the individual at the center of our research and try to elucidate the most important moments from which it arises."[18] To Piaget, *speech follows cognitive development that has already taken place within the individual.* To Vygotsky, *speech is the social tool that allows cognitive development to take place at all.* Put more simply, for Piaget individual thought precedes speech; for Vygotsky, the social tool of speech engenders thought. To pursue in even more detail the social constructivist position about language and learning on the concrete-affiliative landscape, let us turn to the Systemic linguistics of Halliday[19] and Bernstein,[20] two sociolinguists whose works have had marked effects on learning theory in the last several decades.

Systemic linguistics insists that the socialization of the child is brought about primarily by language. The child learns society, as it were, by learning society's language, says Bernstein in one of his early works wherein he traced the linguistic development of a boy named Nigel from birth to about four years old.

> As the child learns his speech or, in the terms used here, learns specific codes which regulate his verbal acts, he learns the requirements of his social structure. The experience of the child is transformed by the learning which is generated by his own apparently voluntary acts of speech. The social structure becomes the substratum of his experience essentially through the consequences of the linguistic process. From this point of view, every time the child speaks or listens, the social structure of which he is a part is reinforced in him and his social identity is constrained. The social structure becomes the child's psychological reality by the shaping of his acts of speech.[21]

Halliday picked up this theme when he wrote that before she ever comes to school, the child has learned about her social universe because she has learned how to talk. The child "has accumulated a vast store of information about these things," which is all the more amazing because "it is not as if anyone teaches a child the mysteries of the social system," yet the child does have this knowledge very early on, "and [s]he has learnt it largely through language: through the small change of everyday speech, the casual linguistic interaction at home, the street and the neighbourhood."[22] The child's internalization of social meanings and *mores*, on one hand, and her waxing facility with language, on the other hand, are so organically interwoven that it is pointless to try to say where one leaves off and the other begins. To see how social "semiotics" (or, the social meaning-system) takes root and grows in a child is in many ways equivalent to seeing how her language grows.

The concrete-affiliative perspective offers us the clearest vision, then, about how language grows and identity forms in the context of proto-scientific rules and basic social roles. Two major curricular implications follow from this third-landscape vantage-point on the formation of language, thought, and identity in the child—implications that relate not only to the child but all learners.

Culturally Sensitive Curricula

The first implication is that generalized, context-free knowledge, although able to serve certain limited functions, is not essentially what learning is about in this socio-cognitive territory. As Brown and his associates claimed, "activity and situations are integral to cognition and learning.... [B]y ignoring the situated nature of cognition, education defeats its own goal of providing useable, robust knowledge."[23] Lively and durable knowledge is learned not as sterile abstractions with no relation to the situation at hand; it comes, rather, from grasping ideas and mastering skills that are organically related to the context in which one presently finds oneself and the roles one is playing—or learning to play. Mariana Hewson has pointed out that sensitivity to cultural affiliation must even characterize teaching the so-called "context-free, hard sciences," and that this is especially so in developing countries, where

> group differences which may be based on history, religion, geographic location, socioeconomic status, or culture, may well be factors that play a role in the development of particular conceptions.... [S]tudents do not enter the classroom as a *tabula rasa,* but come to instruction with a knowledge base which may prove to be in conflict with the subject matter being taught. In such cases, their learning of West-

ern science may be hindered, and students' alternative conceptions may persist in the face of instruction.[24]

This is particularly true when it comes to issues regarding language and literacy, for the interaction between literacy and cultural identity is psychosocially complex and emotionally charged. Literacy "in large part, involves facility in manipulating the symbols that codify and represent the values, beliefs, and norms of the culture—the same symbols that incorporate the culture's representations of reality."[25] The concrete-affiliative ramifications of this fact are many for the teacher and curricularist.

> *Becoming* literate means developing mastery not only over processes, but also over the symbolic media of the culture—the ways in which cultural values, beliefs, and norms are represented. *Being* literate implies actively maintaining contact with collective symbols and the processes by which they are represented. Thus, literacy goes beyond superficial transaction with a printed or written page and extends into the ability to comprehend and manipulate its symbols—the words and concepts—and to do so in a culturally appropriate manner.... So it is that literacy instruction can constitute a profound form of socialization.... In the case of a majority child attending majority schools, this is essentially transparent in that neither educator nor pupil need consciously attend to the ways in which they are engaged in a process of cultural transmission.... For members of cultural minorities, the potential conflicts will be greater, as will the salience of group membership.[26]

Au and Kawakami have shown how powerful such culturally congruent approaches to literacy can be in a short but intriguing article entitled "'Talk Story' and Learning to Read." In it, they recount their experiences teaching reading to low-SES Hawaiian children. These authors wanted to devise culturally sensitive ways of teaching standard content. Casting off what they call "conventional school practices" in reading instruction, the authors decided instead to "talk story." "Talk story" is

> an important nonschool speech event for Hawaiian children.... During talk story, the children present rambling narratives about personal experiences, often joking and teasing one another. The chief characteristic of talk story is

joint performance, or the cooperative production of responses by two or more speakers.... Thus, there are few times during talk story when just one child monopolizes the right to speak.... [W]hat is important to Hawaiian children in talk story is not *individual performance* in speaking, which is often important in the [traditional] classroom, but *group performance* speaking.... [T]alk story-like reading lessons...are not exactly like nonschool talk story events. They are easily recognized as reading lessons in purpose, because discussion is focused closely on the text and text-related topics. In practice, then, talk story-like reading lessons are actually hybrid events, having the same goals for instruction as other classroom reading comprehension lessons, but making use of different rules for participation.[27]

The Classroom as a Community of Learners

In addition to the multicultural pedagogies that grow out of third landscape soil, a second major educational implication of social constructivism is that *all* learning is a social act, involving all of the child's primary generalizations about her socio-physical world. This is simply to make the commonsense point that we generally learn best when we learn with others in situations that we enjoy and with things that we like. We solve problems more creatively when we join our skills with those of others to create a whole which is greater than the sum of its parts. Herein lies the power of Vygotsky's idea of the *Zone of Proximal Development.* This is the idea that cognitive growth occurs in the form of "development as determined through problem solving under adult guidance or *in collaboration with more capable peers.*"[28] Development is not "passive maturation," as Vygotsky characterized Piaget's view. It is dynamic, task-specific, and involves group effort and mutual instruction. For this reason, Resnick argued that the most successful educational environments "involve socially shared intellectual work, and they are organized around joint accomplishment of tasks, so that elements of the skill take on meaning in the context of the whole."[29] "We must concern ourselves much less with symbol manipulation," said Resnick, echoing the "project-centered" Progressive pedagogies of the earlier part of the 20th century, "and much more with contextualized reasoning."[30] But this can only occur if the teacher provides "authentic activities in which students, mutually inspired, can jointly interrogate and invent their communal world(s)."[31]

Landscape Three, Reference Group Theory, and Academic Failure

The concrete-affiliative landscape is the plain on which many curriculum theories and instructional practices die because they run counter to the demands of certain roles that the child perceives as central to her cultural identity. In the terms of educational sociology, this is an instance of the "contextual effects of primary socialization" undermining the official curriculum. As Bocock has written, "students respond to the norms, performance standards, and rewards that are salient to the student body of which they are members, or to certain other students who serve as role models."[32] Reference group theory forwards the simple but powerful idea that

> people behave according to the norms of their membership groups. In the case of racial or socioeconomic context, [this] refers to the "unofficial" norms of the school. These are different from the "official" teacher-directed norms. [Reference group theory thus helps us understand] the values of youth cultures, a set of contextual norms that are often anti-intellectual and that act as an obstacle to learning in most cases.[33]

Wilber has called these primary-role issues "mythic-membership" issues because they involve accepting the foundational narratives (or *myths*) and fulfilling the social roles that make one a *member* of a particular group.[34] As Coleman demonstrated over four decades ago in his classic study of peer groups in schools, *The Adolescent Society,* the mythic-membership issues that define and drive adolescents and their various peer-groups frequently sabotage the official curriculum in complex and highly effective ways.[35]

An illustration of this is found in Wax and his associates' analysis of the failure of Great Society educational reforms among Oglala Sioux children in reservation schools in the 1960s.[36] Wax examined the process of subordinate-culture resistance to the values of a dominant culture as those values form the subtext of the official curriculum that is being taught by teachers who are themselves members of the dominant group. Until the age of about eight, these Indian children generally did quite well academically; after that time, however, they came to understand that embedded in the official curriculum of the public schools was the hidden message that White, Anglo-Saxon, middle-class culture was superior to their own, and that to succeed academically and socially would entail renouncing their Sioux identity. Out of this growing collective awareness various peer groups arose that functioned, both on the school grounds and off, to discourage anyone from trying to succeed academically—and to ostracize the occasional child who did.

A decade later, Paul Willis, studying middle-class boys in an English school in *Learning to Labour,* demonstrated that the "lads," as they called themselves, interpreted academic success as a threat to virtually every norm of the proletariat subculture from which they came. Ranging from matters of discourse to intercourse, the lads perceived (usually quite accurately) that the ideas and behaviors that the school and its staff advocated contrasted sharply with those that determined their cultural identities.[37]

Margaret Gibson[38] advanced this line of research concerning peer pressure and academic success in the 1980s by employing Ogbu's notion of "sojourning" versus "caste-like" minorities in her analysis of the differential performance of the children of Sikh immigrants and Mexican American children at a central California high school.[39] What she found was that the different attitudes of the Sikh and Mexican American peer groups regarding schooling were largely responsible for the contrasting academic performance of those two groups. Moreover, these peer-group attitudes resulted from each group's status as either a sojourning minority or caste-like minority.

Sojourning (or "immigrant") minorities are those which have just arrived in the U.S. They still have an intact culture and language upon arriving here; they generally view the United States as a land of great opportunity relative to their limited socio-economic opportunities "back home"; and many comfort themselves with the idea that if things ever get too culturally difficult in the United States, they can go back home. Sojourning-minority families and students, therefore, tend to see schools as essentially (although far from completely) positive places which do not necessarily pose an overwhelming threat to their cultures. Accordingly, the peer groups that form among these students generally value and encourage academic success among their members. There is a relatively low degree of dissonance among their cultural affiliations and the culture of the school, and the result (for the most part) is academic success.

On the other hand are the "caste-like" minorities—African Americans, Hispanic Americans, and Native Americans being the most prominent. These minorities are different in almost every essential respect from their sojourning counterparts: their culture has been assaulted in various ways over generations of systematic oppression and exclusion; their language has been denigrated by the dominant culture as at best inferior and at worst a sociolinguistic disease that needs to be eradicated by the strong medicine of English-only policies; their experience of the presumed economic bounty of the U.S. is what sociologists call "perceived relative deprivation"—that is, they feel that they have only the remotest chances, if any, of ever truly experiencing the American dream that so many others (mostly from the dominant group) seem to be enjoying. And unlike, say, the immigrant student from Hong Kong, the Native American student obviously does not have a "home" to return to. This *is* her home.

Understandably, these students and their parents often view schools as the pedagogical agent of an unjust society and experience a wide range of emotions regarding public schooling, from embarrassed unease to conflicted uncertainty to seething bitterness.[40] The peer groups that form among these caste-like students in the schools can be psychologically, socially, and sometimes even physically punishing to the member who succeeds academically. The peer group thus demands an alternative "subcultural curriculum" of academic failure which its members must follow as the only subculturally legitimate response to the institutional curriculum. Resistance and failure thus become the students' primary means of exposing the cultural irrelevancy and danger of the official curriculum—and indeed all of what they believe to be the educational system's hollow promises.

In addition to these concrete-affiliative interpretations of minority-student failure, several other interpretations along the same lines are also prominent. For instance, it has been noted that lower SES black students often do significantly better academically in Catholic schools than public schools.[41] This improvement may be because Catholic schools are better than the public schools (especially inner city ones) at inculcating and reinforcing those basic rules and roles in the child so necessary to psychosocial efficacy.

> Thus it appears that Catholic schools are able to overcome this general incompatibility between educational quality and equality. Coleman, Hoffer, and Kilgore (1982) concluded that this two-fold effectiveness of Catholic schools was due to a combination of stronger academic demands, a more disciplined and orderly environment, [school uniforms that minimize visible SES differences among students], and less tracking or differentiation of students. In later work, Coleman and Hoffer (1987) argue that these

> schools policies are the result of a more effective authority
> and control structure that is made possible through the exis-
> tence of functional and values communities that are shared
> by parents, students and teachers in Catholic schools.[42]

The relative absence of tracking, the wearing of school uniforms, the sharing of values (and their consistent enforcement), and a school spirit in which every child is seen as valuable and capable—all of these elements come together to form a concrete-affiliative school culture that the child and her parents may now see as a solid, legitimate, and positive cultural option for the student. Parents and children may "buy into" this academic culture because it not only does not pose a threat to their subcultural identities but may actually *become* one of those identities. To be sure, higher order socio-cognitive dynamics will eventually need to be stressed at such a school, but this will happen all the more readily as the school culture itself becomes one of the student's mythic-membership commitments.

Ironically, it is also for concrete-affiliative reasons that such alternative routes to academic success for marginalized students sometimes do *not* work. In attempting to understand why so many inner-city black families do not send their children to the suburban schools which voucher programs would enable them to attend, Wells and Crain found that "what is most striking about the city students and their discussions of why they choose to stay in their neighborhood schools is the degree to which they are attracted to that which is familiar and comfortable."[43] These students also do not want to abandon their "comfort zones" because of their suspicion that they will experience various forms of bigotry once they leave the enclaves of cultural safety that their communities represent for them. So powerful is the pull of mythic-membership, in brief, that, in order to retain one's membership status, one may choose to remain in an oppressive situation. These dynamics also help us understand why African American students (especially African American *males*) in integrated classes often show only slight improvement academically but decline in terms of self-esteem.[44] We are fundamentally social creatures who spend a good deal of our lives seeking each other out in various ways and diverse corners of the concrete-affiliative landscape. Educational scenarios that do not accommodate this fact will almost always fight an uphill battle.

Mythic Membership and the "Values Curriculum"

As she learns to fill the roles of the third landscape, the individual also begins to understand that those roles are not "set in stone"—that one can occupy various roles and that a certain role can mean different things to different people. Nevertheless, this understanding—still in its earliest formative stages—is quite limited at this point. Indeed, according to developmental theorists such as Kohlberg, few people ever fully attain the capacity to venture very far beyond the narrow circles of concrete-affiliative conventionality.[45] Kohlberg's developmental model of "moral reasoning" has been charged with having a male, Eurocentric bias regarding what constitutes "normal" cognitive and ethical development, yet it has nevertheless been highly influential in the construction of many values curricula. Therefore, it is necessary to spend some time looking at the Kohlbergian picture of the development of the ability to think through moral dilemmas. The model moves from what Kohlberg has called "pre-conventional" moral reasoning to "conventional" moral reasoning and finally—for a few people—to "post-conventional" moral reasoning. Examining Kohlberg's hierarchy in terms of the three landscapes that we have already visited will help to clarify it and understand its educational implications.

A person at the pre-conventional level of moral reasoning is operating on organismic and transferential ground. Responding merely to the prospect of rudimentary physical and emotional rewards and punishments, a person at this stage judges the appropriateness or inappropriateness of an act on the basis of whether or not that act will immediately result in basic forms of pleasure or pain. Stealing a cookie is bad because, if you get caught, mommy will call you a bad girl and spank you. But if you don't get caught, stealing the cookie is good because chocolate chips are so delicious! (By the way, this example should not lead us to believe that pre-conventional moral reasoning exists only in children. There are even presidents of the United States who seem to believe that burglary and vandalism of the opposite party's headquarters or wanton sexual behavior in the Oval Office are bad only if you get caught doing it. There has been some talk lately of the post-modern presidency, but perhaps we should be more concerned with the pre-conventional president.)

Conventional moral reasoning, the next step up in Kohlberg's ethical hierarchy, rests squarely on the affiliative assumption that something is good if it results in social approval and bad if it results in social censure. Affiliative curricula prize attitudes and behaviors that most members of the society believe to be necessary for its smooth functioning. For example, theft is morally unacceptable because people will think that you are bad if they discover that you have done it. At a slightly higher affiliative level of conventional moral reasoning, theft is also bad because "our society" could not function smoothly if property rights were not honored.

Chapters 4 and 5, containing the interpretive-procedural curriculum and the Existentialist curriculum, deal with the final Kohlbergian levels of moral reasoning—the post-conventional stage—so a full discussion of that stage must await those chapters. Suffice it to say at this juncture that post-conventional moral reasoning goes beyond affiliative, socially constructed norms because it discovers and follows so-called "universal moral principles" that (it is claimed) span all (or at least, most) cultures and periods. It thereby claims to transcend the instrumental-advantage perspective of pre-conventional reasoning and the social-harmony perspective of conventional reasoning. For our purposes at this point, it is enough to understand that many values curricula in the schools are designed to help the child transition smoothly from what Wilber calls the bio/ego-centrism of preconventional moral reasoning on the organismic and transferential landscapes to the more socially functional realms of conventional moral reasoning on the concrete-affiliative landscape.[46]

Although the person on the third, affiliative landscape is learning how to take perspectives on roles *within* her own social environment, she cannot yet relativize the value of that environment in comparison with other, very different social systems. This is the limitation of many values-inculcation curricula: they simply support the political *status quo*. That is to say, the student can now begin to understand that she could be both a worker in a factory or the CEO of a major corporation, depending upon the circumstances of her birth, the nature of her education, and the degree to which she has applied herself to achieving corporate success. She can even understand what it would take for her to move from worker to owner status, and to start making the necessary steps to accomplish that goal. What she *cannot* do from this vantage point is question the corporate system *as such* in which she is embedded, nor can she critique the extreme socioeconomic divisions that it contains, for that is "just how things are" in "my society," which is, by definition, "the best society." To go beyond that point of view would require crossing over into the fourth and fifth landscapes, where, as we shall see, one learns not only to understand one's own system but to see it as relative to alternative systems which may, in some or even many respects, be better than one's own.

It is in this light that we can better understand such high school history books as Harold Rugg's *Changing Governments and Changing Cultures* (1932)[47] and, later, Howard Zinn's (1990) *People's History of the United States*.[48] These works were unique in the history of American history textbooks in that they asked the student to transcend the strictly affiliative belief that American history and its governing ethos of capitalist individualism are somehow beyond reproach—beyond the need for serious critique and reform. What Rugg and Zinn both attempted was to challenge students to rise above the socio-centric bounds of their affiliative, nationalist assumption that the United States was so specially favored that radically critiquing it should be—quite literally—unthinkable.

Between the Affiliative and Interpretive Landscapes

Some people and curricula on the third landscape do occasionally cross over into the next curricular landscape—namely, the interpretive one. As we shall see in much greater detail in the next chapter, the goal of many "classical" curricula is to encourage students to relinquish their local, concrete perspectives in order to achieve less context-specific ones. The ability to see oneself and one's groups from multiple perspectives is a momentous change, but it certainly does not happen all at once, nor does everyone develop this skill to the same extent. It is a continuum, with some people able to socially decenter almost at will, others only occasionally, and some seemingly unable to ever do so.[49] Where the narcissistic personality disorders are an extreme form of the inability to decenter personally (that is, to leave the first and second landscapes), xenophobia is the inability to decenter socially (to cross over from the third to the fourth landscape).

For one who is able to do so, however, the burgeoning capacity to decenter emotionally and socially also begins to extend to cognitive and moral domains. Such a person is learning how to take multiple perspectives on many cognitive and moral issues. Moving from Piaget's concrete operations to formal operations, she is now growing ready for what Eisner calls the cognitive-developmentalist curriculum, which we may therefore locate somewhere between the affiliative and interpretive landscapes.[50] According to standard developmental theory, these changes begin at the farthest reaches of the concrete-affiliative domain because of the embryonic emergence (at about twelve years old in most standard developmental theories) of hypothetico-deductive reasoning and the search for categorical truths.

> Unlike the concrete operational child, the adolescent is able to approach a problem by trying to imagine all the possible relationships among items in a given body of data. Then, through a process that combines logical analysis and experimental verification, he or she can determine which of the possible relationships actually holds true. In short, the adolescent becomes more capable of hypothetico-deductive reasoning, which is much like the reasoning of the scientist.[51]

In other words, although the child is still largely socio-centric, she is beginning to rise above her local affiliations. She also begins to be able to take the point-of-view of her dialogical partner—although usually only to the extent that that other person shares her social standards and values.[52] This "plate tectonic" tension on the border of the third and fourth landscape can result in psychic earthquakes for the person who is making her first attempts at crossing over. To discuss how the teacher can address these problems, let us turn to the work of the psychotherapists Aaron Beck and Weishaar[53] and Judith Beck.[54]

Some Concrete-Affiliative Dysfunctions— and Their Educational Implications

According to script theory, as one develops through adolescence she internalizes many rule/role "scripts" about who she and others are and should be. These scripts become the criteria against which she evaluates herself and others on the third landscape. When a person's scripts are realistic, appropriate, and productive, then she can negotiate her psychosocial world with relative ease. However, if those scripts are unrealistic, impractical and destructive, then the result is neurosis. A therapeutically powerful way of understanding and treating neurosis, in fact, is to approach it as a "script pathology."[55] Judith Beck even makes the stronger claim that rule-role script distortions are a component of all psychological problems and that "enduring improvement results from modification of the patient's underlying dysfunctional beliefs."[56]

Many approaches to curriculum and instruction focus on this stage—especially those that aim at fostering self-esteem in the student. These pedagogies are attempting to help the student rewrite and internalize a new script or set of scripts about herself because the old ones no longer serve—if they ever did. Brophy's *Motivating Students to Learn*, for instance, provides a superb example of curriculum and instruction at this level.[57] Brophy offers many sound theoretical constructs and practical strategies that teachers can use to aid students who come to the classroom with a low sense of efficacy and a high sense of helplessness. He does this by showing the teacher how to help the student reframe her vision of herself by enabling her to take a broader, more reasoned perspective on both her problems and potentials. This raises the student onto higher cognitive ground and thus frees her from those outdated images and roles that she has heretofore used to define herself in limited concrete and affiliative terms.

Imagine a student who is not particularly good at spatial reasoning. After learning that she had failed a very difficult geometry test, she might consciously or unconsciously conclude: "I'm no good at this stuff at all. I'm a dummy. I always fail and I always will fail at geometry. All the really smart kids are always getting good grades in geometry and I never do. The teacher must think I'm a total jerk. But I do study. It's just hopeless—that's all!" According to the cognitive therapies, this student is operating off a script that abounds with distorted ideas about herself as a learner. For instance, there is the problem of *selective filtering*. This is when someone only allows herself to register evidence that supports a negative view of herself and refuses to see evidence of positive characteristics. In the present case, the student is discounting the fact that her average score for the first half of the term was "C+". Clearly, she is no geometry whiz, but she does seem to have average ability with geometry, a fact that she has nevertheless selectively filtered out. This has led to another script pathology—*catastrophizing*. On the basis of this single failure, the student has rushed to the conclusion that she will now always fail. She is also certain that the teacher will think she is stupid, which is the script pathology of *mind reading*—assuming (usually incorrectly) that you know what a person is thinking.

The cognitive therapeutic armamentarium offers various ways to help the student to see her "F" in a different light by *rescripting*. The teacher can help the student see that, although it is true that she is not a geometry genius, it is not true that she is a failure at it. In fact, all of her grades except for the most recent one point to average ability. Perhaps she will have to learn to live with the fact that she is average in geometry—maybe even a little below average. The teacher has heard that the student is exceptional at music and also quite good in her history classes. Furthermore, he tells her that it is just not true that all of the "really smart" kids do well in geometry. The teacher has had many students who have been average or even below average in geometry but have gone on to do notable things in other fields. The teacher says that he knows she has worked hard to maintain her C average and respects her for this. This test was especially difficult. What the student needs to do—and he promises to help her—is break down some of the tasks involved in this test into smaller, more manageable units and simply proceed more slowly.

In this example, the teacher is helping the student to update, rewrite, and introject this new script so that her self-talk might be more fruitful. Curricula and instruction which aim at helping the student healthily reframe script problems are often so effective because they are sensitive to the psychodynamics of the transition from the third to fourth landscapes.

Concrete-Affiliative Dimensions of American Progressivism

So far in this chapter our focus has been on essentially "instructional" issues. Let us now pull the camera back dramatically so that we can take a more panoramic view of a few broader issues in American educational history—but still using the concrete-affiliative lens. In doing this, I hope to shed some light on an important phenomenon in American educational history, but I also want to offer an example of how the curricular model that I am proposing might offer useful terms and vantage points in the historical analysis of American education in general as it does in curriculum analysis.

The period from the opening years of the 20th century to the launching of Sputnik in 1957 witnessed the rise and decline of the Progressive movement in American education. As Cremin,[58] Tyack,[59] Kliebard,[60] and Ravitch[61] have shown, a very influential branch of Progressivism in the first half of the 20th century wanted curricula that aimed at "adjusting" the child to her "probable station" in society—and doing so in a manner that was administratively efficient. In order to fill her slot in the burgeoning American economy, the child was to learn (through the combined force of the official, operational, extra, hidden and null curricula) those "rules" and "roles" that would "train" her to fill her destined slot and make her a productive "worker-citizen."[62]

This branch of Progressivism—which Kliebard calls the "social-efficiency" branch—focused on basic affiliative issues of social and corporate loyalty. It is in these terms that we can best appreciate Wil-

liam Torrey Harris's Hegelian vision of schooling as the primary instrument of preparing students to be serviceable tools of the state. At
about the same time in France, we also see the pioneering sociologist
Emile Durkheim offering similar arguments about how schools should
function as servants of the state. As Harris, the U.S. Commissioner of
Education, wrote in an 1874 pamphlet entitled *The Theory of Education
in the United States of America:*

> Military precision is required in the maneuvering of
> classes. Great stress is laid upon (1) punctuality, (2) regu-
> larity, (3) attention, and (4) silence, as habits necessary
> through life for successful combination with one's fellow
> men in an industrial and commercial civilization.[63]

Today many of us look with great suspicion upon such martial
rhetoric to promote educational programs, and we are right to do so. On
the other hand, we must avoid the historiographic fallacy of "presentism." Presentism is the rather self-indulgent mistake of using our current constructs and experiences to render judgment on a time and place
that had not had those experiences and in which those constructs may
not have applied—or indeed even existed. For, in the context of the expansive optimism and expanding might of the United States in the last
decades of the 19th century, such statements undoubtedly seemed less
threatening and more reasonable to many people than they do to us today. Certainly, it was such pronouncements that won Theodore Roosevelt the presidency and kept him there through two terms as an enor-
mously popular and charismatic figure, which is a fair indication of
how widely held those values were.[64] This was a time, in other words,
when there was a conservative social premium placed on cultural cohe-
siveness and economic order—all understandable enough in a society
that was taking some of its initial, *post-bellum* steps as one of the first
truly "modern" nations and as the emerging military-industrial colossus
of the approaching century. Little wonder, then, that Harris's view of
public schooling reflected these important historical developments, the
legitimacy of which is easier to appreciate as a concrete-affiliative phenomenon. A "holistic historiography" helps us both identify and honor
what was valuable in this early 19th-century vision of the role of
schools. This is by no means to say that Harris's corporate vision of
schooling was without problems. It is to say, however, that we must
analyze those problems with a certain historical humility and sensitivity

that comes from recognizing the concrete-affiliative hopes and fears of that time.

Indeed, it is even possible—using the terms that I have already introduced and anticipating a few that will soon appear—to understand some of the critiques of Harris's vision of education that were forwarded by Dewey, Counts, Rugg and other Progressives who demanded curricula that encouraged students to question and change social structures, not neatly fit into them.[65] Where Harris wanted an essentially *affiliative* system of public schools, the liberals wanted a primarily *interpretive* approach to education. Harris envisioned public schooling largely on the third landscape; Dewey, Counts and Rugg on the fourth. This tension is especially clear in the controversy that swirled around "life-adjustment" curricula.

The purpose of the life-adjustment curricula was to identify the student's "probable station" in life and then guide her into a scholastic track that would best prepare her for her future position in society. One of the earliest and most influential statements of this educational agenda issued from the NEA in 1918 in its document *Cardinal Principles of Secondary Education*. Having already touched upon this document in preceding chapters, it is now time to cite a few passages from it at some length. According to the authors,

> in order to determine the main objectives that should guide education in a democracy, it is necessary to analyze the activities of the individual. Normally, he is a member of a family, of a vocational group, and of various civic groups.... It follows, therefore, that worthy home-membership, vocation, and citizenship, demand attention as three of the leading objectives. Aside from the discharge of these specific duties, every individual should have a margin of time for the cultivation of personal and social interests.... The unworthy use of leisure impairs health, disrupts home life, lessens vocational efficiency, and destroys civic-mindedness.... To discharge the duties of life and to benefit from leisure, one must have good health. The health of the individual is essential also to the vitality of the race and to the defense of the Nation. Health education is, therefore, fundamental. There are various processes, such as reading, writing, arithmetical computations and written expression, that are needed as tools in the affairs of life. Consequently, command of these fundamental processes, while not an end in itself, is nevertheless an indispensable objective. And fi-

nally, the realization of the objectives already named is dependent upon ethical character, that is, upon conduct founded upon right principles, clearly perceived and loyally adhered to. Good citizenship, vocational excellence, and the worthy use of leisure go hand in hand.[66]

This is an organismic/concrete-affiliative agenda *par excellence.* Education is now to revolve exclusively upon the needs of "the Nation." Membership is, indeed, the key word throughout this document: membership in the family, in a vocational group, in various civic organizations. Even one's leisure time does not escape the demands of membership; for, leisure must not be simply *enjoyed* but *cultivated* to enhance one's moral and physical health, thereby transforming the student into an even better member of the political and industrial order. Whatever contributes to this overarching goal becomes, by this affiliative definition, "educative." Watras's brief summary of the social studies section of the NEA document captures the group-loyalty spirit of the document in general. "Students would develop loyalties to their city, state, and their nation that were tempered by a sense of membership in the world community."[67]

Twenty two years later, in 1940, The American Council on Education, in *What the High Schools Ought to Teach,* echoed the previous call to curricular action of *Cardinal Principles,* as did another influential document produced by the Vocational Education Division of the United States Office of Education in 1944 entitled *Vocational Education in the Years Ahead.* Charles Prosser, lobbyist for the National Society for the Promotion of Industrial Education, headed the committee, which would now codify what had already become the widely accepted "formula" for what percentage of students should occupy which curricular tracks.

The vocational school of a community will be able to prepare 20 percent of the youth of secondary school age for entrance upon desirable skilled occupations; and...the high school will continue to prepare another 20 percent for entrance to college. We do not believe that the remaining 60 percent of our youth of secondary school age will receive the life-adjustment training they need and to which they are entitled as American citizens—unless and until the administrators of public education with the assistance of the vocational education leaders formulate a similar program for this group.[68]

In the teeth of considerable opposition, proponents of such curricula argued that they were highly democratic because they did not impose a body of elitist knowledge upon a child—as in the European tradition of classical education—but rather tailored the child's school experience to what she would *really* need and want to know in order to perform her allotted role as a citizen.

However, critics argued that life-adjustment curricula were profoundly *anti*-democratic. For what criteria, these detractors asked, did educators use in identifying a child's "probable station" in life if not primarily the occupation and socioeconomic status of her parents—i.e., her current concrete-affiliative contexts and constraints? "Life-adjustment," they maintained, despite its democratic rhetoric, obviously meant nothing more than tracking children into courses of study that would merely keep lower-SES students caught in their concrete-affiliative chains.

Interestingly, this critique of the life-adjustment curriculum as an insipid tool of political disempowerment can be found on both the Left *and* the Right today. On the conservative side, Ravitch has insisted that the life-adjustment curriculum spelled the end of Progressivism's initially democratic ideal of providing all children with access to the same socially empowering bodies of knowledge which exist, as we shall see, on the next landscape—the interpretive-procedural.[69] On the Left, Bourdieu has said that the socio-economic *habitus*—or social, cultural and economic background from which a student comes—provides her with certain kinds and amounts of "cultural capital" that will ultimately determine where she is academically tracked.[70] According to him, differentiated curricula amount to nothing more than the institutional legitimation and educational perpetuation of a student's affiliative capital—or lack thereof. As such, these curricula do not teach the student "knowledge"—just the "knowledge" that will keep her in the same socioeconomic location that she occupied to begin with.

But whether one evaluates the life-adjustment curriculum movement (and its current restoration in the form of school-to-career curricula) as good, bad, or neutral, Kliebard has shown that there were compelling historical circumstances that stimulated its growth in the first half of the 20th century. Not least of these were the First and Second World Wars and their cultural and economic aftermaths, for wars are times when concrete-affiliative imperatives are understandably paramount.

> Industrial arts courses were revised to take into account armament needs. Consumer education and home-management also received increased attention in order to assist the citizenry to live under wartime conditions.... As the hostilities wore on, more and more attention was given [to this and] not so much [to] what changes ought to be wrought in the postwar system of American schooling. In wartime, when criticism of the American social structure, such as that advanced by the social reconstructionists, could be construed as unpatriotic, and with child-centered education increasingly being attacked on all sides as lacking in social commitment, it was once more social efficiency that moved to center stage.... [I]t was life-adjustment education that emerged in the mid-1940s as the sauce that captured the attention of the professional education community.[71]

Of course, this did not mean the classical liberal-arts curriculum—complete with Latin, German, French, Spanish, trigonometry, calculus, physics, biology, and the canonical literary works—was dead. It simply meant that it would be accessible only to those relatively few whose socioeconomic status (and thus "probable station") earmarked them for loftier curricular tracks than their poorer classmates were fated to occupy.

Additionally, many school people were alarmed at declining enrollment rates, which they attributed to low birthrates during the Depression, military enlistment, and the attractiveness of abundant and high paying employment in the defense industries. These educationists believed that the best way to lure young people back into the schools was by offering practical curricula that would pay occupational dividends immediately upon graduating—and this, of course, meant an occupationally stratified curriculum.[72] The threat to the "American way of life" that the 1957 launching of Sputnik represented to many Americans reinforced the appeal and increased the influence of concrete-affiliative curricula. For, although the "Red Scare" curricula were meant to promote higher order cognitive skills, they were doing so in order to produce scientists and soldiers who would be able to protect "our way of life."

A concrete-affiliative perspective gains us a unique understanding of some of the most interesting philosophical assumptions, historical determinants, internal tensions, and pedagogical implications of the "social efficiency" wing of American Progressivism in the early decades of the 20th century.[73]

Conclusion

In this chapter we have examined a few of the multifaceted educational manifestations of the concrete-affiliative perspective.

First, we looked at some of the classical Piagetian theories about how students' concepts change, or resist change, in the course of instruction. We then turned to the social constructivist challenge to Piaget with its insistence that all knowledge is mediated by both the immediate and larger social contexts in which the individual exists—her concrete-affiliative milieu.

Second, we examined the role of language as the primary concrete-affiliative mediator of knowledge, an idea that originated in the Sapir-Whorf hypothesis toward the turn of the 20th century and that reached its climax in the Systemic linguistics of Halliday and Bernstein.

Third, we looked at the rise of multiculturalism and multicultural approaches to curriculum and instruction as educational attempts to be sensitive to the concrete-affiliative situation of the child. We also discussed the related pedagogical vision of the classroom as a community of learners—an idea that rests squarely on Vygotsky's idea of the Zone of Proximal Development.

Fourth, the concrete-affiliative dynamics of the child's reference-group identification(s) were invoked as a powerful way of explaining how and why certain students reject the official curriculum of the school and thus fail academically.

Fifth, moving into the realm of educational psychology we examined concrete-affiliative psychological dysfunctions as they manifest themselves in "script pathologies"—and how to address them in the classroom by helping the student "rescript."

Finally, we moved from the micro-world of the child's classroom and local environment into a macro-analysis of William Torrey Harris and his vision of education in the service of the state. Using the terms and vantage points provided by the concrete-affiliative approach, it was possible both to holistically appreciate *and* critique the causes and effects of the social efficiency approach to education that characterized a significant branch of early 20th-century American Progressivism. Moreover, we saw how the curriculum model being proposed in this book can function as a device for understanding educational issues at the individual, classroom, cultural, and historical levels.

Topics for Discussion

1. In the controversy between "hard" individual constructivism (i.e., the view that there are invariant and universal developmental sequences in the growth of consciousness) and "hard" social constructivism (i.e., the view that the growth of consciousness is totally mediated by constraining social factors), where do you stand—at one of the extreme poles or somewhere in between? After having read this chapter, have your views on these epistemological matters changed? If so, what might be some of the practical consequences of this change in your present teaching or administrative role?

2. In your own experience as a student, teacher, or administrator, what have been some of the major volitional reference groups that have had an impact on you personally and the school in general? What were those effects?

3. Can you think of a student in your own teaching experience who might benefit from cognitive rescripting? What kind of dysfunctional scripts regarding your class and subject-matter do you think the student might have? How would you help the student "rewrite" and internalize more productive scripts?

Topics for Research

1. Review some of the major articles in Conceptual Change Theory literature over the past 20 years. Do you see a trend toward hard individual constructivism, hard social constructivism, or some synthesis?

2. What is the current state of Reference Group Theory in educational sociology? What are some of the major volitional reference groups (i.e., Goths, Granolas, Jocks, etc.) in public schools today as defined by educational sociologists and anthropologists, and what impact are they having on the school's official curriculum?

3. Present some of the major arguments that were offered in the early 20th century *pro* and *con* regarding the idea of the "life-adjustment curricula" of the Progressive movement. Do you feel that life-adjustment

curricula represented pedagogical sensitivity to the differential needs of students or do you feel that they simply tended to reproduce socioeconomic inequalities?

Notes: Chapter 3

1. K. Wilber, *A Brief History of Everything* (Boston: Shambhala, 1996).
2. J. Conger and J. Galambos, *Adolescence and Youth: Psychological Development in a Changing World* (New York: Longman, 1997).
3. C. Riordan, *Equality and Achievement: An Introduction to the Sociology of Education* (New York: Longman, 1997).
4. J. Nussbaum, "The Earth as a Cosmic Body," in *Children's Ideas in Science,* eds. R. Driver, E. Guesne, and A. Tiberghein (Philadelphia: Open University Press, 1985).
5. G. Posner, K. Strike, P. Hewson, and W. Gertzog. "Accommodation of a Scientific Conception: Toward a Theory of Conceptual Change," *Science Education* 67(4) (1982): 212-213.
6. S. Toulmin, *Human Understanding: The Collective Use and Evolution of Concepts* (Princeton, N.J.: Princeton University Press, 1972).
7. M. McCloskey, "Naive Theories of Motion," in *Mental Models,* eds. D. Gentner and A. Stevens (Hillsdale, New Jersey: Erlbaum, 1983): 317.
8. C. Bereiter, "Towards a Solution of the Learning Paradox," *Review of Educational Research* 55(2) (1985): 201-226.
9. W. Winn, "Some Implications of Cognitive Theory for Instructional Design," *Instructional Science* 19 (1990): 59.
10. L. Vygotsky, *Mind in Society: The Development of Psychological Functions* (Cambridge, Mass.: Harvard University Press, 1986).
11. J. Brown, A. Collins, and P. Duguid. "Situated Cognition and the Culture of Learning," *Educational Researcher,* January-February (1989): 32-42.
12. M. Hewson, "The Ecological Context of Knowledge: Implications for Learning Science in Developing Countries," *Journal of Curriculum Studies* 20(4) (1988): 317-326.
13. Vygotsky, p. 50.
14. Ibid., 56.
15. Ibid., 56-57.
16. Ibid., 61.
17. B. Rogoff, *Apprenticeship in Thinking: Cognitive Development in Social Context* (New York: Oxford University Press, 1990).
18. J. Wertsch, *Vygotsky and the Social Formation of Mind.* (Cambridge, Mass.: Harvard University Press, 1985), 61.
19. M. Halliday, *Language as Social Semiotic* (London: Edward Arnold, 1978).
20. B. Bernstein, *Class, Codes, & Control: Volume 1* (London: Routledge & Kegan Paul, 1971).

21. Ibid., 124.
22. M. Halliday, *Learning How to Mean* (London: Edward Arnold, 1975), 120. See also: C. Mayes, "The Social Foundations of Systemic Linguistics," *The Sugiyama Journal* 18(1) (1987): 41-75. C. Mayes. "The Tristratal Model of Language in Systemic Linguistics," *The Sugiyama Journal* 17(1): 105-117. C. Mayes, "The Idea of Register and Code in Systemic Lingustics," *The Nagoya Gakuin University Round Table on Literature and Linguistics* 14(3) (1986): 138-155.
23. Brown et al., 32.
24. Hewson, 185.
25. B. Ferdman, "Literacy and Cultural Identity," *Harvard Educational Review* 60(2) (1990): 187.
26. Ibid., 188-189.
27. K. Au and A. Kawakami. "Research Currents: Talk Story and Learning to Read," *Language Arts* 62(4) (1985): 407-410.
28. Wertsch, 67-68. Emphasis added.
29. L. Resnick, "The 1987 Presidential Address: Learning in School and Out," *Educational Researcher* 16 (9) (1987): 18.
30. Ibid., 15.
31. Brown et al., 34.
32. S. Boocock, *Sociology of Education: An Introduction.* 2nd edition, (Boston, Houghton Mifflin, 1980), 194.
33. Riordan, 127.
34. K. Wilber, *Integral Psychology: Consciousness, Spirit, Psychology, Therapy* (London: Shambhala, 2000).
35. J. Coleman, *The Adolescent Society,* (New York: Free Press, 1961).
36. M. Wax, R. Wax and R. Dumont, Jr. *Formal Education in an American Indian Community: Peer Society and the Failure of Minority Education.* (Prospect Heights, Illinois: Waveland Press, 1964).
37. P. Willis, *Learning to Labour* (Aldershot: Gower, 1977).
38. M. Gibson, *Accommodation without Assimilation: Sikh Immigrants in an American High School* (Ithaca, New York: Cornell University Press, 1988).
39. J. Ogbu, "Variability in Minority School Performance: A Problem in Search of an Explanation," *Anthropology and Education Quarterly* 18 (1987): 312-334.
40. Riordan.
41. A. Byrk, V. Lee, and M. Driscoll, *Catholic Schools and the Common Good.* (Cambridge: Harvard University Press, 1993).
42. Riordan, 14.
43. A. Wells and R. Crain. "Consumers and Urban Education," in *The Structure of Schooling: Readings in the Sociology of Education,* eds. R. Arum and I. Beattie (London: Mayfield, 1997), 316.
44. Riordan.

45. L. Kohlberg, *The Meaning and Measurement of Moral Development* (Clark Lectures: Clark University, 1979).

46. Ibid.

47. H. Rugg, *Changing Governments and Changing Cultures: The World's March toward Democracy* (New York: Ginn, 1932).

48. H. Zinn, *A People's History of the United States* (New York: Harper Perennial, 1990).

49. Kohlberg.

50. E. Eisner, *The Educational Imagination: On the Design and Evaluation of School Programs* (New York: Macmillan, 1985).

51. J. Conger and J. Galambos, *Adolescence and Youth: Psychological Development in a Changing World* (New York: Longman, 1997), 103.

52. K. Wilber, *Brief History.*

53. A. Beck, and M. Weishaar. "Cognitive Psychotherapy," in *Current Psychotherapies,* eds. R. Corsini and D. Wedding (Itasca, Illinois: Peacock Publishers, 1995): 229-261.

54. J. Beck, *Cognitive Therapy: Basics and Beyond* (New York: Guilford Press, 1995).

55. Wilber, *Integral Psychology.*

56. J. Beck, *Cognitive Therapy.*

57. J. Brophy, *Motivating Students to Learn* (Boston: McGraw-Hill, 1994).

58. L. Cremin, *The Transformation of the School: Progressivism in American Education, 1876-1957* (New York: Vintage Press, 1964).

59. D. Tyack, *The One Best System: A History of American Urban Education* (Cambridge, Mass.: Harvard University Press, 1974).

60. H. Kliebard, *The Struggle for the American Curriculum: 1893-1958* (New York: Routledge, 1986), 206.

61. D. Ravitch, *The Troubled Crusade: American Education, 1945-1980* (New York: Basic Books, 1983).

62. J. Spring, *Educating the Worker Citizen* (New York: David McKay Co., Inc. 1972).

63. W. T. Harris, "The Theory of Education in the United States of America," in G. Willis, W. Schubert, R. Bullough, Jr., C. Kridel, and J. Holton, eds. *The American Curriculum: A Documentary History* (London: Praeger, 1994).

64. R. Hofstadter, *The American Political Tradition* (New York: Vintage Books, 1958).

65. Ravitch.

66. "Cardinal Principles of Secondary Education," as excerpted in G. Willis, W. Schubert, R., Bullough, Jr., C. Kridel, and J. Holton, eds. *The American Curriculum: A Documentary History* (London: Praeger, 1994): 153-162.

67. J. Watras, *The Foundations of Educational Curriculum and Diversity: 1565 to the Present* (Boston: Allyn and Bacon, 2002),

68. C. Prosser, "Vocational Education in the Years Ahead," as excerpted in W. Willis, Schubert, R., Bullough, Jr., C. Kridel, and J. Holton, eds. *The American Curriculum: A Documentary History* (London: Praeger, 1994).
69. Ravitch.
70. P. Bourdieu, "Cultural Reproduction," in *Power and Ideology in Education,* eds. J. Karabel and A. Halsey (New York: Oxford Press, 1977): 487-507.
71. Kliebard, H. *The Struggle for the American Curriculum: 1893-1958* (New York: Routledge, 1986).
72. Ibid.
73. Ibid.

4

THE INTERPRETIVE-
PROCEDURAL LANDSCAPE

Pivotal Themes in Chapter 4

*The advent and importance of metacognition—the ability to think about thinking.

* The ability to interpret certain social conventions relativistically—and thus to transcend them.

* The academic-rationalist curriculum as situated on this landscape. Scientific reasoning in its classical hypothetico-deductive forms as the primary tool of discovery and expression at this level.

* Lipman's view of the student as a "philosopher," even in the earliest grades.

* The student as "cognitive apprentice" in a classroom that is a "community of discourse."

* Jerome Bruner's "Structure-of-the-Discipline" approach to curriculum, in which the student learns how to think like an "expert" in a

given field. "Schema" pedagogy—or helping the student internalize the cognitive schema which the "expert" uses in asking questions and finding answers in a given domain.

* Cybernetic theories of mind as mechanistic examples of schema theory. Chomskyan Transformational-Generative linguistics, and its pedagogical implications.

* The conservative Progressives who felt that a standard academic-rationalist curriculum—and not a differentiated curriculum adjusted to the student's "probable vocational destination"—was most democratically empowering.

Thinking about Thinking

The interpretive-procedural landscape is the home of hypothetico-deductive reasoning. It is also the final step in Piagetian cognitive development, which Piaget called "formal operations"—or the ability to make and evaluate abstract logical propositions. The leap from a concrete-affiliative orientation to an interpretive-procedural one might be pictured as a "grammatical transition" from the "indicative" (with its fixed attention on things *as they are*) into the subjunctive (with its fluid ability to imagine things *as they might be*). On the fourth landscape, one can picture constructs and systems that do not exist, or do not exist *yet*—and are not tied in to concrete realities, local conditions or personal affiliations. Interpretive-procedural consciousness often asks "what if" and imagines "as if" in ways that may challenge the student's personal and cultural affiliations. Part of this ability consists in *metacognition*—the capacity to think about thinking. Interpretive-procedural consciousness observes itself in order to critique and transform itself. It also scrutinizes social and philosophical "givens" that it had previously just accepted at face value.

Adolescence is typically the period for the emergence of this type of cognition. Coming into their own in terms of interpretive-procedural abilities, adolescents are therefore often irritating to adults, whose social and ethical worlds adolescents are learning how to deconstruct with reckless abandon and (most galling of all!) occasional accuracy. An interpretive-procedural perspective is the cognitive passport that allows consciousness to leave the socio-centric confines of the third landscape.

Interpretive-procedural consciousness thus analyzes and manipulates the signs and symbols that functionally but sometimes naively organize its immediate sensory, biological, emotional, cognitive and social worlds. On the interpretive-procedural landscape, the individual can relativize and manipulate signs and symbols in order to see how his universe is socio-linguistically constructed. This enables the person to understand the contingency of his ethnocentric views—and as such is one of the goals of multicultural education.[1]

Metacognition is the highest level of consciousness in classical developmental theory—corresponding to Piaget's formal operations, Kohlberg's post-conventional moral reasoning, Beck's systematic-relativistic consciousness, Wilber's rational-reflexive consciousness, Neumann's ego consciousness, and Steiner's rational soul. Here the individual begins to look for ways of approaching and encoding truths that supersede cultural norms and linguistic conventions that now emerge in plain view as having been relative all along.

Interpretive-procedural analyses often take the form of a search for Kant's "categorical imperatives"—those universal ethical principles that anyone can supposedly discover simply by consulting his intuition. It is the intuitive accessibility and ethical primacy of the categorical imperatives that ultimately allow no excuse for the plea of the affiliatively obedient concentration camp guard that he "was just following orders." Post-conventional reasoning is the summit of Aristotelian ethics, too, as both critics and adherents of Kohlberg have noted. What differentiates these and similar developmental theories from more recent transpersonal developmental theories is that conventional developmental theory "maxes out" at this stage whereas transpersonal theory sees it as the springboard into transpersonal, transrational ways of seeing and being.[2] This is a point that I examine in depth in Chapter 6.

The Interpretive-Procedural Curriculum:
Foundations and Examples
Since this is the landscape on which occurs the search for generalizable interpretive strategies and universal moral imperatives, it is here that we must place what Eisner has dubbed the "academic-rationalist" curriculum. Here also resides Ornstein and Hunkins' "intellectual-academic" curriculum and its assumption that syllogistic processes lead to the upper-limits of human knowing.[3]

As Ornstein and Hunkins have noted, Dewey's instructional theory paralleled interpretive-procedural methodologies, for Dewey pictured effective thinking as: "1. becoming aware of a difficulty (or a felt difficulty), 2. identifying the problem, 3. assembling and classifying data and formulating hypotheses, 4. accepting or rejecting the tentative hypotheses, 5. formulating conclusions and evaluating them."[4] Note the similarity here between the Deweyan model of effective thinking and the early conceptual change theories of the 1980s. Early conceptual change theorists held that the most pedagogically effective and psychologically authentic curricula would teach students to think like scientists. This would mean showing students how to identify "anomalous" data, modify their existing conceptual paradigms in order to handle those anomalies, and finally test and, if necessary, further revise those theories. The results of this process would count as "knowledge" until the appearance of another anomaly, when the recursive process would begin again in order to reveal new "knowledge." Miller has dubbed this the "cognitive processes" approach to curriculum. Because such educational models stop at this point, they have been challenged by feminist theorists, postmodernists, and transpersonal developmentalists alike with the very legitimate charge that our lives are made of more exotic political, emotional and spiritual stuff than just syllogisms.[5]

Still, Aristotle was undoubtedly right that, whatever else we are, we are the animals that reason. It is impossible to gainsay the value of what Noddings calls the "formal conversation" of rational academic discourse[6] and what Miller terms "curriculum as transaction."[7] It is difficult to imagine an education that can claim adequacy if it has not familiarized students with the conventions and potentials of formal academic discourse. As some conservative educationists correctly point out, a curriculum that does not do this but cavalierly dismisses all canonical education as merely "patriarchal white discourse" is, no matter how politically correct, also politically disempowering for precisely those students who need such knowledge in order to advance in a society that will always value it.[8] Proponents of interpretive-procedural, "critical thinking" curricula are many, but I shall focus on the curriculum theory of Matthew Lipman because I feel it best represents most of the major features of curricula on the fourth landscape.

Lipman, Philosophy, and the Child

According to Lipman, many of the world's woes can be attributed to the fact that teachers and administrators have not fashioned classrooms into communities of rational discourse—those Deweyan laboratories of democracy where students learn how to create knowledge that rationally moves the collective body forward into ever newer realms of social possibility. In perhaps an excessive act of professional contrition, Lipman proclaims that "as educators, we have a heavy responsibility for the unreasonableness of the world's population."[9] "The greatest disappointment of traditional education has been its failure to produce people approximating the ideal of reasonableness."[10]

How can we as educators atone for this personal and historical failure? We must bring philosophy and its saving power to even the earliest grades of the schools. "Even young children can enter into such dialogue," asserts Lipman, for "doing philosophy is not a matter of age but of ability to reflect scrupulously and courageously on what one finds important."[11] That reflection, which will of course include "classical rhetoric and dialectic," is suitable even for young children so long as they are "given practice in discussing the *concepts* they take seriously."[12] Not only is such instruction possible, even at the earlier levels, it is necessary—so necessary, in fact, that it should become "the core or armature of the curriculum."[13] "Because philosophy is the discipline that best prepares us to think in terms of the other disciplines, it must be assigned a central role in the early as well as in the late stages of the educational process."[14] Of the thirty critical skills that Lipman wants student to acquire, he particularly stresses:

> (1) concepts; (2) generalizations; (3) cause-effect relationships; (4) allogistic inferences; (5) consistencies and contradictions; (6) analogies; (7) part-whole and whole-part connections; (8) problem formulations; (9) reversibility of logical statements; and (10) application of principles to real-life situations.[15]

There are many implications here for all aspects of the educational process—from teacher education to student assessment.

> The irrationalities or "socially patterned defects" that permeate education have to be rooted out because they do not die out on their own: they have a marvelous capacity for self-perpetuation. This involves our bringing a greater degree of order into the curriculum, into the methodology of teaching, into the process of teacher education, and into the procedures of testing.[16]

Although Lipman's vision of curriculum relies heavily on syllogistic thinking, we must be careful not to ascribe to Lipman a slavish adherence to it. His proposals for creating the "reasonable curriculum" are more than just a pedagogical outgrowth of formal logic, for thinking *reasonably* also means thinking *creatively*. It means using the imagination to envision new worlds. Yet, this is something that the student will never fully do, Lipman reminds us, if that student is forced to consider issues that he thinks are personally and socially irrelevant.

Here again, as in the last chapter, we see the unmistakably interpretive-procedural core of much of liberal Progressive pedagogy; indeed, Lipman is very clear that his primary pedagogical alliance is with Dewey's liberal progressivism and its current incarnation as social constructivism, which generally holds that emotionally and politically vital types of learning can only occur in classrooms where the individual's cognition is situated in a community of learners engaged in interesting tasks.[17] As did Dewey, Lipman hopes that such curricular changes will ultimately work massive social transformations.

> There is good reason to think that the model of each and every classroom—that which it seeks to approximate and at times becomes—is the community of inquiry. By inquiry, of course, I mean perseverance in self-corrective exploration of issues that are felt to be both important and problematic.... If we begin with the practice in the classroom—the practice of converting it into a reflective community that thinks in the disciplines about the world and about its thinking about the world, we soon come to recognize that communities can be nested within larger communities and these within larger communities still, if all hold the same allegiance to the same procedure of inquiry. There is the familiar ripple effect outward, like the stone thrown in the pond: wider and wider, more and more encompassing communities are formed, each community consisting of individuals committed to self-corrective exploration and creativity. It is a picture that owes...much...to John Dewey....[18]

With this declaration we come full circle in Lipman's vision of the curriculum: he begins by attributing much of humanity's "fall" into unreasonableness to the schools, and he concludes with the promise of social salvation through the broadly "rational" curriculum. Lipman's theory meets in every particular the requirements of Miller and Seeler's "curriculum as transaction," which are that curricula be dialogic, rational and active, fostering cognitive processes and democratic ideology.[19]

The Student as a Cognitive Apprentice

Although it does not generally make such grand socially redemptive claims, much recent conceptual change theory rests on similar notions of education as a discursive process of socially negotiated cognition. According to this view, the best teacher will draw students subtly together as they collectively pose questions and create knowledge in an ongoing classroom process. In this way, too, teachers can acquaint their students with the issues and strategies of larger communities of discourse, thereby transforming them into "cognitive apprentices."

> Unfortunately, students are too often asked to use the tools of a discipline without being able to adopt its culture. To learn to use tools as practitioners use them, a student, like an apprentice, must enter that community and its culture. Thus, in a significant way, learning is...a process of enculturation.[20]

In short, effective fourth-landscape teaching is a gentle art of "cognitive negotiation" between teacher and student—with the teacher serving as master "cognitive artisan" teaching his "cognitive-apprentices" how to inquire and create like people in various professions and disciplines do.[21,22] This current trend in instructional theory is genealogically related to such earlier approaches as Bruner's structure-of-the-discipline theory, where the teacher, by both explicit instruction and implicit modeling, shows students how to define and solve problems in a given field by learning how "experts" in that field do their work—but always, Bruner adds, in ways that are developmentally appropriate to the child's present stage. The "structure of knowledge" in a discipline must thus form the pedagogical basis for the "structure of instruction and learning." As one of the leading theorists on the fourth curricular landscape, Bruner explained four decades ago how the structure of virtually any discipline could be tailored to the capabilities of virtually any age group. What was required was simply that the discipline's "mode of representation, economy, and power" be adapted to the capacities of that particular developmental and/or ability group. Bruner explained:

> Any idea or problem or body of knowledge can be pre-
> sented in a form simple enough so that any particular
> learner can understand it in a recognizable form. The struc-
> ture of any domain of knowledge may be characterized in
> three ways, each affecting the ability of any learner to mas-
> ter it: the *mode of representation* in which it is put, its
> *economy,* and its effective *power.* Mode, economy, and ef-
> fective power vary in relation to different ages, to different
> "styles" among learners, and to different subject matters.
> Any domain of knowledge (or any problem within a do-
> main of knowledge) can be represented in three ways: by a
> set of actions for achieving a certain result (enactive repre-
> sentation); by a set of summary images or graphics that
> stand for a concept without defining it fully (iconic repre-
> sentation); and by a set of symbolic and logical proposi-
> tions drawn from a symbolic system that is governed by
> rules or laws for forming and transforming propositions
> (symbolic representation).... Much of Piaget's research
> seeks to discover just this property about children's learn-
> ing and thinking.[23]

The best curriculum in any domain, Bruner asserted, is a developmentally appropriate one that shares the domain's assumptions, mirrors
its structures, and uses its processes. This helps the student (to the
maximum practical extent) assume the role of a practitioner in that particular domain. Bruner's famous anthropology curriculum, *Man: A
Course of Study,* attempted to translate this theory of curriculum into
practice. The specific form of an interpretive-procedural curriculum
will naturally vary according to the histories, world-views, and objectives of the specific discipline, as well as the inclinations and objectives
of the teacher; but whether the subject matter of the curriculum is physics or literature, psychodynamics or auto mechanics, the generally accepted texts, standard evaluative procedures, and received evidentiary
criteria of the discipline as practiced by "experts" should, according to
Bruner, drive the curriculum.

Experts, Schemas, and Thinking Machines

Bruner's approach is but one of many interpretive-procedural approaches to curriculum which aim at getting students to examine their
own cognitive "maps" in order to make them more closely match the
maps that the "experts" in a field presumably carry around in *their*
brains. In cognitive psychology, these cognitive maps are called

"schemas," and theories of learning that revolve around cognitive schemas are called schema theories. Rummelhart, a leading schema theorist, defines a schema theory as

> a theory about how knowledge is represented and about how that representation facilitates the *use* of knowledge in particular ways. According to schema theories, all knowledge is packaged into units. These units are the schemata. Embedded in these packets of knowledge is, in addition to the knowledge itself, information about how this knowledge is to be used. A schema, then, is a data structure for representing the generic concepts stored in memory. There are schemata representing our knowledge about all concepts: those underlying objects, situations, events, sequences of events, actions and sequences of actions. A schema contains, as part of its specification, the network of interrelations that is believed to normally hold among the constituents of the concept in question. A schema theory embodies a *prototype* theory of meaning. That is, inasmuch as a schema underlying a concept stored in memory corresponds to the *meaning* of that concept, meanings are encoded in terms of the typical or normal situations or events that instantiate that concept.[24]

Note the Piagetian premium placed here upon internal, individual processes, as opposed to Vygotskyan social constructivism with its stress on social dynamics. This individualistic orientation characterizes most of the curricula which revolve around the idea of "concept mapping."[25]

A related approach to these "expert-referenced" pedagogies grew out of cybernetics. Originating in the 1950s and 1960s, when computers were beginning to enter the scene, the cybernetic approach initially represented an attempt to break free of the superficiality of behaviorism and create a model of mind that was rational and "deep." Since computers were being heralded as the ultimate thinking machines, it seemed reasonable to attempt to fashion a theory of mind around them. The ultimate tool designed to serve us would now become a symbol by means of which we could interpret ourselves *to* ourselves.

In linguistics, Chomsky made notable strides in this direction with the publication of *Aspects of the Theory of Syntax*—a cybernetic approach to grammar which was particularly influential in the fields of first- and second-language learning in the 1960s and 1970s.[26] Chomsky argued that the surface phenomena of spoken or written speech were ultimately "generated" (hence the term "Generative grammar") from fundamental grammatical structures in the person's mind which operated according to binary ("yes/no") algorithms—just like a computer. In *Aspects*, these relations and algorithms were presented in terms of grammatical categories, choices and transformations. As Transformational-Generative grammar developed, however, Chomsky came to believe that fundamental grammatical relationships were themselves merely secondary products of transformations that had already occurred at even deeper cognitive levels. With this, Transformational-Generative semantics was born.

The basic tenet of Transformational-Generative semantics was that, even deeper than the cognitive stratum of grammatical forms and choices, lay the bedrock of purely abstract logical categories along with the ground rules of how they could interact. The rules of cognition paralleled the rules of logic, and grammatical structures were merely encodings of these deeper semantic processes. As those processes began to near the "surface," further phonemic, morphemic, lexical, syntactic and graphemic rules of transformation would determine—again in a binary way—how the core message could be intelligibly presented in either spoken or written form. In first- or second-language curricula and instruction that followed Chomskyan theory, the student learned the phonological, morphological, and syntactic rules of a language as a series of transformations that emanated from the deepest semantic levels and finally emerged at the surface level of actual speech or writing.

Transformational-Generative grammar seriously challenged the then prevailing Structuralist approach to language learning, whose very practical motto was "Teach the language, not about the language."[27] Structuralist second-language teaching was also called the *Aural-Oral* or *Mim-Mem* approach because of its tenet that students learned both their own and other languages through *mim*icry and *mem*orization of the surface structures (i.e., actual utterances) that they actually *heard* and *spoke*—not by analyzing semantico-grammatical rules as in the Transformational-Generative approaches.[28] There was no room in the commonsensical Structuralist view for language learning that dealt with grammatical abstractions and hypothetical "deep semantic structures." With its practical emphasis on language as a primary form of socialization accomplished through emotional attachment and obedient repetition, and its rejection of procedural reflectivity, Structuralism can best be characterized as a concrete-affiliative approach to language learning.

It rejected Chomsky's program of placing language learning on the fourth curricular landscape with its interpretive-procedural orientation, preferring to stay put on the more familiar territory of actual linguistic exchanges in practical settings on the third landscape. Chomsky's cybernetic framework in linguistics provided the scaffolding upon which later "cybernetic pedagogies" (as I shall call them) could build their actual curricula. A good example of a cybernetic approach is Chi and his associates' influential study, "Categorization and Representation of Physics Problems by Experts and Novices," in which they presented an example of how their instructional approach might work in teaching about the concept of momentum in physics.[29]

Assuming that mind, like the computer, has only so much memory and so many slots into which information can be put, Chi concluded that bits of information must be synthesized—"chunked" together—and contained in schemas that then occupy the precious mental slots. Abstraction is essentially a space-saving technique. However, as information increases, the schemas will also begin to proliferate and exceed available space. They must themselves, therefore, be subsumed under even higher power schemas. This process can go on indefinitely, limited only by the life-span and intelligence of the individual. Indeed, the ability to chunk is a good functional definition of intelligence in the cybernetic pedagogies. The degree to which one possesses this ability is the essential difference between the novice and the expert. Hence, Chi stresses at every step "the importance of categorizing in expert problem solving."

> Expert-novice differences may be related to poorly formed, qualitatively different, or non-existent categories in the novice representation. In general, this hypothesis is consistent with the "perceptual chunking" hypothesis for experts (e.g., Chase and Simmons, 1973), and its more general cognitive ramifications, which suggest that much of expert power lies in the expert's ability to quickly establish correspondence between externally presented events and internal models for these events.[30]

Whereas Bruner argued that the gap between the expert and the novice could best be spanned by strategies of communal discovery, Chi seems to be taking a much more classically Piagetian approach in which the goal is to get the "schema" of the student to conform to that of the expert in a fairly linear, step-by-step, individualistic manner. For all their differences, however, both Piaget and Chi are trying to help the student reflect on his own thinking in such a way as to bring that thinking more into line with the way expert practitioners in a discipline (presumably) think. Despite their usefulness in cognitive mapping and their historical importance as a challenge to what was, in the 1950s, the dictatorship of behaviorism, the cybernetic pedagogies still have a fundamental flaw and contradiction—and that is in their governing metaphor of the brain as a computer. Paradoxically, in attempting to offer a humane alternative to behaviorism in curriculum and instruction, the cybernetic pedagogies reflected, even magnified, the very depersonalization that they were attempting to address.

> This point could be expressed in a different way: Cognitive Science theorists attempt to model or recreate the child's activity in a [mechanistic] medium that is different from the child's mind. If, when realized on a machine, the model "behaves" in the same way that the child behaves, then the model suits its purpose. Thus, the model is primarily descriptive. "Why" a child behaves in a particular way is left more to an elaborate description of "how". In other words, the primary goal of the [cognitive science] theorist would seem to be to represent the child's activity in terms of a model, not to explain the activity that is involved in her construction of representations. The child's "personal relationship" to her representation is incidental.[31]

In his discussion of the learning paradox, Bereiter has echoed the same cautionary note, saying that the conundrum of how we learn anything at all "cannot be overcome by theories that treat the human mind as merely a computational device—that an adequate theory must embrace a much larger range of mental resources."[32] And Winn despairs of the ability of any mental model that is strictly propositional and rigidly procedural to deal with such fourth-landscape issues as metacognition, emergent properties of cognition, situated cognition, individual differences, and chaos theory, for all of the above "provide evidence that human behavior is indeterminate and far from predictable."[33]

American Progressivism on the Fourth Landscape

Turning once again from specific instructional issues to broadly historical ones, we see that American curriculum history contains many instances of the attempt to define curriculum in those classical, disciplined-centered terms that fit so well into the contours of the fourth curricular landscape.

For instance, relying upon the then popular notions of faculty psychology, the authors of the *Yale Report of 1828* declared that the best curriculum encouraged the student to master not only subject matters but also research procedures that would reveal general truths and lift the student above the confines of merely local experience:

> The two great points to be gained in intellectual culture are the discipline and the furniture of the mind; expanding its powers, and storing it with knowledge. The former of these is, perhaps, the most important of the two. A commanding object, therefore, in a collegiate course, should be to call into daily and vigorous exercise the faculties of the students. Those branches of study should be prescribed, and those modes of instruction adopted, which are best calculated to teach the art of fixing the attention, directing the train of thought, analyzing a subject proposed for investigation; following, with accurate discrimination, the course of argument, balancing nicely the evidence presented to the judgment; awakening, elevating, and controlling the imagination; arranging, with skill, the treasures which memory gathers; rousing and guiding the powers of genius.[34]

Sixty-five years later, in 1893, the NEA published the *Report of the Committee of Ten on Secondary Schools*. In many ways, this report represented a radical departure from the *Yale Report*, attempting to move the curriculum away from the *Yale Report's* single-mindedly classical orientation toward a focus on greater contemporary relevance and disciplinary variety.

> In part the [NEA] Report was a response to the growing number of academic disciplines, represented by the emergence of some forty associations in different disciplines, such as the National Geographic Society, in the second half of the nineteenth century. In part it was a response to school leaders who were upset about the huge variation in expectations by colleges as represented by questions on college entrance examinations. Still another part of the impetus for the Report was the desire by Charles W. Eliot (1834-1926), the Committee's Chair and President of Harvard, and by other educators to loosen the hold of classical

studies...on collegiate entrance requirements and thereby
promote the elective system, which Eliot himself had introduced at Harvard in 1884.[35]

In this sense, most contemporary analyses of the NEA report of
1893 are right in claiming that it foreshadowed the nearly total emphasis on practical social relevance in the NEA report, issued 26 years
later, *Cardinal Principles of Secondary Education,* which we examined
in the preceding chapter in concrete-affiliative terms.

Surprisingly, however, what is often missed in current analyses of
the *Report of the Committee of Ten on Secondary Schools* is that, for all
of its functionalist foreshadowings, it nevertheless revolved around an
essentially fourth landscape commitment to traditional skills and
knowledge. For regardless of both the child's concrete-affiliative point
of social origin and his "probable station" at the end of his schooling,
the authors of the 1893 document insisted that all children, college-
bound or not, should be treated and educated similarly, receiving essentially the same curriculum that would teach them the *procedural* skills
and canonical knowledge necessary for every individual to *interpret*
himself and his society in a principled, "objective" way. Anything less
than this would be undemocratic in that it would provide certain groups
of children access to empowering knowledge and deny it to others. Not
only that, but giving all students access to this kind of knowledge was
the only way of providing them with a fair shot at winning admission
into America's increasingly accessible universities.[36] What this all
boiled down to, said the authors of the report, was that, although not all
students would be going on to college, they should all be educated *as if*
they were:

> The secondary schools of the United States, taken as a
> whole, do not prepare boys and girls for college.... At the
> same time, it is obviously desirable that the colleges and
> scientific schools should be accessible to all boys and girls
> who have completed creditably the secondary school
> course.... In order that any successful graduate of a good
> secondary school should be free to present himself at the
> gates of the college or scientific school of his choice, it is
> necessary that the colleges and scientific schools of the
> country should accept for admission to appropriate courses
> of their instruction the attainment of any youth who has
> passed creditably through a good secondary school course,

no matter to what group of subjects he may have mainly
devoted himself in the secondary school.[37]

The Committee therefore recommended that the secondary school
curriculum revolve around the following subjects for all students:
Latin, Greek, English (and other modern languages), Mathematics,
Physics, Chemistry, Astronomy, Natural History, History, Civil Government, Political Economy, and Geography.

In short, the *Report of the Committee of Ten*, although justifiably
interpreted as a significant step toward the affiliative, social-
membership "functionalism" of *Cardinal Principles of Secondary Education,* represented at the same time a commitment to pedagogical principles and philosophical assumptions that underlie many interpretive-
procedural pedagogies. Now, the fact that this curricular vision strad-
dled two landscapes need not disconcert us—that is, if we take the integrative view that a curriculum, like any complex organism, can (and
given the complexity of things, usually *does*) embody and promote
more than one set of legitimate purposes at the same time. The special
power of holistic theory and practice is that it not only recognizes this
fact but cultivates its interactive potential instead of creating unnecessary oppositions.

Similarly, it is possible to interpret Boyd Bode's 1937 classic, *Democracy as a Way of Life,* as a balancing act—an attempt to respond to
some of the concrete-affiliative excesses of social-efficiency Progressivism with a counterbalancing emphasis on the need for interpretive-
procedural education. For it was this that would, according to Bode, allow a student to transcend socio-centric biases and attain broader
views. Bode said that it was only such a curriculum—at once socially
functional and intellectually strong—that would forge a society that
was not only unified but also enlightened:

> We can at least hold that the pupils coming to school are
> entitled to learn what the issue of fixed versus flexible pat-
> terns is all about. The cultural outlook which they uncon-
> sciously absorb is dominated by fixed patterns—fixed pat-
> terns in religion, in ethics, in art, in science, in economics
> and in government. They are in no position to realize that
> any other point of view is possible. If our present conten-
> tion is sound, *viz.,* that the democratic point of view is a
> challenge to the whole mass of tradition, it follows that no

school can claim to be truly democratic if it does not accept the clarification of this issue as a major responsibility.[38]

Bode certainly prefigures Lipman's later declaration that "the irrationalities or 'socially patterned defects' that permeate education have to be rooted out because they do not die out on their own: they have a marvelous capacity for self-perpetuation."[39] The interpretive-procedural curriculum also has a "marvelous capacity" to raise students to the higher reaches of hypothetico-deductive reasoning, to allow them to enter a community of discourse, to communally generate and creatively solve problems, and thus to move a democracy forward.

Nevertheless, problems may arise on the interpretive-procedural landscape if one "gets stuck" there and "unholistically" denies the legitimate educational claims and needs of other landscapes. An example of this error is Adler's *Paideia Proposal*.[40] In Adler's view, the Socratic examination of canonical philosophical, literary and historical classics is the *only* really legitimate goal of higher education. But there are many ways of knowing that have great worth but do not fit so neatly into Adler's completely and classically Eurocentric worldview—and some that do not fit it at all. I want it to be clear at this juncture that I do not ally myself with the radical multiculturalist assertion that the canon of texts in the Western tradition represents nothing more than a patriarchal white discourse intent on educationally colonizing people who are already politically oppressed. Far from it. I agree with Barzun that *that* tradition and its standard works are, by and large, a heritage of incalculable worth in understanding ourselves both historically and morally.[41] For it is certainly the case, as T.S. Eliot wrote, that "a people without a history is not redeemed from time."[42] But it is not the *only* way of knowing; it is not always even the *best* way; and it can sometimes be a *destructive* way.

To offer just one pedagogical example of such a danger, I have argued elsewhere[43] that, in Jungian terms, Adler's approach might result in psychological and moral harm to teachers in its overemphasis on the archetype of the teacher as philosopher. There are many other archetypes that power one's decision to become a teacher and then sustain him in his difficult work. Some of these archetypal images (which abound in the literature on teacher reflectivity) include the teacher as a priest, poet, therapist, mother, revolutionary, trickster, and wise old woman or man. Limiting a teacher's role to a facilitator of Socratic discourse is psychologically and pedagogically problematic for such teachers, who generally have a wide range of psychological, ethical and spiritual reasons for being teachers.[44]

To begin exploring some of those reasons, we must journey to the next curricular landscapes—starting with the Existential landscape. And this we will do in the next chapter.

Conclusion

In this chapter, we examined the interpretive-procedural worldview and the educational approaches it entails. First, we saw that this is the territory on which arises metacognition—the ability to think about thinking. Second, it here that students are encouraged to see certain social phenomena relativistically—and in so doing, to transcend them. Third, we noted that this is the place where what is generally called the academic-rationalist curriculum, or curriculum-as-transaction, exists. This type of curriculum prizes and cultivates hypothetico-deductive thinking as its primary instrument of discovery and expression. Fourth, we examined the image of the student as a "cognitive apprentice." Fifth, we looked at Bruner's "Structure-of-the-Discipline" approach, Rummelhart's Schema Theory, Chi's Expert-Novice distinction, Chomsky's Generative Semantics, and Lipman's Student-as-Philosopher model as distinct yet interrelated instances of interpretive-proceduralism. Finally, as in the previous chapter, we used the seven-part curricular model to approach a few important questions and controversies in American educational history.

Topics for Discussion

1. Is the interpretive-procedural curriculum basically a white patriarchal discourse, as such feminist theorists as Kristeva and Cisoux have claimed? And even if it does have legitimate academic uses, does the interpretive-procedural approach to curriculum run counter to what Belenky has called "women's way of knowing"—which values relationship and care over analysis and control—and does it thereby push women to the margins of academic discourse?

2. What are your first impressions of Lipman's claim that the child can be taught to think like a "philosopher" insofar as the child can determine what is valuable to him, find evidence to support or contradict those value claims, and think about ways to put those values into ac-

tion? What are some psychological, ethical, and perhaps even spiritual consequences—positive and/or negative—of focusing on such issues and ways of thinking so early on in the child's education?

3. What do you think about the claim that a classical curriculum (i.e., one in which the students read canonical texts and learn traditional interpretive procedures) is ultimately the most socially empowering form of study for students from oppressed minorities?

Topics for Research

1. This chapter looked at how cybernetic psychologies are related to Chomskyan linguistics and its approach to creating foreign-language curricula in the 1960s and 1970s. Examine the role that behaviorist psychology played in the rise of Structuralist linguistics and its approach to second-language acquisition—i.e., the Mim-Mem/Aural-Oral approach of Lado, Fries, and others—in the 1940s through the 1960s.

2. Look at Bruner's structure-of-the-discipline curriculum *Man: A Course of Study*. What kind of success or lack of success did this curriculum meet with, and why?

3. Diane Ravitch, the conservative American educational historian, has recently argued that the conservative Progressive educationists of the early 20th century do not generally receive sufficient attention in the current study of U.S. educational history because of the postmodern biases of the current academic environment. Thus, read Bode's *Democracy as a Way of Life* (1937) and Bagley's *Education and Emergent Man* (1934). Discuss how these texts offer a pedagogical and historical perspective that you have perhaps not seen adequately or fairly represented in your studies.

Notes: Chapter 4

1. J. Banks, *Teaching Strategies for Ethnic Studies* (Boston: Allyn and Bacon, 1997).
2. J. Ferrer, *Revisioning Transpersonal Theory: A Participatory Vision of Human Spirituality* (Albany, New York: State University of New York Press, 2002).

3. A. Ornstein and F. Hunkins. *Curriculum: Foundations, Principles, and Issue,* (Boston: Allyn and Bacon, 1988).
4. J. Dewey as quoted in Ornstein and Hunkins, 79.
5. J. Miller, *The Educational Spectrum: Orientations to Curriculum.* (New York: Longman, 1983).
6. N. Noddings, "Stories and Conversations in Schools," In *Education, Information, and Transformation: Essays on Learning and Thinking,* ed. J. Kane, Columbus, Ohio: Merrill (1999): 319-336.
7. J. Miller. *The Holistic Curriculum* (Toronto, Ontario: The Ontario Institute for Studies in Education, 1988).
8. D. Ravitch, *Left Back: A Century of Failed School Reforms* (New York: Simon and Schuster, 2000).
9. M. Lipman, *"From* Philosophy Goes to School." *Philosophical Documents in Education* (New York: Longman, 1996), 250.
10. Lipman, 251.
11. Lipman, 249.
12. Lipman, 249. Emphasis added.
13. Lipman, 249.
14. Lipman, 252.
15. Ornstein and Hunkins, 98.
16. Lipman, 252.
17. J. Brown, A. Collins and P. Duguid, "Situated Cognition and the Culture of Learning," *Educational Researcher,* January-February (1989): 32-42.
18. Lipman, 252.
19. J. Miller and W. Seller, *Curriculum: Perspectives and Practice* (New York: Longman, 1985).
20. L. Resnick, "The 1987 Presidential Address: Learning in School and Out," *Educational Researcher* 16 (9) (1987): 33.
21. M. Hewson, "The Ecological Context of Knowledge: Implications for Learning Science in Developing Countries," *Journal of Curriculum Studies* 20(4) (1988): 324.
22. Brown et al., 32-42.
23. J. Bruner, *The Process of Education* (New York: Vintage, 1960), 44-48.
24. D. Rummelhart, "Schemata: The Building Blocks of Cognition," In *Theoretical Issues in Reading Comprehension,* eds. R. Spiro, B. Bruce, & W. Brewer (Hillside, New Jersey: Lawrence Erlbaum Associates 1980): 125-167.
25. J. Novak, "Concept Maps and Vee Diagrams: Two Metacognitive Tools to Facilitate Meaningful Learning," *Instructional Science, 19,* 29-52.
26. N. Chomsky, *Aspects of the Theory of Syntax* (Cambridge, Mass.: MIT Press, 1968).
27. R. Lado and C. Fries. *English Sentence Patterns: Understanding and Producing English Grammatical Structures* (Ann Arbor, Michigan: University of Michigan Press, 1958).

28. W. Rivers, *A Practical Guide to the Teaching of English as a Second or Foreign Language* (New York: Oxford University Press, 1978).

29. M. Chi, P. Feltovich, and R. Glaser, "Categorization and Representation of Physics Problems by Experts and Novices," *Cognitive Science* 5: 121-152.

30. Chi et al., 122-123.

31. R. Orton, *Constructivist and Information Processing Views of Representation in Mathematics Education.* A Paper Presented at the Annual Meeting of the American Educational Research Association.

32. C. Bereiter, "Towards a Solution of the Learning Paradox," *Review of Educational Research* 55(2) (1985): 205.

33. W. Winn, "Some Implications of Cognitive Theory for Instructional Design," *Instructional Science* 19 (1990): 63.

34. *The Yale Report of 1828* as excerpted in Willis et al., 1997, 28. See also: J. Brubacher and W. Rudy, *Higher Education in Transition: A History of American Colleges and Universities* 4th edition. New Brunswick, New Jersey: Transaction Publishers, 1997.

35. Willis et al., 1997, p. 85.

36. J. Brubacher and W. Rudy, *Higher Education in Transition: A History of American Colleges and Universities.* 4th Edition. New Brunswick, New Jersey: Transaction Publishers, 1997.

37. *Report of the Committee of Ten,* 1893, cited in Willis et al., 1997, 92-93.

38. B. Bode as quoted in Willis et al., 1997, 247.

39. Lipman, 252.

40. M. Adler. *The Paideia Proposal: An Educational Manifesto* (New York: MacMillan, 1982).

41. Barzun, J. (2000). *From Dawn to Decadence: 500 Years of Western Cultural Life* (New York: HarperCollins).

42. T.S. Eliot, *T.S. Eliot: The Complete Poems and Plays: 1909-1950* (New York: Harcourt, Brace and World, Inc., 1971).

43. C. Mayes, "The Teacher as an Archetype of Spirit," *Journal of Curriculum Studies,* 34(6) (2002): 699-718.

44. P. Joseph and G. Burnaford. *Images of Schoolteachers in Twentieth-Century America: Paragons, Polarities, Complexities* (New York: St. Martin's Press, 1994).

5

THE PHENOMENOLOGICAL LANDSCAPE

Pivotal Themes in Chapter 5

* The ability of consciousness to relativize even rationality as merely another event among many in consciousness.

* Consciousness as self- and world-forming.

* "Meaning" as the function of consciousness constantly "discovering itself" as Heidegger's *Dasein* (literally, a "Being-There") on a primal ground of Being.

* The basic Existentialist imperative for the individual to create herself in acts of freedom and authenticity. Self-awareness and self-actualization as the highest Existentialist goals.

* The educational impact of Maslow's ideal of self-actualization as the ultimate psychological and ethical goal in life. The phenomenological foundation of Existentialist philosophy and pedagogy.

* Noddings's notion of "ontological care" as the teacher helping the student self-actualize. Greene's use of art in the curriculum to "defamiliarize" the student's world, thereby awakening the student to the strangeness of existence and the primacy of her consciousness as it confronts that existence. Eisner's aesthetic view of curriculum theory.

* Huebner's vision of the curriculum as creating a "language of empowerment" in the classroom—enabling the student, through the subject matter, to discover new aspects of her consciousness and new ways to act on that heightened awareness in responsible freedom.

* Buber's notion of the existentially authentic *I-Thou* relationship, and its uses as a model for existentially authentic teacher-student interaction.

* Postmodern educational theory as essentially an Existentialist development in what Giddens has called "late modernity."

* The fifth landscape as the foundation of politically liberating pedagogies.

* The teacher reflectivity movement as a fifth-landscape event—in which teachers think deeply about the psychological, political, and pedagogical roots and implications of their sense of calling and classroom practice.

* The Existentialist/phenomenological approach as existing on the threshold of the spiritual domain.

The Phenomenological Turn

The fifth landscape is the place where consciousness begins to take *transrational* metaperspectives. This means that one comes to view any sign, symbol, concept, or system as fundamentally just one "event" in consciousness among many other "events." Any patterns we might impose on those inner events are ultimately reflections of our own need for order and not evidence of some external pattern. Such an external order of things may or may not exist, but it is beyond our capacity to know whether it does, and, if it does, what it is.

Indeed, consciousness even problematizes its own "unity" on the fifth landscape by seeing the "self" as continuously deconstructing and reconstructing itself in ongoing acts of existential freedom—a freedom limited only by death. To engage fully and authentically in such acts is, in Existentialist terms, to pursue one's unique "existential project" in "good faith."[1] In Heideggerian terms, it is to know oneself as *Dasein*—as an irreducible "Being-There" of awareness on the primal Ground of existence.[2] To fail to achieve and act on this existential awareness is the ethical error of living in "bad faith," which, because of its psychological inauthenticity and ineffectiveness, is the root of neurosis.[3]

In this realm of inner experience, the focus is not on "absolute objects"—what Kant called the thing-in-itself and what Sartre called the unknowable *etre-en-soi* (or "being-in-itself"). Rather, the focus is on the individual's thoroughly subjective, ultimately incommunicable *experience* of existence, which allows the individual to become a "being-for-herself"—the Sartrian *etre-pour-soi*. The emphasis on the fifth plain, then, is on consciousness-in-the-world and the-world-in-consciousness. At its outer reaches the fifth landscape may even begin to verge on the border of the more mystical sixth landscape vision of the world-*as*-consciousness.

According to Camus and Sartre, the only productive response to the specter of nihilism which haunted the 20th century was authentic being-in-the-world. One lives authentically in the world when, in full and frank awareness of her (and every human being's) limitations in an indifferent universe, a person courageously discovers and pursues those life-projects that are most meaningful to *her* until death irrevocably forecloses the process. As Camus insisted, the fundamental choice in life is whether or not to commit suicide. One is free to do so and it may be a valid choice, but if one does not, then the decision to live necessarily implies that one has a felt reason for continuing. In order to live authentically, one is ethically bound to discover and act on this reason for going on—this "existential project"—in the mature acceptance of one's mortality. This is mature living in "good faith." Living in "bad faith" is the neurotic attempt to escape the overwhelming truth of one's human limitations in an indifferent universe by concocting or buying into an evasive, deluded project of immortality. Such misguided projects are psychologically *unhealthy*, according to Existentialist psychotherapy, because they are existentially *unreal*.[4]

The primary danger of getting stuck on this landscape is the quagmire of existential despair. Because all signs, systems, rules and roles are seen merely as psychosocial constructs with no absolute validity, consciousness may easily fall into the disastrously counter-intuitive belief that, since there no longer seem to be any fourth-landscape universals, no worldview is preferable to any another. This psychologically and ethically unproductive result is the conclusion that any worldview is just another "text" in an ontological library where there is no reason to "check out" one book instead of another. Its newly found power to relativize *everything* can lead consciousness into a neurotic, nihilistic inability to commit to *anything*. Thus, in its less affirmative forms, postmodern thought teeters dangerously on the brink of a paralyzing self-absorption, as in Deleuze and Guattari's tendency to romanticize the schizoid state.[5]

In a more positive vein, it is also true that consciousness at this point can, if it chooses, begin "to go transrational" (to use Ken Wilber's phrase). But this does *not* mean that consciousness becomes "irrational." Rather, the phenomenological approach simply means that consciousness, retaining all of its rational powers, is able to "bootstrap" itself to higher ground from which it can view and evaluate rationality as just one of many ways of knowing—a useful way in certain contexts and for certain purposes but not "the last word" epistemologically. Indeed, the phenomenological turn insists that logic is often epistemically limiting, for "both rationalism and empiricism fail to depict thought as it occurs in lived or 'inner' time. The phenomenological investigator questions how phenomena...present themselves in the lived experience of the individual, especially as they present themselves in lived time."[6]

However, the phenomenological turn need not result in such self-consuming dead ends. As Sartre showed in his passionate involvement with Marxism, the Existentialist-phenomenological approach can be vitally engaged not only with matters of individual consciousness but also with issues of political importance, for in its most creative moments "human consciousness moves *toward* the world, not away from it.... Phenomenologically understood, consciousness is characterized by intentionality...."[7] In this light we may better understand the meaning of the famous Existentialist motto: "Existence precedes essence." Being, and one's experience *of* it at any *acutely lived* (as opposed to merely endured) moment, precedes any systematic statements we might make *about* it. The living and reflecting are all. At least, they are all one can *truly* know. "The more...commentary and analysis are undertaken, the more the inquiry becomes hermeneutical, narrative, or even practical," as indeed it is on the third and fourth landscapes.[8]

Yet the fundamental inadequacy of propositional language to capture and certify the nature of deeply lived experience does not mean that we are left mute in the face of such experience. For on this fertile landscape artistic expression flowers as the primary means of celebrating the freshness of Being-as-such. Art does this by "bracketing out" a piece of our taken-for-granted world so that we can see it fresh, as if for the first time, and thus respond to it creatively. This bracketing process should occur in curriculum making no less than in making or appreciating a piece of art. What Ezra Pound said about good poetry is also true of the good Existentialist curriculum: it "defamiliarizes" and breaks up a part of our world, and then makes us put it back together again in novel ways. This causes us to invest ourselves in that recreated portion of our reality with enhanced intellectual perceptivity, emotional immediacy, and moral validity. The great aesthetician Theodore Meyer Greene, writing about this interconnection of the ontological, aesthetic, and phenomenological realms, proclaimed that "a work of art is a unique, individual whole—a self-contained artistic 'organism' with a 'life' and 'reality' of its own.... The competent critic...apprehends the individual work of art in all its self-contained uniqueness through sensitive artistic re-creation."[9] Similarly, the teacher must help the student "recreate" the subject being studied in such a way that the student experientially makes it her own.

Curriculum and instruction that attend to the aesthetic-phenomenological realm have five major characteristics according to Van Manen, which begin to lead us into the *trans*-rational, or spiritual.

> (1) Phenomenological research investigates lived experience. The phenomenological investigator studies the life-world as it is immediately experienced, presumably before we conceptualize it.... (2) Phenomenological research seeks the essence of experiences, employing an "eidetic reduction" to "bracket" the "natural attitude," or to reflect on one's taken-for-granted commonsensical views of things.... (3) Phenomenological research is the conscious practice of "thoughtfulness...." Thoughtfulness is defined as "minding," a "heeding," for Heidegger, an "attunement" to what it feels like and means to be alive. Phenomenological pedagogy becomes an expression of "thoughtfulness...." (4) Phenomenological research does not produce knowledge for knowledge's sake; rather it produces knowledge to disclose what it means to be human. The phenomenological researcher works to comprehend the meaning of being in

the world, as man, woman, child. Such knowledge requires knowledge of historical, cultural, and political traditions.... (5) Phenomenological research always embodies a poetic quality..... Like poetry, phenomenology attempts an incantational, evocative speaking, a primal telling, wherein the phenomenologist aims to utilize the voice to an original singing of the world...."[10]

Noddings and the Curriculum as Ontological Caring

Echoing the dean of Humanist psychology, Abraham Maslow, Eisner characterized Existentialist approaches to education as self-actualization curricula.[11] Maslow, who was instrumental in defining education as the quasi-therapeutic pursuit of the student's existential identity and project, declared that

> if we want to be helpers, counselors, teachers, guides, or psychotherapists, what we must do is to accept the person and help him learn what kind of person he is already. What is his style, what are his aptitudes, what is the person good for, not good for, what can we build upon, what are his good raw materials, his potentialities?... Above all, we would care for the child, that is, enjoy him and his growth and his self-actualization.[12]

Dewey also said that the purpose of education should not be primarily to acquire information but to seek "self-realization." Likewise, Maxine Greene asserted that *that* curricula should offer the student the "possibility for him as an existing person [to make] sense of his own life-world."[13] This is, I believe, the heart of Noddings's vision of "caring." The caring teacher helps the student identify and realize herself and her project as an "existing person" with "[her] own life-world." Teachers often say the same thing with the simple statement, "I teach students, not subjects."

This does not mean that one minimizes the cognitive, social and historical import of what one is teaching. But it does mean that one is *primarily* concerned with teaching subject matter in such a way that it promotes the psychosocial health and potential of the child; and it also means that the teacher avoids presenting subject-matter to the student in a way that is irrelevant and dull. Noddings's caring is an *ontological caring*, not a *sentimental psychologizing*. It does *not* mean using sweet, "Hallmark" language or evoking mere emotionalism in class, as might happen if one takes a simplistic view of Noddings's complex notion of ontological care. Indeed, the teacher-language of love may be quite ethically demanding and conceptually subtle, it may even seem hard at times, but it is loving because it *cares* for the student *ontologically.*

For Noddings, the pedagogical and ethical imperative to care "is anchored in feminist perspectives. An ethic of care is thoroughly relational. It is the *relation* to which we point when we use the term 'caring'."[14] Her pedagogy, stemming from a feminist "relational ontology," is thus Existentialist through and through because

> it does not posit a source of moral life beyond actual human interaction. It does not depend on gods, nor eternal verities, nor an essential human nature, nor postulated underlying structures of human consciousness. Even its relational ontology points to something observable in this world—the fact that *I* am defined in relation."[15]

Curriculum is the marble on which teacher and student, fellow artists in a joint commission, freely, carefully, and dialogically conceive, carve out, and complete the figures of their individual and shared identities in the studio of the classroom.

Phenomenological curricularists often use artistic creativity as a model, metaphor and means of education when it is personally and interpersonally generative. This is especially true in the earlier work of Maxine Greene, where the synthesis of the phenomenological and aesthetic offers the student ample curricular "occasions for ordering the materials of [her unique] world, for imposing 'configurations' by means of experiences and perspectives made available for personally conducted cognitive action."[16] But before reconstructing our world, we must first deconstruct it by exploding the comfortable geometries of our ordinary existence. This aesthetic goal, which underlay Cubist painting, is translated by Greene into educational terms as the "Cubist curriculum."[17] Its purpose is to move the teacher and student beyond the easy, standard interpretations of the subject matter; to confront the issues under discussion with the same intensity, curiosity and creativity with which one confronts a piece of art for the first time. The teacher, no less than the student, must come face to face with the subject matter with the emotional clarity and moral sincerity that a good critic employs in evaluating a piece of art. When this happens, classroom discussion promotes self-awareness and humane action—both in the classroom and beyond.

This emphasis on the aesthetic dimension of phenomenologically valid curricula follows quite naturally from the very nature of the phenomenological endeavor, for phenomenological research "is that form of interpretive inquiry that focuses on human perceptions, particularly on the aesthetic qualities of human experience. As such, it is that form of interpretive inquiry that comes closest to artistic inquiry...."[18] Greene turned to certain art curricula to show how both teacher and student may best discover themselves and each other by authentic engagements with a piece of art.[19] Primarily, she focused on literature and literary criticism to make her pedagogical points. Ornstein & Hunkins have termed this and similar arts-based approaches to curriculum *"Humanist-Aesthetic."*[20] However, it would be a mistake to conclude that only art classes promote the "expressive outcomes" of "aesthetic" curricula. Any classroom can become an aesthetically and phenomenologically lively zone.

> Any activity—indeed, at their very best, activities that are engaged in to court surprise, to cultivate discovery, to find new forms of experience—is expressive in character. Nothing in the sciences, the home or mechanical arts, or in social relationships prohibits or diminishes the possibility of engaging in expressive outcomes. The education problem is to be sufficiently imaginative in the design of educational programs so that such outcomes will occur and their educational value will be high.[21]

To achieve this almost alchemical transformation of the ordinary classroom into the existential gold of poetic presence is the goal of Existentialist curricula.

It is not only in making and teaching a curriculum that the aesthetic dimension comes into play. It may also guide curriculum theorizing itself.

> We may want to study the aesthetic qualities of a textbook series, or of a series of deliberations and discussions leading to curriculum change, of a given teacher's classroom, or of a full degree sequence that we may be planning to alter.... The important point is that aesthetic inquiry into a curriculum problem must above all leave us free to *respond to qualities that may take us by surprise;* our response to these qualities will be helped and shaped by our training and experience in seeing these qualities....[22]

The phenomenological curriculum—highlighting personal exploration and expression—educationally embodies the existential ideal of living in good faith.

The Language of Empowerment

Duane Huebner's work continues to set the standard for any curriculum theorizing that aspires to experiential, aesthetic, and existential depth. Huebner was key in formulating the "Reconceptualist" notion that any curriculum is a text that may be interpreted in order to evaluate its psychological, political, existential, and spiritual assumptions.[23] Since curriculum is a "text," and since a text encodes some form of discourse, then we cannot possibly engage in curriculum studies without acknowledging its fundamentally linguistic nature. "Our teaching space is a text that constantly has to be read, interpreted, written, and rewritten."[24]

Classroom language through which the student enters into true relationship with the teacher, her classmates, and the subject matter is language that ultimately guides her into her own depths. As Marx insisted, we only know ourselves in relationship to others, and therefore alienation from others must lead to self-alienation. Teacher-language that promotes deep communication in the classroom sustains the student in her classroom journey of discovery of self and other—of discovery of self *through* the other. Emotionally and socially fed on this rich classroom discourse, the student is strengthened to engage in ethical action both in the classroom and the world.

Drawing on Heidegger, Huebner says that existentially careful, compassionate, and creative teacher language is poetic. Poetry is not simply language that follows certain conventions of meter and rhyme. When language is only that, it is a parody of poetry—and is just another linguistic object among many lifeless linguistic objects, signifying little more than a television commercial or a traffic sign. On the other hand, any dialogical moments of existential presence in the classroom *are* poetry. There thus emerges into even sharper focus the moral gravity of the teaching situation. St. John, at the outset of his gospel, tells us that God created the world by the force of His Word. In like manner, the teacher, godlike, creates classroom universes through her empowering or disempowering language.

The teacher's language largely determines whether the cosmos of the classroom is a life-affirming space, mindfully constructed to generate psychological, intellectual and ethical possibilities for the students, or whether it is an academic and emotional wasteland, where institutionally surviving by being anonymous or merely obedient is the student's number one goal. The moral potential of authentic teacher talk lends it an entirely different significance than the instrumental, competency-based, object-talk that both neo-liberal and neo-conservative "reformers" seek to impose on teachers and students. The object-talk that the corporate educational agendas prize—with their single-minded focus on the bottom-line of efficiency and expansion—reflects and promotes the object-fetishism that lies at the heart of capitalism itself. "In the technical-bureaucratic 'Newspeak' which dominates schooling, the future is expressed in watered-down language as objectives or goals. Image or vision, in contrast, is necessarily poetic and in large measure personal."[25]

Thus, on the fifth landscape, one's primary task is not the teaching of an established subject. This is not to deny the high importance of subject matter. However, the teacher—precisely *in order to* engage her students in subject matter most powerfully—should invite them to join her in a pedagogical song of discovery of self, other, and the world. And it is important to state again that these classroom incantations can occur as readily in a science class as a literature class, for pedagogical poetry is not a set of prefabricated skills, nor is it a practice that is limited to the privileged precincts of certain types of knowledge only.

A beautiful example of this comes from Martin Buber's essay "On Teaching," in which he asks the reader to imagine a young substitute teacher entering a classroom full of boys at the beginning of a geography class. The students are noisy, some are rude, a few even seem to be poised on the edge of their seats to catch the teacher in the smallest mistake. It hardly seems a likely venue for the birth of a poetic *I-Thou* relationship. Understandably defensive, the teacher is at once inclined to bark out orders,

> to say No, to say No to everything rising against him from beneath.... And if one starts from beneath one perhaps never arrives above, but everything comes down. But then his eyes meet a face which strikes him. It is not a beautiful face nor particularly intelligent; but it is a real face, or rather, the chaos preceding the cosmos of a real face. On it he reads a question which is something different from the general curiosity.... And he, the young teacher, addresses this face. He says nothing very ponderous or important, he

puts an ordinary introductory question: "What did you talk about last in geography? The Dead Sea? Well, what about the Dead Sea?" But there was obviously something not quite usual in the question, for the answer he gets is not the ordinary schoolboy answer; the boy begins to *tell a story.* Some months earlier he had stayed for a few hours on the shores of the Dead Sea and it is of this he tells. He adds: "And everything looked to me as if it had been created a day before the rest of creation." Quite unmistakably he had only in this moment made up his mind to talk about it. In the meantime his face has changed. It is no longer quite as chaotic as before. And the class has fallen silent. They all listen. The class, too, is no longer a chaos. Something has happened. The young teacher has started from above.[26]

The teacher assumes the poet's mantle whenever she galvanizes the student to the possibility for lived experience in the material at hand. Such singing can be heard as easily in a special education class— in the high hopes and wizened care that a teacher communicates to a marginalized student—as in an AP English class discussion of Dylan Thomas. Indeed, some of the most poetic teachers with whom I have the privilege to work, teach in programs and schools that are also the least prestigious in my community. But this should not be surprising, for great poetry has often come from the outskirts of polite society— and, in like manner, may emerge from the margins of educational respectability, too.

Existentially valid teacher talk is politically engaged, for it stands in opposition to the pseudo-speech of alienation that makes up the glossy jargons and slick slogans of corporate capitalism. The teacher and students linguistically call a politically alternative world into existence in the classroom and thus create a space that sparks with compassion and creativity, and which therefore always threatens to set surrounding spaces of alienation and servitude on fire. Socrates was politically dangerous precisely because he was pedagogically great.

In sum, our acts of teaching are moral when they permit rich relationships between people. Immoral teaching prevents authentic relationship by turning the student into a mere object of someone's corporate agendas, institutional objectives or personal lusts. When "the relationship between the teacher and student is one of *pure dialogue,*" language is aesthetically and morally life-giving.[27]

I have focused so far on how teacher language enables the student's being, but classroom also language shapes the *teacher's* being, for "teaching is fundamentally an act of being."[28] Or rather, teaching is fundamentally an act of being *or* non-being, depending on the teacher's use of either psychologically generative or destructive language. Authentic being as a teacher and authentic talking as a teacher go hand-in-hand for the person who has become a teacher out of a sense of "vocation"—that is, a felt moral mission to generate and cultivate personally and politically liberating conversation in the classroom.[29] And, truly, how could it be otherwise for the great teacher? How could we separate that teacher's language from her being, and how could we separate both from how, and how much, the student grows in the classroom? A teacher who is not teaching and talking out of a sense of calling cannot speak in a poetic voice, for a teacher's voice is the fruit of her ethical commitments.

Teaching *with* and *to* the whole person is emotionally and morally risky for the teacher—an existential gamble, entailing public acts of self-disclosure. Teaching with the whole person involves the possibility (even the inevitability) that we will sometimes be *dramatically and publicly* wrong—and *that* in full view of the very people whom we are trying to guide! "To accept teaching as a vocation" is not for the faint of heart, for to put on the teacher's mantle "is to acknowledge a fundamental fallibility, hence a fragility and insecurity."[30] But to be existentially meaningful, an act *must*, by definition, be performed in the arena of one's limitations. Paradoxically, laying oneself bare in this way—becoming vulnerable—is the teacher's greatest act of existential courage, for it is the precondition of what the Existentialist Protestant theologian Paul Tillich called "the courage to be"—and it is a valor that stems from true care for one's students, one's subject matter, and oneself.

Idle Talk/Non-Apocalyptic Talk
Nothing inhibits ethical classroom conversation so much as what Huebner has called "reckless language" and "obstinate language." Reckless language haphazardly treats the subject-matter as cold capital to mechanically deposit in the student's passive brain, not as a living medium of psychic, moral, and spiritual exchange between teacher and students. Subject-matter, deeply understood, has its own organic, evolving, independent existence that must itself be engaged in living and respectful encounter. Reckless language can neither grasp nor result in anything very deep, memorable, or relevant about the subject it is ostensibly researching.

Reckless language is toxic because it can poison subject matter—can make it seem deadly and distasteful to the student. Like a work of art, the subject matter under discussion in the classroom should be approached with humility. Careless language violates both student and subject matter. *Care-full* language, on the other hand, has reverence for the history embedded in and the possibilities engendered by the subject matter. At the same time, however, careful language unsentimentally probes the subject matter in order to root out whatever inhumane biases and intellectual arrogance it may harbor as it is presently constituted. Van Manen beautifully captures the necessity of existential humility before a subject matter that, like any living being, embodies a history, exists in a problematic present, and projects itself toward a largely indeterminate future:

> It is probably less correct to say that we learn *about* the subjects contained in the school curriculum than that the subjects let us know something. It is in this letting us know that subject matter becomes a true subject: a subject which makes relationship possible. The subject calls upon us in such a way that its otherness, its it-ness, turns into the dialogic Other: the "you." In this way our responsiveness, our "listening" to the subject, constitutes the very essence of the relationship of a student with subject matter.[32]

Idle talk is also wrong because it is *non-apocalyptic.* I am using the word "apocalypse" in its original sense as an "uncovering," a "revealing." *Engaged* teacher talk *is* apocalyptic because it is a conversational attempt to *reveal* in each existentially authentic classroom moment the teacher's and students' personal and collective histories and potentials. "History is continually unconcealing. In specific situations, in a classroom for instance, we attune ourselves in order to see that which our everyday eyes do not see. We must close these eyes, listen and discover what lies concealed."[33] In this light, curriculum becomes an apocalyptic occasion for personal and social discovery and action in the institutional space of the school. This, I believe, brings us close to Pinar's idea of the curriculum as *currere,* "the investigation of the individual experience of the public.... *Currere,* historically rooted in the field of curriculum, in Existentialism, phenomenology, and psychoanalysis, is the study of educational experience."[34]

The phenomenological curriculum is neither a document nor an agenda (although it may sometimes crystallize in that form); neither is it only a codified or quantified product (which by itself would only serve to *cover* the teacher's and student's ethical possibilities); rather, it is a pedagogically embodied act of and plea for the existential liberation of the teacher, the student, and, finally, the world.

Obstinate Talk/Power Trips

Another species of non-poetic teacher language, says Huebner, is obstinate talk. Whereas idle talk is a discursive sin of omission by the teacher who fails to inject any reality into classroom discourse, obstinate talk is a discursive sin of commission in which the teacher goes on "power trips." Power talk is obscure, unnecessarily technical, and arrogant. For the student, it is disempowering and demeaning. A teacher uses power talk to glorify herself and colonize the student psychologically, politically, and morally. "The natural educative consequences of conversation are broken when the power relations between speaker and listener are unequal and when power is used [by the teacher] to impose an interpretation...."[35] Freire speaks of the moral ugliness of power talk.

> The teacher who does not respect the student's curiosity in its diverse aesthetic, linguistic, and syntactic expressions; who uses irony to put down legitimate questioning...; who is not respectfully present in the educational experience of the student, transgresses fundamental ethical principles of the human condition.[36]

Drawing on Kohut's psychoanalytic theories, I have tried to demonstrate elsewhere that teacher power-talk often reflects infantile object-relations problems in the teacher.[37] At any rate, as a fundamental violation of the psycho-spiritual needs and spaces of the student, power talk is simply abusive—a pernicious example of what Buber called the *I-It* pseudo-relationship. "If a man lets it have the mastery, the continuing growing world of *It* overruns him and robs him of the reality of his own *I*, till the incubus over him and the ghost within him whisper to one another the confession of their non-salvation."[38] When this happens, the classroom becomes a psycho-spiritual killing-field. There is simply no evading the inescapable moral necessity that the teacher must speak the language of love, using the relational grammar of *I and Thou*. The teacher who furthers the student's existential "salvation" (even if only to a small degree) has, by her creative and caring use of language, resisted the wicked delights of domination that power language provides. She has said "No!" to the perverse appeal of what my religion calls "unrighteous dominion."[39]

Naturally, the teacher who uses language to enliven and empower a student inspires trust—trust that is all the more precious because it transcends the boundaries of that particular classroom and becomes

> trust in the world because this [teacher] exists—that is the most inward achievement of the relation in education. Because this human being exists, meaninglessness, no matter how hard pressed you are by it, cannot be the real truth. Because this human being exists, in the darkness the light lies hidden, in fear salvation, and in the callousness of one's fellow-men the great Love.[40]

Created by language, this trust also preserves language.

> Language is entrusted to the teacher until the student can receive it as his trust, and thus assume guardianship of it. Teachers guard and serve language by being alongside of it concernfully, by being with others in it conversationally, and by dwelling in it thoughtfully and poetically.[41]

Critical Theory and Postmodernism on the Fifth Landscape

On the fifth landscape, the postmodern approaches to curriculum theory also begin to show up on the map. This is unsurprising if (as Giddens has very perceptively suggested) we view postmodernism as largely a variation on earlier 20th-century Existentialism.[42] Both Existentialism and postmodernism revolve around the process of radical deconstruction/reconstruction of the self and society in ongoing questioning of all "master narratives." In the more affirmative varieties of postmodernism—such as that forwarded by Slattery—the ontological adventures of the self are not solipsistic—not divorced from the passionately felt need to question institutions and *mores* in order to shape them into more emotionally hospitable and politically liberating forms.[43] This is Kelly's ideal of curriculum as a continual dynamic of self and social redefinition—as a "process and development" in which the individual and society continuously (re)construct each other in an existential synergy that has come to be called "radical democracy."[44] The postmodern curriculum rests on the idea that the student's "development is a continual process of reconstruction, of submitting one's personal and private thoughts to public scrutiny."[45] According to most

postmodern curricularists, we only know ourselves as individuals insofar as we negotiate our being with others in various acts of mutual
shaping. We are existentially free (and, in fact, existentially obliged) to
democratically invent our *selves* and communities in ways that are individually and collectively unfettering. Perhaps the most important
20th-century educational prophet of this dual existential vision of personal and political freedom was Paolo Freire, who insisted that

> in truth, it would be incomprehensible if the awareness that
> I have of my presence in the world were not, simultane-
> ously, a sign of the impossibility of my absence from the
> construction of that presence. Insofar as I am a conscious
> presence in the world, I cannot hope to escape my respon-
> sibility for my action in the world.... At the heart of the ex-
> perience of coherently democratic authority is a basic, al-
> most obsessive dream: namely, to persuade or convince
> freedom of its vocation to autonomy as it travels the road of
> self-construction, using materials from within and without,
> but elaborated over and over again. It is within this auton-
> omy, laboriously constructed, that freedom will gradually
> occupy those spaces previously inhabited by dependency.[46]

Here is Freire's well known pedagogical practice of *conscientizacion,* which I would roughly translate as "consciousness-raising." It
is easiest to understand *conscientizacion* in light of what it is *not,* for although Freire was a Marxist, he was quite adamant that *conscientizacion* was *not* identical to the classical Marxist practice of "ideological
critique." Ideological critique occurs when a teacher moves into a site
of oppression in order to *tell* her students (in the standard Marxist terms
of class conflict) what is wrong with their political situation and then
instruct them about what they need to do in order to *correct* the situation. This is not *conscientizacion.* Indeed, it is psychologically insensi-
tive and ethically indefensible because it objectifies the very people
whom it purports to be liberating, positing a curricular *essence* that precedes (and thus negates) the personal *existence* of the oppressed students—and which, by being *imposed* on the students, objectifies and
dehumanizes them. This existential inauthenticity is a pedagogical and
political contradiction.

How does a curriculum of ideological critique objectify students?
It does so because it sees and treats them as mere instances of an *a priori* political analysis and thus misses the local texture of *their particu-*

lar conditions of oppression; it does so because it does not consult the people themselves about their lived experience of oppression—what, *in their views,* the oppression consists of, and what, *in their views,* would make it better; it does so because it is fundamentally oxymoronic, claiming to make people free by imposing on them a body of knowledge and a collection of skills without consulting them about whether they believe the knowledge and skills will be useful in their specific situation as it is presently constituted and *as they perceive it*; and, therefore, it destroys freedom in the name of freedom because it replaces the fiscal tyranny of the landlord with the ideological tyranny of the teacher. In fact, ideological critique simply shifts the locus of power from the landlord to the teacher. In both cases, the peasant/student is prohibited from taking part in the redefinition of self and society. She is constrained to listen and obey—always, of course, "for her own good." From all of this it follows, says Freire, that *conscientizacion* can occur only in the classroom where teacher and student freely and jointly identify and act upon their own felt needs, problems and goals at both the personal and collective levels.

Another salient feature of most postmodern approaches to the curriculum is the challenging of traditional definitions of subject-matter. With some postmodernists, this type of analysis is lively, compelling, and constructive, stimulating us to question what should count as knowledge in light of our individual and historical life-worlds. Slattery offers an excellent example of affirmative postmodernism, and I will therefore quote him at length.

> Humanity must transcend modernity...in ways that include the following features: a post-anthropocentric view of living in harmony with nature rather than a separateness from nature that leads to control and exploitation; a post-competitive sense of relationships as cooperative rather than as coercive and individualistic; a post-militaristic belief that conflict can be resolved by the development of the art of peaceful negotiation; a post-patriarchal vision of society in which the age-old religious, social, political, and economic subordination of women will be replaced by a social order based on the "feminine" and the "masculine" equally; a post-Eurocentric view that the values and practices of European tradition will no longer be assumed to be superior to those of other traditions...; a post-scientistic belief that while the natural sciences possess one important method of scientific investigation, there are also moral, re-

> ligious, and aesthetic intuitions that contain important
> truths that must be given a central role in the development
> of worldviews and public policy; a post-ecologically inde-
> pendent view of the cosmos rather than the mechanistic
> perspective of a modern engineer controlling the universe;
> and finally, a post-nationalistic view in which the individu-
> alism of nationalism is transcended and replaced by a
> planetary consciousness that is concerned about the welfare
> of the earth first and foremost. In short, postmodernism re-
> gards the world as an organism rather than as a machine...,
> and persons as interdependent rather than as isolated and
> independent.[47]

Knowledge domains should not be fixed, serving one group and marginalizing another. They should be evolving, interpenetrating, and interdefining so as to allow teachers and students to communally generate questions and projects that are psychosocially compelling. This kind of curriculum is a socially constructed conversation that draws upon the past but always in the service of present and future needs and possibilities. In this postmodern approach to the curriculum as process, "students learn not only how to operate within [knowledge domains] but also how to change them."[48] Van Manen exemplifies the reverence that this enterprise both inspires and requires.

> In listening and submitting to what it is that something lets
> us know, we (children or adults) enter a relationship with
> the things of the world about which we learn. To know a
> subject does not only mean to know it well and to know it
> seriously in the fundamental questions it poses. To know a
> subject also means to hold this knowledge in a way which
> shows that the knowledge is indeed a subject loved and re-
> spected for what it lets itself be known for.[49]

However, in its less constructive forms, postmodern curriculum theory dismisses the very notion of subject-matter and suicidally obliterates the very idea of curriculum and curriculum theorizing itself. It does so because it views not only traditional knowledge domains but even newly constructed ones as merely tools that one group of people will use to oppress others. This approach obviously relies heavily on the extreme postmodern notion that any social regulation is ultimately oppressive.[50]

Certainly, the idea that social forms often serve vested interests of some groups at the expense of others is not new. The whole sociological enterprise began with this assumption. But I firmly agree with Best and Kellner's argument that the extreme deconstructionist's project of reducing *all* institutional forms to *nothing but* instances of surreptitious psychic and political control is immature and even shrill.[51] It is reductionistic in its irresponsible disregard for the necessary and healthy purposes that institutions and institutional knowledge sometimes *do* in fact serve; it verges on paranoia in its excessive fear that lurking around every institutional corner or under every discursive bush is some monster of psychosocial catastrophe and control; and it evidences what can only be called an ongoing oedipal rage against the personal and archetypal father.

Postmodernism has performed the important service to curriculum studies of revealing how curricula can subtextually legitimate certain forms of "knowledge" that aggrandize some people and marginalize others. This is an important—indeed a crucial—component of any curriculum theory that aspires to psychological, intellectual, social, moral, and spiritual validity. The blanket condemnation of schools and curricula, however, as always and only instruments of some ubiquitous form of oppression (discernible everywhere but located nowhere in particular) is neither accurate nor helpful. We must dismiss as irresponsible, therefore, such sweeping postmodern condemnations as Popkewitz's pronouncement that curricula since the Reformation have *merely* represented a "disciplinary technology," an especially insidious "form of social regulation."[52] Some *have* been that—but they have been many other things, too. Curriculum theory has a great deal to learn from the postmodern turn, but we must be discriminating and, for the sake of the children whom we ultimately serve, embrace only the constructive aspects of postmodern curriculum theory—and leave the rest to die the natural death which they slowly seem to be doing.

The Reflective Practitioner

The fifth-landscape stress on self and social deconstruction/reconstruction is also the basis of the growing movement toward *teacher reflectivity* over the last two decades.[53] Teacher reflectivity encourages both prospective and practicing teachers to examine themselves at deep existential levels about the biographical and political forces at play in why and how they teach. The goal is to bring these largely subconscious ideas and images regarding teaching to the surface so that teachers may renew themselves, their curricula, and their practice.[54] The reflectivity movement arose as a rejoinder to the depersonalization of technical, competency-based approaches to teacher education that are rooted in behaviorism and the search for corporate profitability. In *technist* "pre-service" teacher "training," student teachers learn a set of predetermined "competencies."

Let me be clear here that I do not think that learning useful skills as a prospective teacher is bad. It would be impractical to deny that becoming familiar with some time-honored, concrete "tricks of the trade" has a pragmatic role to play in teacher education—and may help lessen some of the anxieties of the prospective teacher about how she will handle her first classes. However, I *am* arguing that a skills-based curriculum as the core of a teacher preparation program inevitably minimizes and ultimately negates each teacher's existential uniqueness. It is a curriculum of bad faith because it turns teachers into objects of an institutionally defined notion of "efficient practice"—and thereby turns them into uncritical agents of society. And not only are such approaches rife with moral and political danger; they are also psychologically dangerous because their anonymity does fundamental violence to each teacher's unique sense of calling.

As Van Manen has observed, we must not expect that society will always, or even often, understand our calling. Some people will even make light of it, especially those who see teaching as merely keeping children in line, pounding cultural platitudes into them, or priming them to make money.

> We must acknowledge that some people, some parents, some teachers may not heed or attend to the call of pedagogy. We may even acknowledge ourselves of having been deaf to the calling of parenting or teaching. And if we haven't heard its calling, how then can we comprehend its nature? For those who cannot hear, reflecting on pedagogy as a calling is just sentimental nonsense, or at best a useless exercise.[55]

This should not cause us to despair, however. And what is more, with biographical and critical reflectivity we need not do so! They help the teacher explore and cultivate her unique sense of calling in ways that promote her and her students' holistic growth. Thus, what Pinar has called "ontological autobiography" is a potent antidote to the poisonous objectification of teachers and students.[56]

How does a teacher engage in such existential reflectivity on her craft? She begins by asking herself questions. As I have written elsewhere:

> Examples of questions that a teacher engaging in biographical reflectivity might ask herself, are: *What psychological dynamics (i.e., personal needs, hurts, hopes, potencies and fears) were involved in my decision to become a teacher in the first place? (How) are these dynamics and needs getting addressed and expressed in my classroom? Are they changing as I develop as a teacher? Is my development as a teacher affecting them? Are they benefiting me and my students—or are they ever destructive or inappropriate?*
>
> Slightly different examples of questions at the personal level that have a more explicitly "pedagogical" ring, are: *How have my own experiences as a student shaped my images and models of good and bad teaching? Are these images and models empowering for me as a teacher or limiting? If they are positive, how can I cultivate them? If they are limiting, how can I eliminate them or harness them to better serve me and my students?*
>
> Biographical reflectivity—typically in the form of journal work, group processing, and contemplative techniques—provides a way to approach these questions.... Examples of questions that a teacher might ask himself/herself along these lines are: *Do the texts, curricula, and programs assigned have embedded in them problematic conclusions that serve the interests of a certain dominant class, race, ethnic group, or gender at the expense of another? Do I consciously or unconsciously share the dominant perspectives and interests so that I teach the required curriculum, text, and other materials in a way that uncritically reflects that agenda? And if my answer is "yes," then how, specifically, am I imposing all of this on students from the disempowered groups, thereby becoming an agent of their oppression instead of an agent of their liberation? In short, what can I do to raise my students' and my own political consciousness?*[57]

These psychologically, ethically, and politically rich approaches to teacher education, rooted in the teacher's reflection on her craft, are some of the best fruits that have appeared over the last several decades in the fields of teacher education and curriculum studies—and it is a harvest that has taken place of the fifth landscape.

The Threshold of the Transpersonal

The fifth landscape provides fertile ground for some of the best statements and practices in Existentialist/postmodern education—cultivating presence, fostering freedom, and celebrating personal and social diversity.

Furthermore, the fifth landscape often borders on *the transpersonal landscapes* of spiritual approaches to curriculum, which are the topics of chapters 6 and 7. For Gardner is certainly right: the fifth landscape curriculum is proto-religious in its stark confrontation with our epistemological limitation, our temporal bracketing as mortal beings, and the reality of our moral agency.[58] However, insofar as consciousness stops here, it does not attain that *trajectory toward transcendence* that characterizes fully spiritual world-views—and fully spiritual curricula.[59]

This landscape is also proto-religious because consciousness begins to see its "self" as a continuous creation, forever sloughing off any fixed properties or characteristics that would make it static. In the poet Wallace Stevens's terms, the self is revealed on the fifth landscape as "the supreme fiction"—and a paradoxical one, too, both because it *does not exist* as a stable entity and also because it *does exist* as an ongoing narrative self-invention. The discovery that the self is ephemeral is certainly at the heart of Buddhist psychology—a point that some Existentialist philosophers examined in considerable depth in the 1960s, when Zen Buddhism was becoming popular in the West.[60] This highlights from yet another angle the claim that the phenomenological turn takes us to the very threshold of spirituality, beginning with the sixth curricular landscape—the unitive spiritual landscape. Accordingly, it is to that penultimate landscape that we now turn.

Topics for Discussion

1. What are some situation-specific examples that you have experienced or which you might imagine of a teacher living in "bad faith" in the classroom? Of a student living in "bad faith" in the classroom? What does it mean for you—given your past experiences, present needs, sense of calling as a teacher, subject-matter, and institutional constraints at your school—to engage in your teaching practice in

"good faith"? What constitutes "good faith" in a student? Is it even possible for teachers in the public schools—increasingly pressured as they are by public criticism, institutional demands, and legislative/judicial guidelines—to teach in "good faith?"

2. Do you agree that the essence of the best teacher-student relationships is that they operate on an *I-Thou* basis? Are there other criteria that you feel are more important in evaluating the success of a teacher-student relationship? Are there some moments or subject-matters where an *I-Thou* relationship is more appropriate than others? Are there some when it is less so?

3. As you reflect on your sense of calling and classroom practice as a teacher and/or educational leader, what are some of the major psychological, political, cultural, and spiritual factors that have been or are especially important to you?

Topics for Research

1. Survey some of the major journal articles on teacher reflectivity over the last 20 years. What are some of the major issues with which it deals? What directions does it seem to have taken and to be taking? How widespread does teacher reflectivity actually seem to be in teacher education programs?

2. What have been some of the major responses over the last decade—*pro and con*—to Noddings's notion of teaching as care?

3. Compare Freire's 1970 work *Pedagogy of the Oppressed* with his 2001 *Pedagogy of Hope.* Do you see any changes in his thinking?

Notes: Chapter 5

1. J. Sartre, *Being and Nothingness: An Essay on Phenomenological Ontology* (New York: Philosophical Library, 1956).
2. M. Heidegger, *Being and Time* (New York: Harper and Row, 1964).
3. R. May and I. Yalom, "Existential Psychotherapy." In *Current Psychotherapies* ,eds. R. Corsini and D. Wedding. Itasca, Illinois: F.E. Peacock Publishers (1995): 262-292.
4. May and Yalom, 262-292.

5. G. Deleuze and F. Guattari, *A Thousand Plateaus* (Minneapolis: University of Minnesota Press, 1987).

6. W. Pinar, W. Reynolds, P. Slattery and P. Taubman, eds. *Understanding Curriculum: An Introduction to the Study of Historical and Contemporary Curriculum Discourses* (New York: Peter Lang, 2000), 405.

7. Ibid., 1992, 405-406.

8. P. Willis, *Learning to Labour* (Aldershot: Gower, 1977), 175.

9. T. Greene, "The Function of Criticism." In *The Problems of Aesthetics*, eds. E. Vivas and M. Krieger. New York: Reinhart (1953): 414.

10. M. Van Manen, "Phenomenological Pedagogy," *Curriculum Inquiry* 12(3) (1982): 407.

11. E. Eisner, *The Educational Imagination: On the Design and Evaluation of School Programs* (New York: Macmilllan, 1985).

12. A. Maslow, *Toward a Psychology of Being,* 2nd ed. (Princeton, New Jersey: D. Van Nostrand, 1968), 693.

13. M. Greene, "Cognition, Consciousness, and Curriculum," in *Heightened Consciousness, Cultural Revolution, and Curriculum Theory,* ed. W. Pinar. Berkeley, California: McCutchan Publishing (1974): 69-83.

14. N. Noddings, "Care and Moral Education," in *Critical Conversations in the Philosophy of Education,* ed. W. Kohli, New York: Routledge (1995): 138.

15. Ibid., 139.

16. M. Greene, "Curriculum and Consciousness," in *Consciousness, Cultural Revolution, and Curriculum Theory,* ed. W. Pinar. (Berkley, California: McCutchan Publishing, 1975): 299.

17. Ibid.

18. G. Willis, "Phenomenological Inquiry: Life-World Perceptions." In *Forms of Curriculum Inquiry,* ed. E. Short. Albany, New York: State University of New York Press (1991): 173.

19. M. Greene, "Cognition," 69-83.

20. A. Ornstein and F. Hunkins, *Curriculum: Foundations, Principles, and Issues* (Boston: Allyn and Bacon, 1988), 4.

21. Eisner, 122.

22. E. Vallance, "Aesthetic Inquiry." In *Forms of Curriculum Inquiry,* ed. E. Short. Albany, New York: State University of New York Press (1991): 159-160.

23. W. Pinar, ed., *Curriculum Theorizing: The Reconceptualists* (Berkeley, California: McCutchan Publishing, 1975).

24. P. Freire, *Pedagogy and Freedom: Ethics, Democracy, and Civic Courage* (New York: Rowman and Littlefield, 2001), 89.

25. D. Huebner, *The Lure of the Transcendent: Collected Essays by Dwayne E. Huebner,* ed. V. Hillis (London: Lawrence Erlbaum Associates, 1999), 383.

26. M. Buber, *Between Man and Man* (New York: Vintage, 1985), 112-113.

27. Ibid., 98.

28. T. Aoki, as quoted in Pinar et al., 1995, 427.
29. P. Joseph and G. Burnaford, *Images of Schoolteachers in Twentieth-Century America: Paragons, Polarities, Complexities* (New York: St. Martin's Press, 1994).
30. Huebner, 384-385.
31. Freire.
32. Van Manen, 295.
33. W. Pinar, "'Whole, Bright, and Deep with Understanding': Issues in Qualitative Research and Autobiographical Method," ed. P. Taylor, *Recent Developments in Curriculum Studies* (Philadelphia, Pennsylvania: NFER-NELSON Publishing Co., Ltd, 1986): 31-32.
34. W. Pinar, W. Reynolds, P. Slattery and P. Taubman, eds. *Understanding Curriculum: An Introduction to the Study of Historical and Contemporary Curriculum Discourses* (New York: Peter Lang, 1995), 400.
35. Huebner, 256.
36. Freire, 59.
37. Mayes, C. "Personal and Archetypal Aspects of Transference and Counter-Transference in the Classroom," *Encounter: Education for Meaning and Social Justice,* 15(2) (2002), 34-49. See also: C. Mayes, "Reflecting on the Archetypes of Teaching." *Teaching Education* 10(2) (1999): 3-16. C. Mayes, "The Use of Contemplative Practices in Teacher Education." *Encounter: Education for Meaning and Social Justice* 11(3) (1998): 17-31.
38. M. Buber, *I and Thou* (New York: Vintage, 1965), 46.
39. *Doctrine and Covenants of the Church of Jesus Christ of Latter-day Saints, The,* (Salt Lake City, Utah: The Church of Jesus Christ of Latter-day Saints, 1981), 121: 39.
40. M. Buber, *"Between,"* 98.
41. D. Huebner, *The Lure of the Transcendent: Collected Essays by Dwayne E. Huebner,* ed. V. Hillis (London: Lawrence Erlbaum Associates, 1999), 10.
42. A. Giddens, *Modernity and Self-Identity: Self and Society in the Late Modern Age* (Stanford: Stanford University Press, 1991). See also: S. Best and D. Kellner, *Postmodern Theory* (New York: The Guilford Press, 1991).
43. P. Slattery, *Curriculum Development in the Postmodern Era* (New York: Garland Publishing, Inc., 1995).
44. A. Kelly, *The Curriculum: Theory and Practice* 4th ed. (Thousand Oaks, California: Sage Publications, 1999).
45. W. Doll, "Teaching a Post-Modern Curriculum," in *Teaching and Thinking About Curriculum: Critical Inquiries,* eds. J. Sears and D. Marshall, New York: Teachers College Press (1993): 42.
46. Freire, 26, 87.
47. Slattery, 19.

48. A. Applebee, *Curriculum as Conversation: Transforming Traditions of Teaching and Learning* (Chicago: University of Chicago Press, 1996), 9.
49. M. Van Manen, "Phenomenological Pedagogy," *Curriculum Inquiry* 12(3) (1982): 295.
50. M. Foucault, *Power and Knowledge: Selected Interviews and Other Writings, 1972-1977* (New York: Pantheon Books, 1980).
51. S. Best and D. Kellner, *Postmodern Theory* (New York: The Guilford Press, 1991).
52. T. Popkewitz, "The Production of Reason and Power: Curriculum History and Intellectual Traditions," *Journal of Curriculum Studies* 29(2) (1997): 132.
53. R. Bullough, *First-year Teacher: A Case Study* (New York: Teachers College Press, 1989).
54. R. Bullough and A. Gitlin, A., *Becoming a Student of Teaching: Methodologies for Exploring Self and School Context.* New York: Garland Publishing, Inc., 1995. See also: E. Pajak and J. Blase, "The Impact of Teachers' Personal Lives on Professional Role Enactment: A Qualitative Analysis," *American Educational Research Journal* (26)2 (1989), 283-310. Pinar et al., 1995.
55. Van Manen, 285.
56. W. Pinar, "*Currere*: Toward Reconceptualization." In *Curriculum Theorizing: The Reconceptualists,* W. Pinar, ed., (Berkeley, California: McCutchan Publishing, 1975): 396-414.
57. C. Mayes, "Deepening our Reflectivity," *The Teacher Educator* 36(4) (2001): 251-252.
58. H. Gardner, "Are There Additional Intelligences? The Case for Naturalist, Spiritual, and Existential Intelligences," in *Education, Information, and Transformation: Essays on Learning and Thinking,* ed. J. Kane (Columbus, Ohio: Merrill, 1999): 111-131.
59. P. Berger, *The Sacred Canopy: Elements of a Sociological Theory of Religion* (New York: Doubleday and Company, 1967).
60. D. Suzuki, *An Introduction to Zen Buddhism* (New York: Grove Press, Inc., 1964).

6

THE UNITIVE-SPIRITUAL LANDSCAPE

Pivotal Themes in Chapter 6

* Maslow's early (1968) statements about the need for psychology to transcend merely personal issues and recognize the intrinsic need to connect with a spiritual dimension.

* The growth of Transpersonal psychology. Transpersonal psychology as "religion with a little 'r'"—not requiring any specific doctrinal commitments.

* Assagioli's "Psychosynthesis" and the Buddhistic/therapeutic notion of "disidentifying from subpersonalities" to find a "still point" in consciousness that transcends ego identity and connects with the Ground of all Being.

* Huxley's articulation of "the perennial philosophy"—a presumed mystical core of the world's great religions in which the ego dissolves into the cosmic totality. Its pedagogical and curricular implications and applications.

* The growth of the Holistic Education Movement. The historical roots of holistic education in Rousseau, Pestalozzi, Froebel, Tolstoy and the American Transcendentalists. Examples of holistic schools and curricula.

* Political and curricular implications of holistic perspectives: ecological issues, human-scale institutions, appropriate technology, nonviolence, and androgyny as psychologically optimal.

* The holistic view of adult education. Approaching second-half-of-life issues in terms of cultivating ontological awareness and preparation for passing from mortality into another sphere of existence.

* Images and practices of the teacher as a type of Zen master.

Beyond Self-Actualization: The Transpersonal Threshold

On the fifth landscape, the curriculum begins to problematize the concept of "the person" by picturing the individual as largely a product of social and linguistic factors. It is supposed that this fact negates the idea that there is something that is innate and immutable in each individual that lends him his unique identity. Rather, we should picture the "individual" as a work that is always in progress—a constantly shifting phenomenological zone of changing textures and boundaries. Nevertheless, this continuous deconstruction of the self does not fundamentally challenge the notion of personal identity so much as it attempts to redefine it in more valid ways. It is only on the sixth landscape that we make a quantum leap into the outskirts of the transcendent landscapes, where the self, as we have heretofore know it, dissolves. Wilber has called these outskirts the "threshold of the transpersonal," and they serve as the entrance gate to the "unitive curriculum" of the sixth landscape. We begin the journey on this curricular landscape by going back to the late 1960s in American psychology, when Abraham Maslow, the dean of Humanist/Existentialist psychotherapy in the United States, coined the term "transpersonal."

Maslow came to the conclusion in the late 1960s that psychology needed to go beyond the theoretical constructs and therapeutic modalities of behaviorism, psychoanalysis, and his own Humanist/Existentialist psychology—which he called the first three "forces" of modern psychology. His famous hierarchy-of-needs model, culminating in "self-actualization," was incomplete, he said, because it failed to take into account what he had come to see as a basic human need to access "the naturalistically transcendent, spiritual, and axiological." This he called religion with a little "r," implying that such experience did not necessarily require or lead to formal religious commitments.

> Humanistic, Third Force Psychology [is] transitional, a preparation for a still "higher" Fourth Psychology, transpersonal, transhuman, centered in the cosmos rather than in human needs and interest, going beyond humanness, identity, self-actualization, and the like.... Without the transpersonal, we get sick, violent, and nihilistic, or else hopeless and apathetic.[1]

Similarly, Ron Miller, a leading figure in transpersonal education, has asserted that Existential psychology, despite its undoubted significance as a "break from mainstream culture," is "often missing a sense of *transcendence,* a way of seeing human powers as expressions of something more vast and more mysterious than individual personality or social custom."[2]

Neither transpersonal psychology nor transpersonal curricula require commitment to a specific religious doctrine, for they deal with "levels of functioning of human consciousness that are potentially available in all cultures, with widely varying content and context."[3] Wade suggests that the ideological indeterminacy of the transpersonal realm relates to the fact that it is a "threshold" experience—a bridge between the existential realm and the realm of fully blown religious commitment of some sort. This "ontological neutralism"[4] is characteristic of transpersonal theory because

> conviction of an uncertain but presumably meaningful existence is often initially linked to an agnostic or completely non-theistic stance, but it incorporates a belief—often quite vague—in some existence beyond the physical plane (Wade, 1989). Exactly what this may be, or whether it exists at all, is unknown to [the person of transpersonal consciousness] and unimportant as a motivator, though death is tentatively construed as a transition to some other kind of existence. There is a growing interest in metaphysical issues in response to existential questions, and an openness to unconventional, transcendental concepts....[5]

An important recent development in transpersonal theory is Ferrer's notion of "enactive spirituality," which, like ontological neutralism, acknowledges the subjective validity of many forms of transpersonal experience but then makes the larger point that those multiple forms may also have equally valid *ontological reality*—especially when they are co-created by individuals in an "intersubjective community of belief."[6] Put simply, this is the aphorism that there are many paths up the mountain; some are strictly personal and others are formal—but many of them can get you to the top. Or, rather, to the *tops*—for Reality is a mountain with many peaks, not just one that stands in imperious isolation. Using another metaphor, Ferrer says that

> *the various traditions lead to enactment of different spiritual ultimates and/or transconceptual disclosures of reality.* Although these spiritual ultimates may share some qualities..., they constitute independent religious aims whose conflation may prove to be a serious mistake.... *We could say, then, that the Ocean of Emancipation has many shores.*[7]

It is not so much that there are many *roads to* salvation as that there are many different *kinds of* salvation. Despite the variety of "enactments" in this transpersonal pluralism, however, there do seem to be some common elements.

Common Elements of the Transpersonal Theories

As we saw on the fifth landscape, the "self" is interpreted as an ongoing project of phenomenological re-creation but always in the service and quest of a more actualized self. A fundamental aim of transpersonal theory, however, is (as its name indicates) to *transcend* the merely *personal* in order to find a reality that is higher and more lasting than could ever be found within the narrow boundaries of the existentially limited self. Whereas on the fifth landscape a person is encouraged to make and celebrate her biographical narrative as the ultimate project, the transpersonal theorist, therapist and teacher say that there is yet another project after the biographical one has reached its limit. This project

> is concerned not so much with our stories as with fear and attachment and their release, and with bringing mindfulness

to areas of delusion, grasping, and unnecessary suffering. One can, at times, find the deepest realizations of self and non-attachment through some of the methods of transpersonal psychology.[8]

To reach this supra-individual "disidentification" from the issues that had heretofore defined one's "self," transpersonal theorists insist upon the therapeutic need for some form of meditative practice, which Walsh and Vaughan call the "royal road to the transpersonal."

> Techniques exist for realizing transpersonal potentials. These techniques are part of an art or technology that has been refined over thousands of years, in hundreds of cultures, and constitute the contemplative core of the world's greatest religious traditions. This is the art or technology of transcendence, designed to catalyze transpersonal development.[9]

One of the most immediate effects of regular meditative practice—and one which is a central objective of transpersonal education and therapy—is what the early transpersonal psychiatrist Roberto Assagioli called "disidentification from sub-personalities." Ferrucci, Assagioli's chief disciple, explains:

> One of the most harmful illusions that can beguile us is the belief that we are an indivisible, immutable, totally consistent being.... We can easily perceive our actual multiplicity by realizing how often we modify our general outlook, changing our model of the universe with the same facility with which we change dress.... Our varying models of the universe color our perception and influence our way of being. And for each of them we develop a corresponding self-image, and a set of body postures and gestures, feelings, behaviors, words, habits, and beliefs. This entire constellation of elements constitutes in itself a kind of miniature personality, or, as we call it, a subpersonality.... Subpersonalities are psychological satellites, coexisting as a multitude of lives within the overall medium of our personality. *Each subpersonality has a style and a motivation of its own, often strikingly dissimilar from those of others. Each of us is a crowd.* There can be the rebel and the intellectual, the seducer and the housewife, the saboteur and the aesthete, the

organizer and the bon vivant.... Often they are far from being at peace with each other.[10]

Attaining a sense of the illusory nature of the self by watching
one's many ephemeral selves rise and fall in consciousness during a
meditation session is the crucial first step in dispelling the illusion that
there ever was or ever could be a "self" in the first place. To grasp this
fact is "to go transpersonal."[11] One trains the mind to observe the rising
and falling of these phenomenological clusters called "subpersonalities" with detachment. This leads to greater emotional presence and
practical efficiency.

The therapeutic possibilities of managing psychic pain through objective detachment are enormous, yet after three decades of transpersonal psychotherapeutic research and practice, they have been far from
fully explored.[12] Again Ferruci:

> When we recognize a subpersonality, we are able to step
> outside it and observe it. [This is] *disidentification.* Because
> we all have a tendency to identify with—become one
> with—this or that subpersonality, we come implicitly to be-
> lieve that we *are* it. Disidentification consists of our snap-
> ping out of this illusion and returning to our self. If is often
> accompanied by a sense of insight and liberation.[13]

Deikman, an early researcher in transpersonal states of consciousness, has termed this watching function the "Observing Self," which he
capitalizes in order to suggest that it is *personally* empty and therefore
metaphysically transcendent.[14] "This transparency or self-knowing is at
the same time a self-transcending process whereby knowing liberates
itself from its own ground (often almost immediately) to create new
grounds."[15] These "new grounds" are none other than the sixth landscape.

Freed from the painful illusion of separation and able to witness—
instead of suffer—the reality of impermanence, the Observing or
Transpersonal Self now begins to intuit that it is connected to a supra-
individual, supra-temporal Reality. Indeed, at the farthest Buddhistic
reaches of unitive spirituality, consciousness comes to know not only
that it is *related* to this supra-temporal Reality but that, ultimately and
eternally, it *is* this Reality. The existential self has fully evolved beyond
itself at this point into the realization of its own true nature as the One
Transpersonal Self. This is the Hindu realization: *Thou art the Divine.*

Even in its less rigorously meditative forms, this unitive intuition may bring an immense sense of

> authenticity—that this is one's own knowing; immediacy—there is little or no conceptual mediation; connectedness—the boundaries that separate and create a separate sense of an isolated self seem to dissolve; and transformative capacity—the knower is changed by the knowing and at the same time, openness to change in one's sense of identity opens one to the knowing.[16]

For the experience of the transpersonal to be durable, healing, and life-altering, occasional "peak experiences," as Maslow called them, are not enough. This may be difficult because of the almost literally "entrancing" nature of some of those peak experiences, which exert such a tremendous power to fascinate that they can easily become ends in themselves. Such experiences include the well documented existence of paranormal, psychic and synchronistic events that begin not only to occur on this landscape but even to abound.[17] Some transpersonal scholars and practitioners seem quite content to rest in this territory of spiritual manifestations as sufficient—the end of the journey. Most transpersonalists, however, see these manifestations as, at best, only part of the complete "unitive story"; some unitive "purists" even dismiss such things as more or less distractions on the road to complete enlightenment; others see them as necessary and valuable but secondary stepping stones on the road to the highest states of consciousness. In short, these phenomena—or *Siddhis,* as they are called in Hindu epistemology—are not nearly as important as a vision of the Whole which infuses one's entire life, not just rare and exciting moments. The fruit of such vision is compassion and virtuous living for the benefit of all sentient beings. The point is that the experience of and identification with the unitive Self must inform the "structure" of one's consciousness, not just be an exciting but sporadic "state."[18] Transforming the state into the structure is the goal of transpersonal therapy—and of transpersonal education as well.

As one's life is increasingly lived in the light of the transpersonal, there is a greater sense of the organic interconnection of self, other, nature and cosmos as a dynamic unity in which—to use a Buddhist metaphor—each part reflects all the other parts. Indeed, each part *is* the reflection of all the other parts. Each part, therefore, *is* only insofar as it *is in relationship* with everything else on the primal field of Being. This is what Miller means by "holism," which he identifies as the philosophical foundation of holistic education.

> In atomism the universe is viewed as a collection of atoms; in pragmatism it is seen as an ongoing process; in holism it is perceived as harmonious and interconnected. Holism acknowledges the individual part and that things are in process; however, there is a fundamental unity underlying the process and connecting the parts.[19]

Thus, I have termed this landscape *unitive*; for here each part is in the whole and the whole is in each part. To *know* and, even more profoundly, to *intuit* this wholeness *with* one's whole being and, indeed, *as* one's whole being, is to know the sacred, for the "*sacred* is the innate tendency to experience the world *whole*. It expresses a reverential oneness, a unity among things. Soul is a sacred connection between all things...."[20] And it bears stressing again that in the transpersonal therapies and pedagogies, meditative practices are indispensable in attaining this intuitive vision of ontological unity, for they "help one to *see*.... the interconnectedness of things."[21] This is the paradoxical yet saving wisdom of the unitive spiritual view: the farthest reaches of our subjectivity open out onto the primal landscape of that which fundamentally *is*, and which *is* only *in* and *as* an integral, indivisible unity. At this point, the existential self transcends itself to find itself, reborn, *in, for,* and *as* the Eternal Self.

The unitive view has been popularly summed up in what has become the prime formulation of a great deal of transpersonal theory. This is Aldous Huxley's statement of "the four fundamental doctrines" which characterize "The Perennial Philosophy"—so named because, according to Huxley, it summarizes the enduring essence of the world's greatest wisdom literatures stripped of their doctrinal and cultural differences. Because Huxley's statement of the Perennial Philosophy is so central in unitive theory, therapy, and education, I will cite its four guiding principles in their entirety:

> First: the phenomenal world of matter and of individualized consciousness—the world of things and animals and men and even gods—is the manifestation of a Divine Ground within which all partial realities have their being, and apart from which they would be nonexistent.

Second: human beings are capable not merely of knowing *about* the Divine Ground by inference; they can also realize its existence by a direct intuition, superior to discursive reasoning. This immediate knowledge unites the knower with that which is known.

Third: man possesses a double nature, a phenomenal ego and an eternal Self, which is the inner man, the spirit, the spark of divinity within the soul. It is possible for a man, if he so desires, to identify himself with the spirit and therefore with the Divine Ground, which is of the same or like nature with the spirit.

Fourth: man's life on earth has only one end and purpose: to identify himself with his eternal Self and so to come to unitive knowledge of the Divine Ground.[22]

Although the Perennial Philosophy has a distinctly Eastern orientation, one sees traces of it as well in the mysticism of certain Western religious figures—particularly Hildegard of Bingen, Juliana of Norwich, St. John of the Cross, St. Teresa of Avila, and Meister Eckhardt.[23] Whether in its Western or Eastern forms, however, unitive spirituality as it is currently practiced typically insists upon: 1) "The interconnectedness of reality and the fundamental unity of the universe," 2) "the intimate connection between the individual's inner or higher self and the fundamental unity of the universe," 3) "the cultivation of intuition and insight through contemplation and meditation," and 4) "social action as a means of relieving human suffering."[24]

Clearly, intuitive modes of seeing, being, and communicating are at a premium in transpersonal epistemology. They figure prominently in transpersonal curriculum theory, too, which insists upon the cultivation of intuition as a primary (if not indeed *the* primary) educational task. The transpersonal instructional theorist Reinsmith calls these the "apophatic" modes of teaching and learning.[25] Vaughn has identified four types of intuition.[26] There is *physical* intuition, such as the somatic warning signals that our body sends us when we are in danger; *emotional* intuition, such as the "sense" we have of a person after just meeting her; *mental* intuition, such as the "mere hunch" that leads a scientist to look in an unexpected corner for evidence to confirm or disconfirm a hypothesis; and most importantly for transpersonal therapy and education, *spiritual* intuition: "Here intuition is independent from feelings, thoughts, and sensations.... At the spiritual level intuition moves beyond dualism to experience unity directly.... Meditation is a technique designed to quiet the mind so that spiritual intuition can arise.[27] Feige has thus characterized the transpersonal way of knowing as an "aesthetic epistemology thriving in an aesthetic, ultimately unified world."[28] Although Feige's idea of an aesthetic epistemology bears similarities to Maxine Greene's vision of the aesthetic curriculum, the difference is that Greene is agnostic whereas for Feige the aesthetic curriculum is "redemptive" because it *does* lead the student to an intuition of divinity.

Holistic Education

The educational philosophies and practices that grew out of transpersonal theory in the 1970s called themselves "holistic education"—a phrase that is not used as much as it used to be but which still best captures the world-view embedded in this approach to curriculum. The success of *The Holistic Education Press* and its journal, *Encounter: Education for Meaning and Social Justice* (until several years ago known as *The Holistic Education Review*) along with the advent of other holistic presses and the spate of new studies in holistic education, bear witness to the growing appeal of this approach to curriculum. Holistic theory and practice has increasingly and courageously turned its attention to how to bring its spiritual yet non-dogmatic framework for education to public as well as private schools.

John Miller, a founding theorist of modern holistic education, has defined it in the following way:

> the focus of holistic education is on relationships—the relationships between linear thinking and intuition, the relationships between mind and body, the relationships between various domains of knowledge, the relationship between the individual and the community, and the relationship between self and Self. In the holistic curriculum the student examines these relationships so that he/she gains both an awareness of them and the skills necessary to transform the relationships where it is appropriate.[29]

Miller and Seller speak of the holistic approach to curriculum as "transformation" of the student at all levels—the physical, cognitive, psychological, social, emotional and spiritual.[30] They contrast this with two other forms of curriculum that have dominated 20th-century education. The first is curriculum as transmission—the teacher-centered conveying of facts and standardized assessment of how well the student can recall and reproduce those facts. This would roughly correspond to

Wilber's rule/role curriculum. The second is curriculum as transaction—those dialogical pedagogies that encourage the relativization of knowledge. Holistic curricula integrate the best of transmissional and transactional curricula—but always in the primarily *transformative* service of transcendence, without which, to revisit Maslow, "we get sick, violent, and nihilistic, or else hopeless and apathetic."[31] Sadly, Maslow's diagnosis describes the state of all too many of our students today.

Moffett's[32] and Miller's[33] genealogies of holistic education begin with Rousseau, Pestalozzi, and Froebel, move through both Tolstoy and the American Transcendentalists, and culminate in Montessori, Steiner, Dewey, and A.S. Neill. The pedagogical thread that joins these somewhat disparate educational philosophies is their shared "insistence on the total growth of each person—physical, emotional, social, intellectual, and spiritual."[34] Ron Miller asserts that "the *holistic paradigm*...is in truth a fertile, imaginative, and highly diverse worldview which draws upon serious scholarship, authentic mystical traditions, radical politics, and, above all, a genuine search for personal wholeness and a culture that would truly nurture human potentials."[35]

> An underlying assumption of transpersonal psychology is that physical, emotional, intellectual, and spiritual growth are interrelated, and the optimal educational environment stimulates and nurtures the intuitive as well as the rational, the imaginative as well as the practical, and the creative as well as the receptive functions of each individual. Transpersonal psychology has focused attention on the human capacity for self-transcendence as well as self-realization, and is concerned with the optimum development of consciousness.[36]

Waldorf Schools

Rudolf Steiner's Waldorf Schools are some of the best known examples of holistic education. Especially in the earliest years of a child's Waldorf education, there is ample use of art, music, poetry, myths, and world religions as the tools by which children ultimately learn most of the material that children in the public schools do—in addition to a great deal more than the public school child is ever fortunate enough to encounter. This creates "the imaginative basis for an intellectual understanding."[37]

Waldorf students learn in sequences and paces that are developmentally appropriate, aesthetically stimulating, emotionally supportive, and ecologically sensitive. A Waldorf site often has animals in a mini-farm to which the children attend throughout the day. In this manner, many of the classroom lessons are brought home in tangible ways. The inclusion of such household tasks as baking, sewing, cleaning and repairing also accomplishes these purposes as it cultivates educationally unconventional aspects of the student and fosters in him a sense of solidarity with people engaged in all sorts of work. This was certainly the Deweyan vision of "vocational education." Waldorf children often view and comment on each other's art work as it is displayed around the room without the signatures of the student-artists; this heightens the children's sense of interconnectedness by deemphasizing the standard public school obsession with ownership and competition.

This sketchy portrayal of Waldorf education cannot begin to do it justice. Hopefully, however, it suggests how, in the words of the Waldorf educator Joan Almon, Waldorf pedagogy embodies the holistic goal of fostering "living thinking [which] arises when body, soul, and spirit are allowed to interpenetrate and fructify one another."[38]

Confluent Education

Another example of the holistic curriculum can be found in "confluent education." I will use this model—first developed by Brown, Phillips, and Shapiro in 1976—to frame my remaining discussion of holistic education generally.[39] In this model, the curriculum is seen as "an ecological system" of four concentric circles/domains. Moving from the inner circle outward, these four domains are the intrapersonal, interpersonal, extrapersonal and transpersonal.[40]

The intrapersonal domain includes all sorts of psychological functions that affect the student's classroom performance. These include self-esteem, adequacy and identity issues as well as the psychosexual dynamics of the student-teacher relationship.[41] The Assagiolian notion of subpersonalities is also important in the intrapersonal holistic domain and is used by many holistic teachers in classroom activities (both academic and quasi-therapeutic) that aim to improve the student's scholastic performance and psychic functioning.[42]

One example of an intrapersonal activity is students briefly meditating together before class begins on a particular word such as "beauty," "compassion," "goodwill," "reality," "trust," "serenity," "simplicity," "service," "vitality," "will," or "wisdom."[43] A more clearly scholastic example might be to have students close their eyes and follow the teacher in an English class through a guided fantasy about an alternative course of action that a character in a novel might have taken but didn't. However, "the use of imagery is not limited to language or the creative arts," insists the transpersonal education theorist Thomas Roberts, for

> scientists use dreams, relaxation images, and a state of reverie to make discoveries. Einstein, for example, said he used words only as the very last step in his thinking. He felt the state of his body and used imagery in his original creative thinking. A middle school science teacher uses imagery with good results. Instead of teaching about the water cycle as something "out there," he has students imagine they are molecules of water and he takes them through the entire water cycle.... Guided cognitive imagery is an especially good way to introduce new material.[44]

In a math class, each student might silently develop an image for, say, the concept of irrational numbers or the second derivative of a function, and then share the image with the class. Moving the focus from the student to the teacher, I have also shown how a wide range of Eastern contemplative practices revolving around the twin meditative exercises of "insight" and "focus" meditation can help the prospective teacher contact deep psycho-spiritual images, issues and impulses that are core to her sense of professional calling.[45] I have also employed Jungian archetypal psychology (particularly its analysis of the mythic hero/heroine's journey) as a way to reflect upon some of the professional and relational watershed marks that characterize various teachers' professional lives.[46]

Perhaps the best presentation of intrapersonal holistic theories and strategies in the classroom—and one that is careful not to overstep institutional and legal boundaries regarding spirituality in the public schools—remains the Hendricks and Fadiman classic, *Transpersonal Education: A Curriculum for Feeling and Being.*[47] Claiming in the 1970s that "insights gained from the upsurge of interest in meditation, biofeedback, martial arts, Eastern thought, and altered states of consciousness are finding their ways into the classroom...[and] are accelerating and improving conventional learning, as well as bringing new and more personal areas of learning into the classroom," the authors explored the uses of guided imagery, dream-work, meditation, and mind-body work in even the most conventional public school class-rooms.[48]

The interpersonal domain—the second concentric circle in Brown and his associates' model—deals with

> functioning with others—parents, colleagues, students, or other adults in the world. What happens in and from these interactions is the subject of this area. What occurs in the inner [intrapersonal] circle relates to what occurs in the second [interpersonal] circle. Experiences in the interpersonal relations help shape the contents of the inner circle, affecting intrapersonal experience and learning. Of course, how we are as individuals [also] affects our interpersonal relationships.[49]

The third circle/domain is the focus of most traditional instruction. It is

> the impersonal or extrapersonal, the context in which people learn and experience life, both in and out of school. This circle could include the formal curriculum, the structure of the classroom, the school as a system, the community, and the values, both implicit and explicit, of society. The formal educational process in many schools is most concerned with the contents of this...circle. What is to be learned is emphasized, with less attention focused on the internal world of the student and on [second circle/domain] interactions among students and teachers in the process of learning.[50]

In Eisner's terms, the third curricular domain seems particularly concerned with the official and operational curricula.[51] In their integrative vision, holistic educationists never deny the crucial importance of the *pre-transpersonal* first, second and third domains in the total functioning of the individual and her many socio-cultural contexts. They do, however, insist that those domains must harmoniously and generatively interact not only with each other but, finally, with the most important and inclusive of all the domains—the *transpersonal*—for it is ultimately the transpersonal realm that invests not only our educational processes but our very lives with spiritual significance and hope.

This injunction to "go transpersonal" is more than merely an individual ethical imperative. It is political, too. Holistic educationists emphasize the necessity of an integrative pedagogy by reminding us of the dire ecological and cultural consequences of *not* thinking and acting holistically. According to Moffett, we need

> a new educational system with other social services [that rest upon] a thoroughgoing holistic approach, which tends to be spiritual, whether one thinks of it that way or not, because identifying with other people and creatures, and ultimately with the All, really defines spirituality in a nonsectarian way. The more inclusive the wholes that individuals are in, the holier the society they create together.[52]

Clark has made a very similar point.

> A systemic ecological worldview is now emerging.... This new worldview is global, holistic, and integrative. Its primary mode of thinking is whole-brain thought, incorporating both inductive and deductive strategies, while integrating both rational and intuitive modes of knowing. Although it acknowledges that for certain purposes the concept of objectivity is useful, this perspective affirms that, at its most fundamental level, all knowledge and experience is subjective and value-laden.... This emerging view acknowledges the importance of science and technology, but holds that these must be understood and applied within the context of a global, ecological perspective. This contextual shift reflects...a change in the basic assumptions that have shaped the purposes, goals, and methodologies of education since the early part of this century.[53]

Emphasizing the centrality of the ecological orientation to holistic politics, Bowers argues that we must abandon the anthropocentric, scientistic and colonizing metaphors that have defined Western culture in order to embrace a new metaphor—"the root metaphor of an ecology."

> As a change in root metaphors also changes the way we think about the nature of intelligence, I am proposing that a more adequate root metaphor take into account the way the individual is nested in the symbolic systems of culture and the culture is nested in ecosystems. Thus, these fundamental relationships and sources of dependency should be foregrounded in any discussion of what constitutes intelligence.[54]

According to John Miller, out of the root ecological metaphor grow the four major socio-cultural aims of holistic education—namely to promote: "1) an ecological sense, 2) human-scale organizations, 3) non-violence, and 4) androgyny."[55] In similar strains, Ron Miller observes that "to elevate the masculine and degrade the feminine is a destructive imbalance. An emphasis on rational, utilitarian intelligence, competing for success, and satisfaction of material desires while neglecting compassion, love, justice and peace cannot be a humane way of life." Hence, it is the Green political movement that most closely reflects the purposes and perspectives of holistic education, for it "clearly expresses the connection between a holistic, spiritual image of humanity and a radically democratic social philosophy."[56]

Transpersonal Adult Education

Transpersonal education is not only for children. It is also well suited to adults in their forties and beyond. Arguably, in fact, it is *best* suited to adults.[57] Jung insisted that ideally the person in the second half of life would be engaged in a process of increasing spiritualization, a deepening sense of connection to Something or Someone that transcends bodily death. Having attended to the major *personal* and *social* developmental tasks of the first half of the life that Erik Erikson[58] identified—such as creating an individual identity during adolescence, establishing oneself professionally, negotiating a union with a partner, and making a family between one's 20s and 40s—one now begins to come up against more *supra-personal* issues involving one's diminishing physical capacities, professional limitations, intractable psychological issues, and, ultimately, the increasingly insistent awareness of one's mortality—what T.S. Eliot called "the overwhelming question."[59]

For, neither professional accolades, physical exercise regimens, face-lifts and tummy-tucks, or extra-marital affairs with younger partners can bring eternal youth or dispel the specter of death—a phantom which takes on an increasingly intimate form as we move more deeply into the second half of life. Those *personal* tasks and triumphs that powered the first half of our lives become less significant in the second half of our lives. Or, as Jung liked to put it, the personal psychologies that addressed the needs of the person in the sunrise to noon of his life must give way to a transpersonal psychology regarding the issues of noon to sunset.

According to the transpersonal adult-education theorist V. Quinton Wacks, "full ego- or self-transcendence becomes possible only during the adult and gerontological years…. [B]ecause of life stage or developmental tasks of living, most individuals do not become concerned with such growth needs until the second half of life or later." Most holistic, later life curricula embrace the Transcendentalist tenet "that we are all connected in a common humanity and are part of a larger whole."[60] Curricula that foster this vision of universal interconnectedness promote "a heightened sense of cosmic clarity, altered perception of space and time, an intuitive grasp of the interconnectedness of all things, and a joyful sense of the ultimate perfection of the universe."[61]

This holistic educational view of aging, filled with personally and socially transforming possibilities, contrasts starkly with American "youth worship." Our television and computer screens, CDs and radios sometimes seem to throb and overflow with the seductive cultural message that youth and its sensuality are the one true god; and that aging is the inevitable, inexcusable sin—the Fall from sexual grace which, unlike the Fall in the Judaeo-Christian narrative, comes not at the beginning of life but at its end. Hence, in a commercial for *Pepsi*, Bob Dole, the aged and defeated conservative candidate for president of the United States (who is also in another commercial for the potency enhancing drug *Viagra*), sits alone in a darkened room and wistfully leers at a nubile, semi-clad Britney Spears undulating her hips to sell Pepsi, "for those who think young." He is the postmodern American icon of the superannuated man who may no longer be washed clean of his chronological sin in the saving waters of adolescent sexuality. "A nation that is tyrannically gripped by the spirit of youth will worship it and be addicted to it in a broad variety of forms. It will not be able to satisfy its appetites, live within its means, or set limits upon itself, either material or moral."[62]

The transpersonal educational vision of the maturing adult is not only pedagogically but also politically important, then, for it calls to repentance a culture that disprizes the aged, blithely ignores their wisdom, and only poorly provides for their continuing education. The folly in all of this (outside of the fact that *even we* must someday grow old!) is that we lose the benefit of the ripened vision of the elderly, which could do so much to ripen our own. Indeed, one of the great appeals of holistic educational visions is their stress upon indigenous forms of knowledge and ancient ways of teaching that in almost every case rely upon the wisdom of the elders. This is a wisdom that both *conserves* a culture and opens new possibilities for *transforming* it.

> Part of the unique significance of life's second half is the transcendent function. To transcend means to rise above, to evolve beyond, to see from a broader perspective, and to experience existence and consciousness completely and fully. Whether by evolving through or by experiencing a quantum leap beyond prior conditions or standards, the person expands what has been and what is considered to be normal or possible.[63]

The Teacher as Zen Master

In reflecting on their calling and practice, certain teachers and teacher educators use spiritual imagery. These images embody various aspects of what I have termed "the teacher as an archetype of spirit."[64] These aspects fall into four overlapping but still quite distinct areas: (1) "discursive spirituality" (embodied in images of the teacher as philosopher), (2) "civic spirituality" (embodied in images of the teacher as prophet of democracy), (3) "incarnational spirituality" (embodied in images of the teacher as priest), and (4) "ontological spirituality" (embodied in images of the teacher as Zen master/counselor/mother). It is in this last image of the teacher—that is, as a classroom exemplar of a unitive spirituality of presence—that we see with special clarity the Buddhistic assumptions of most transpersonal approaches to education.

For instance, Reinsmith argues that the teacher as a "Witness or Abiding Presence" is the culmination of great teaching.[65] The Zen teacher—portrayed by Eugen Herrigel in the majestic figure of his Zen archery master in the 1971 classic *Zen and the Art of Archery*—is an example of such a teacher. This type of teacher is a still-point for the student in her turning world of subpersonalities and moral confusion.[66] He is also a flawless mirror for the student, reflecting her to herself with such accuracy and authenticity that she sees herself as if for the first time. But, paradoxically, seeing oneself clearly is to see that one does not really *have* a *self* at all. One discovers instead that one is just a kaleidoscope of shifting phenomenological responses to shifting conditions—or more accurately, that there really is no space between the mental responses and the conditions, for they are finally the same thing in the merger of consciousness and its illusory *objects*.

Looking into the mirror of the teacher, therefore, the student discovers that there is no *one* there: the mirror is empty. The teacher has

drawn the novice out of her illusory mental formations into that absolute negation, that fruitful Void which is self-existent Being.[67] This is
the pedagogical goal of Reinsmith's teacher as Witness/Abiding Presence. Curriculum is the medium but the Great Emptiness is the message. "Teaching in this sense becomes mysterious; the teacher's 'non-
doing' paradoxically brings a feeling of fulfillment unlike that in the
previous forms.... The teacher is moving toward a certain egoless-
ness."[68]

In "Zen and the Art of Teaching," Tremmel discusses how unitive
pedagogy pays rich relational and reflective dividends:

> I am beginning to see that paying attention, not only to what is going
> on around us but also within us, is not only a necessary step towards
> mindfulness and Zen, but it is also the better part of reflective prac-
> tice. For both Zen students and education students, without their pay-
> ing attention, no skillful action of any kind can occur."[69]

The teacher as a counselor and mother—two other images that appear with some frequency in the teacher-reflectivity literature—are
variations on the image of the teacher as Zen master, for their goal is
also the student's psychospiritual nurturance and balance. Most transpersonal educationists quite correctly point to this unique form of presence and nurturance as one of the best fruits of transpersonal approaches to curriculum and instruction.[70]

The Unitive Alternative

In its celebration and integration of various aspects of the learner's
being and needs, its complex vision of the teacher and her craft, its responsiveness to our spiritual cravings, and, finally, its synthesis of the
physical, emotional, intellectual, political and spiritual spheres, there
can be little doubt that the transpersonal, holistic curriculum landscape
is a terrain of great importance. The unitive approaches to education
have immeasurably deepened our vision of the student in her physical,
emotional, intellectual, social and, above all, spiritual aspects. Although
these approaches are varied, they share a commitment to the student as
an integrated being. Yet, for all its fascination and fertility, the unitive
landscape has been far from adequately explored and mapped in most
current educational theory and practice. Indeed, the sixth curricular
landscape unfortunately remains in large measure *terra incognita*. If we
hope for our curricula to have real psychospiritual depths and effects,

we must increase our efforts to explore and map out the unitive, holistic terrain with the seriousness that it deserves.

Topics for Discussion

1. Maslow said that transpersonal psychology and transpersonal educa-tion were not, strictly speaking, *forms of religion* because they were not *formally religious*. Nevertheless, can you foresee any possible legal, political, or institutional problems in using transpersonal activities and approaches in public school classrooms?

2. Can you envisage a curriculum that you are presently teaching, have taught, or anticipate teaching, in the terms that the Confluent Education Model provides? That is, how would you devise a curriculum in your specific field or grade level that would address topics at the interper-sonal, intrapersonal, extrapersonal, and transpersonal levels? Are there some fields to which this model is better suited than others? Are there some fields for which this model would be unsuitable?

3. Do you agree with Reinsmith that "the teacher as abiding witness and presence" is the highest form of teaching? Is this image of the teacher more suitable to certain contexts, subjects, or levels than oth-ers?

Topics for Research

1. Examine the last 20 issues (i.e., the last 5 years) of the journal *En-counter: Education for Meaning and Social Justice*—the most impor-tant American journal in holistic education. (Note that its name used to be *The Holistic Education Review*). What are some of the major themes that you see in reviewing that body of literature? To what uses might you put those themes given your present situation as an educator and educational leader?

2. What are some of the major topics and who are some of the major theorists and practitioners currently in the ecological education move-ment? Be sure to look at the various forms of ecological education, ranging from more conventional forms already in place in many

schools to the "deep ecology" movements that call for a radical restructuring of society in general.

3. Trace the rise and progress of the Waldorf School Movement, or of some other holistic education movement.

Notes: Chapter 6

1. A. Maslow, *Toward a Psychology of Being,* 2nd ed. (Princeton, New Jersey: D. Van Nostrand, 1968), iii-iv.
2. R. Miller, *What are Schools For? Holistic Education in American Culture* (Brandon, Vermont: Holistic Education Press, 1990), 64.
3. B. Scotton, A. Chinen and J. Battista, eds. *Textbook of Transpersonal Psychiatry and Psychology* (New York: Basic Books, 1996), 4.
4. P. Nelson, "Mystical Experience and Radical Deconstruction: Through the Ontological Looking Glass," In *Transpersonal Knowing: Exploring the Horizon of Consciousness,* eds. T. Hart, P. Nelson and K. Puhakka, Albany, New York: State University of New York Press (2000): 57.
5. J. Wade, *Changes of Mind: A Holonomic Theory of the Evolution of Consciousness,* (2001): 171.
6. J. Ferrer, *Revisioning Transpersonal Theory: A Participatory Vision of Human Spirituality* (Albany, New York: State University of New York Press, 2002).
7. Ferrer, 147. Emphasis in original.
8. J. Kornfeld, *A Path with Heart: A Journey through the Perils and Promises of the Spiritual Path* (New York, NY: Bantam Books, 1993), 68.
9. F. Walsh and F. Vaughan, eds. *Paths Beyond Ego: The Transpersonal Vision.* Los Angeles, California: Jeremy P. Tarcher (1993): 47.
10. P. Ferrucci, *What We May Be: Techniques for Psychological and Spiritual Growth through Psychosynthesis* (Los Angeles, California: Jeremy Tarcher, Inc., 1982), 47-48. Emphasis added.
11. K. Wilber, *A Brief History of Everything* (Boston: Shambhala, 1996).
12. B. Cortright, *Psychotherapy and Spirit: Theory and Practice in Transpersonal Psychotherapy* (Albany, New York: State University of New York Press, 1997).
13. Ferrucci, 49.
14. A. Deikman, *The Observing Self: Mysticism and Psychotherapy* (Boston, Mass.: Beacon Press, 1982).
15. Nelson, 2.
16. Ibid, 5.
17. D. Griffin, *Parapsychology, Philosophy, and Spirituality: A Postmodern Exploration* (Albany, New York: State University of New York Press, 1997).

18. K. Wilber, *Integral Psychology: Consciousness, Spirit, Psychology, Therapy* (London: Shambhala, 2000).
19. J. Miller, *The Holistic Curriculum* (Toronto, Ontario: The Ontario Institute for Studies in Education, 1988), 8.
20. B. Samples, "Learning as Transformation," in *Education, Information, and Transformation*, ed. J. Kane. Columbus, Ohio: Merrill/Prentice Hall (1999): 199.
21. J. Miller, 8.
22. A. Huxley, "The Perennial Philosophy," in *Paths Beyond Ego: The Transpersonal Vision*, eds. R. Walsh and F. Vaughan: Los Angeles, California: Jeremy P. Tarcher Publishers (1993), 213.
23. E. Underhill, *Mysticism: A Study in the Nature and Development of Man's Spiritual Consciousness* (New York: E.P. Dutton, 1961).
24. J. Miller and W. Seller, *Curriculum: Perspectives and Practice* (New York: Longman, 1985), 121-124.
25. W. Reinsmith, *Archetypal Forms in Teaching: A Continuum* (New York: Greenwood Press, 1992).
26. F. Vaughan, 1985. *The Inward Arc: Healing and Wholeness in Psychotherapy and Spirituality.* Boston, Massachusetts: New Science Library.
27. J. Miller, 76-77.
28. D. Feige, "The Legacy of Gregory Bateson: Envisioning Aesthetic Epistemologies and Praxis," in *Education, Information, and Transformation*, ed. J. Kane, Columbus, Ohio: Merrill/Prentice Hall (1999): 87.
29. J. Miller, 3.
30. J. Miller and W. Seller, *Curriculum: Perspectives and Practice* (New York: Longman, 1985).
31. A. Maslow, *Toward a Psychology of Being*, 2nd ed. (Princeton, New Jersey: D. Van Nostrand 1968), iii-iv.
32. J. Moffett, *The Universal Schoolhouse: Spiritual Awakening through Education* (San Francisco, California: Jossey-Bass Publishers, 1994).
33. J. Miller.
34. J. Moffett, *The Universal Schoolhouse: Spiritual Awakening through Education* (San Francisco, California: Jossey-Bass Publishers, 1994), 9.
35. R. Miller, *What are Schools For? Holistic Education in American Culture* (Brandon, Vermont: Holistic Education Press, 1990), 58.
36. W. Schutz, "Education and the Body," in *Transpersonal Education: A Curriculum for Feeling and Being*, eds. G. Hendricks and J. Fadiman, Englewood Cliffs, New Jersey: Prentice-Hall (1976): 4.
37. R. Trostli, "Educating as an Art: The Waldorf Approach," in *New Directions in Education: Selections from Holistic Education Review*, ed. R. Miller, Brandon, Vermont: Holistic Education Press (1991): 345.
38. J. Almon, "From Cognitive Learning to Creative Thinking," in *Education, Information, and Transformation: Essays on Learning and Thinking*, ed. J. Kane, Columbus, Ohio: Merrill (1999): 259.

39. G. Brown, M. Phillips, and S. Shapiro, *Getting It All Together: Confluent Education* (Bloomington, Indiana: Phi Delta Kappa, 1976).
40. Ibid.
41. C. Mayes, "Reflecting on the Archetypes of Teaching," *Teaching Education* 10(2) (1999): 3-16.
42. D. Whitmore, *Psychosynthesis in Education: A Guide to the Joy of Learning* (Rochester, Vermont: Destiny Books, 1986).
43. Whitmore, 107.
44. T. Roberts, "Expanding Thinking Through Consciousness Education," *Educational Leadership* 39(1) (1981): 53.
45. C. Mayes, "The Use of Contemplative Practices in Teacher Education," *Encounter: Education for Meaning and Social Justice* 11(3) (1998): 17-31. See also: T. Roberts, "States of Consciousness: A New Intellectual Direction, a New Teacher Education Direction," *Journal of Teacher Education* 36(2) (1985): 55-59.
46. Mayes, 1999; Mayes, 2002.
47. G. Hendricks and J. Fadiman, eds. *Transpersonal Education: A Curriculum for Feeling and Being* (Englewood Cliffs, New Jersey: Prentice-Hall, Inc., 1976).
48. Ibid., vii.
49. Brown et al., 1976, p. 11.
50. Ibid.
51. E. Eisner, *The Educational Imagination: On the Design and Evaluation of School Programs* (New York: Macmillan, 1985).
52. Moffett, xix.
53. E. Clark, Jr. "The Search for a New Education Paradigm: The Implications of New Assumptions about Thinking and Learning," in *New Directions in Education: Selections from Holistic Education Review,* ed. R. Miller, Brandon, Vermont: Holistic Education Press (1991): 17.
54. C. Bowers, "Why Culture Rather than Data Should be Understood as the Basis of Intelligence," in *Education, Information, and Transformation,* ed. J. Kane, Columbus, Ohio: Merrill/Prentice Hall (1999): 34.
55. J. Miller, 48.
56. R. Miller, 60, 61.
57. A. Chinen, *In the Ever After: Fairy Tales and the Second Half of Life* (Wilmette, Illinois: Chiron Publications, 1989).
58. E. Erikson, *Childhood and Society* (New York: Norton, 1963).
59. T.S. Eliot, *T.S. Eliot: The Complete Poems and Plays: 1909-1950* (New York: Harcourt, Brace and World, Inc., 1971).
60. V. Wacks, Jr. "A Case for Self-Transcendence as a Purpose of Adult Education," *Adult Education Quarterly* 38(1) (1987): 52.
61. R. Walsh and F. Vaughan, eds. *Paths Beyond Ego: The Transpersonal Vision.* (Los Angeles, California: Jeremy P. Tarcher, 1980).
62. M. Gellert, *The Fate of America: An Inquiry into National Character* (Washington, D.C.: Brassey's, Inc, 2001), 22.

63. Wacks, 46.
64. C. Mayes, "Aspects of the Teacher as an Archetype of Spirit." *Journal of Curriculum Studies,* 34(6) (2002), 699-718. See also: P. Joseph, and G. Burnaford, *Images of Schoolteachers in Twentieth-Century America: Paragons, Polarities, Complexities* (New York: St. Martin's Press, 1994). M. O'Reilley, *Radical Presence: Teaching as a Contemplative Activity* (Portsmouth, New Hampshire: Boynton/Cook Publishers, 1998).
65. Reinsmith.
66. E. Herrigel, *Zen and the Art of Archery* (New York: Vintage Book, 1971).
67. D.T. Suzuki, *An Introduction to Zen Buddhism* (New York: Grove Press, Inc., 1964).
68. Reinsmith, 140.
69. R. Tremmel, "Zen and the Art of Reflective Practice in Teacher Education," *Harvard Educational Journal* 63(4) (1993): 447.
70. D. Whitmore, 1986; T. Roberts (ed.), *Four Psychologies Applied to Education: Freudian, Behavioral, Humanistic, Transpersonal* (Cambridge, Massachusetts: Schenkman Publishing Company, 1975). T. Roberts, T. and F. Clark, *Transpersonal Psychology in Education.* (Bloomington, Indiana: The Phi Delta Kappa, 1975).

7

THE DIALECTIC-SPIRITUAL LANDSCAPE

Pivotal Themes in Chapter 7

* Basic principles of dialectic spirituality—and how it differs from unitive spirituality. The focus on a personal God. The individual in the process of establishing an eternal personal identity, not fusing with an impersonal Ground of Being.

* Kierkegaard and Buber as representatives of dialectic spirituality. Some of the pedagogical implications of their thought.

* Some major figures of dialectic spirituality in 20th century curriculum theory: Phenix, Macdonald, and especially Huebner.

* Corporate educational agendas as a threat to the dialogical relationship between teacher and student that is at the core of dialectic spirituality and pedagogy.

* Curriculum as a "living presence" through which the teacher and student enter into relationship. Dialectical approaches to the teaching of

science, not only the humanities and arts. The prophetic role of the teacher.

Basic Differences between Unitive and Dialectic Spirituality

In the classical texts, theologies, and practices of the unitive view, the idea that one is separated from God is considered the root illusion of human existence and the cause of all human pain. When we learn how to meditatively distance ourselves from those ever shifting mental constructs that we call our "self," we come to see that we are not any of those waves of the phenomenological sea but are, instead, the sea itself. This transpersonal "Self," as opposed to personal "self," is the still-point of consciousness that dispassionately observes the incessant rise and fall of our unreal "selves." To discover that non-attached center of consciousness—to *become* that center—is to awaken from the nightmare that one ever was or could be anything other than precisely this Divine Awareness of the illusoriness of all existence; this Divine Awareness is, in the last analysis, Awareness of Itself.

In Hindu philosophy, the illusion of estrangement from the Primal Ground is called *Maya*, the veil of lies that masquerade as substantial reality in order to blind us to the only eternal fact—namely, that our existence *in* and *as* the Imperishable Center of Divine Consciousness is eternally assured despite our momentary forgetfulness. One therefore must sacrifice one's impermanent, personal "self" (usually on the altar of meditation) to find one's eternal, impersonal "Self" as the Eternal Unchanging Consciousness. The purpose of reincarnation in many of the Eastern systems is to burn off the illusion of a separate self, with all its fear, grasping, appetite, and lust, in order to see that one is nothing other than this eternally "still point of the turning world," as T.S. Eliot put it.[1]

This Eternal Center is often called the Void—not because it is empty of significance but simply because of the inability of any propositional thought to grasp its nature. Anything we might say about the Void is necessarily an inadequate artifact of our bounded, contingent consciousness and therefore is *not* the Eternal Consciousness Itself. Our thoughts, utterances, and actions regarding the Divine are inherently doomed to come no closer to it than a dream apple is to actual fruit. As one comes to understand (and, more importantly, to meditatively *experience*) this psychological and ontological fact, then one's "personal" consciousness begins to identify with and dissolve into the purity of Divine Consciousness. In this process you do not so much discover God as you discover that you *are* God.

The picture of God is fundamentally different in the major monotheistic, dialectic spiritualities: Islam, Judaism, and Christianity. There are some forms of spirituality which, although nominally dialectic, are actually unitive. In the Christian tradition, for example, there is St. John of the Cross' idea of the "Dark Night of the Soul." Here, the renunciant, seeking to know God, attempts to divest herself of every sensual, conceptual, emotional, or spiritual predisposition or hope. This is very similar to the Buddhist meditative attempts to enter the Void. Conversely, some nominally unitive religious expressions are essentially dialectic. Thus, certain forms of worship in Hinduism focus on the personality of an incarnated divinity who is the object of a devotee's passionate attention and with whom the worshipper wishes to enter into relationship. In this chapter, however, I will not deal with these rather anomalous forms of each type of spirituality but will refer to the unitive and dialectic religions in their more generally understood and practiced senses.

Whereas the practitioner of a unitive spirituality attempts to *experientially discover* divinity as *her true Self*, the adherent of a dialectic spirituality attempts to *dialogically encounter* divinity by entering into conversation with Him as *the Eternal Other*. Although eternally distinct from and superior to the human being, this God nevertheless loves and claims each human being as His unique child, expressly created in His image. In the dialectic religions, it is God's love for us as His children that bridges what would otherwise be a fatal schism between the Creator and His children, all of whom have, to some degree or other, used their agency to deny Him and their dependence on Him. To address this rift between God and the individual, each dialectic religion proposes and practices some sacrificial means of reconciling the person to God so that, having risen to her destined stature as a divine and eternal individual, she may now fully enjoy eternal fellowship with Him.

The dialectic spiritualities assert that our destiny is to be in eternal relationship with God. But relationship can only occur between beings who, however fused in love, nevertheless remain distinct as persons. Eternal relationship requires eternal difference and eternal *conversation*, which is why I call this form of spirituality "dialectic." Spirit, according to Buber, is both the condition and the result of loving encounter between two eternal, and eternally free, beings.

> Spirit in its human manifestations is a response of man to
> his *Thou*,...the response to the Thou which appears and ad-
> dresses him out of the mystery .... Spirit is not in the *I* but
> between *I* and *Thou*. It is not like the air that circulates in
> you, but like the air in which you breathe. Man lives in the
> spirit if he is able to respond to his *Thou*. He is able, if he
> enters into relationship with his whole being. Only by vir-
> tue of his power to enter into relation is he able to live in
> the spirit.[2]

Most dialectic spiritualities stress the infinitely unique potential of
the individual as much as the divine individuality of God. Indeed, we
would not each be unique (or, at least, that uniqueness would not be
eternally consequential) if each person's identity and possibilities did
not flow from or matter to a God who is Himself the epitome of identity and possibility. Hence, when Moses asks the Lord how he should
refer to Him when speaking to the children of Israel, He identifies himself simply as "I am." Kierkegaard understood in this "I am" the message that abstract reasoning and empirical evidence can never reveal ultimate truths, for the ultimate human truth is one's *personal encounter*
with God, not *impersonal speculations* about Him. "God is a subject
and therefore exists only for subjectivity in inwardness," declared
Kierkegaard:

> *When the question of truth is raised subjectively, reflection*
> *is directed subjectively to the nature of the individual's re-*
> *lationship: if only the mode of relationship is in the truth,*
> *the individual is in the truth, even if it should thus happen*
> *to be related to what is not true.* Objectively, [the knowl-
> edge of God] is related to the problem of whether this ob-
> ject is the true God; subjectively, reflection is directed to
> the question whether the individual is related to a some-
> thing *in such a manner* that his relationship is in truth a
> God-relationship.... That very instant he has God, not by
> virtue of any objective deliberation but by virtue of the in-
> finite passion of inwardness.... God is precisely that which
> one takes *a tout prix,* which in the understanding of passion
> constitutes the true inward relationship to God.[3]

God, as *the Immortal Person*, calls on every one of His mortal
children to *transcend* themselves so as to become transfigured into *immortal persons*. This is a process which begins and ends in what

Kierkegaard called a "primitive gripping" of the individual *as* an individual by God.[4]

Commitment to this presently unseen God—Luther's *Deus absconditus*—is not a betrayal of one's higher intellectual capacities. It is a finding of one's *total* self in a moral process that involves the whole person, not *just* the intellect. "By relating itself to its own self, and by willing to be itself," insisted Kierkegaard, "the self is grounded transparently in the Power which constituted it."[5] This process of the self "willing to be itself" by willing to be "grounded transparently" in God, is *faith*. That is why true faith can never rest on merely logical deduction but must engage—and in engaging, transfigure—the whole person, *including her reason*. According to Buber this faith is freedom, for

> the free man is he who wills without arbitrary self-will. He believes in reality, that is, he believes in the real two-fold entity *I* and *Thou*. He believes in destiny, and believes that it stands in need of him. It does not keep him in leading-strings, it awaits him, he must go to it, yet does not know where it is to be found. But he knows that he must go out with his whole being.[6]

This faith also results in what is perhaps the most transformative mystery of all dualistic spirituality: by seeing oneself as having one's being in God, by coming to know *with* one's whole being one's utter insignificance *before* God, there is born a humility that is, paradoxically, the first real step on the road to one's exaltation. Thus we read in *The Pearl of Great Price* that Moses, having been granted a vision of the endless worlds that God had created and knowledge of their glorious destinies, was overcome and fell to the ground,

> and it came to pass that it was for the space of many hours before Moses did again receive his natural strength like unto man; and he said unto himself: Now, for this cause I know that man is nothing, which thing I never had supposed. But now mine eyes have beheld God; but not my natural, but my spiritual eyes, for my natural eyes could not have beheld, for I should have withered and died in his presence; but his glory was upon me; and I beheld his face, *for I was transfigured before him.*[7]

This, then, is the pattern of spiritual growth in the dialectic religions: one is seized by God, one finally comes to see His personal greatness and one's own personal littleness, and this vision paradoxically provokes a mysterious transfiguration of the self—a self which now begins the eternal process of evolution into its own godlike status.

The opposite of this intensely personal process of maturation in faith is despair. Kierkegaard insisted that

> every human existence which is not conscious of itself as spirit, or conscious of itself before God as spirit, every human existence which is not thus grounded transparently in God but obscurely reposes or terminates in some abstract universality (state, nation, etc.), or which, in obscurity about itself, takes its faculties merely as active powers, without in a deeper sense being conscious whence it has them, which regards itself as an inexplicable something which is to be understood *per se*—every such existence, whatever it accomplishes, though it be the most amazing exploit, whatever it explains, though it were the whole of existence, however intensely it enjoys life aesthetically— every such existence is after all in despair.[8]

Dialectic Spirituality and Dialectic Teaching

Current educational discourse rarely concerns itself with the pedagogical implications of dialectically spiritual world-views but tends to stress Buddhistic or transpersonal views. What Ferrer has observed of transpersonal theory in general applies equally well to curriculum theory when it deals with spiritual matters—namely, that a non-dual, monistic metaphysic is the spiritual orientation of choice.[9] Dialectic spirituality is mentioned—if at all—typically through the lens of unitive assumptions. The spiritual statements of certain Western religious figures such as Hildegard of Bingen, Teresa of Avila, and Meister Eckhardt tend to be the focus because they are sometimes consistent with a unitive view in certain limited respects. The purpose of this section, therefore, is not so much to survey the literature on the dialectic spiritual landscape in education, for there is not a great deal to survey. Rather, it is to begin to imagine what some of the general contours of such a theory of curriculum might be.

To say that there have been few dialectic statements regarding dialectic religion and the curriculum over the last several decades is not to say that there have been none. What is lacking in quantity is more than compensated for in quality. Martin Buber and Duane Huebner are without doubt the two most important figures who, like Shakespeare's

Caesar, bestride this world like Colossi. And as I have already said, the work of Soren Kierkegaard provides fertile ground for various types of curricular fruit. Parker Palmer has also helped to open up scholarly conversation about the educational dimensions of monotheistic spirituality. Furthermore, the writings of two 20th-century Protestant Existentialist theologians—Paul Tillich and Reinhold Niebuhr—are rich with implications for curriculum theory. To a more limited extent, one finds certain dialectic notions in the work of Philip Phenix and James McDonald. It is to all of these theorists that I will turn in this concluding discussion of the seventh curricular landscape.

The educational implications of dialectic spirituality are nowhere more clearly laid out than in the work of Martin Buber, who saw the *I-Thou* relationship between the teacher and the student as not only the foundation of great teaching but also of the individual's personal relationship with God.

> The extended lines of relation meet in the eternal *Thou:* Every particular *Thou* is a glimpse through to the eternal *Thou;* by means of every particular *Thou,* the primary word addresses the eternal *Thou.* Through the mediation of the *Thou* of all beings, fulfillment, and non-fulfillment, of relations comes to them: The inborn *Thou* is realized in each relation and consummated in none.[10]

In Buber's pedagogy, the miracle of authentic dialogue between the teacher and student is that it may ultimately result in encounter with God. It is true that in both unitive and dialectic teaching the teacher and student, entering into ever closer relationship, simultaneously move closer to the timeless. However, in dialectic spirituality the purpose of this proximity is personally creative relationship with God as the sovereign dialogical Other. The dialectic educational enterprise aims at discovery of one's transfigured, eternal self *as a self* in the grace and embrace of the Divine Person. Thus, even in the darkness of their mortal limitations, the teacher and student can begin to perceive some of the features of their own and each other's eternal individuality.

There are no specific techniques that can insure the attainment of this goal. However, as Phenix has put it, "a curriculum of transcendence *does* provide a context for engendering, gestating, expecting, and celebrating the moments of singular awareness and of inner illumination when each person comes into the consciousness of his *inimitable personal being.*"[11]

According to Kierkegaard, this "singular awareness" is most conducive to "ethical contemplation," for

> there is only one kind of ethical contemplation, namely, self-contemplation. Ethics closes immediately about the individual, and demands that he exist ethically; it does not make a parade of millions or of generations of men; it does not take humanity in the lump any more than the police arrest humanity at large. If God knows how many hairs there are on each man's head, the ethical knows how many human beings there are; and its enumeration is not in the interest of a total sum, but for the sake of each individual. The ethical requirement is imposed upon each individual, and when it judges, it judges each individual by himself.[12]

This is not to say that one's ethical deliberations cannot involve political issues (although they admittedly run a very distant second in Kierkegaard's writings). However, each individual must ultimately confront those political issues, generate answers, and engage in action on the basis of *individual* analysis and in the light of her *individual* relationship with God. The educator's task is to help each student wrestle with personal and political questions so as to devise courses of action that she finds morally satisfying and transformative. The student can do this all the more effectively as she sees the teacher model such behavior by publicly struggling with the historical, psychological, ethical, aesthetic, and ontological complexities of any subject under analysis—and doing so in authoritative yet respectful dialogue with her students. When this happens, it satisfies Buber's primary pedagogical imperative that "the relation in education [be] one of pure dialogue."[13]

According to Buber, Socrates was a teacher who fostered pure dialogue. His purpose was not so much to lead his student to a particular truth as it was to help the student *find himself* by arriving at a personally resonant truth deep *within himself.* How did Socrates do this? Primarily by being so personally, intellectually, and ethically genuine that the student, following Socrates' model and thus becoming morally "magnetized," was inexorably drawn into authentic dialogue with him.

> How lovely and how fitting the sound of the lively and impressive *I* of Socrates. It is the *I* of endless dialogue, and the air of dialogue is wafted around it in all its journeys, before the judges and in the last hour in prison. This *I* lived continually in the relation with man which is bodied forth

in dialogue. It never ceased to believe in the reality of men and went out to meet them. So it took its stand with them in reality, and reality forsakes it no more. Its very loneliness can never be forsakenness, and if the world of man is silent, it hears the voice of the *daimonion* say *Thou.*[14]

Socrates was a dialectically religious teacher, for "the educator who helps to bring man back to his own unity will help to put him again face to face with God."[15]

Each student will come to this divine encounter—if she comes to it at all—in her own way. In reading the four gospels as well as the other canonical literature in my church, I have always been struck by how Jesus as teacher and healer responds in different ways to individuals who have the same problem. For instance, one blind person he will heal by simply placing His hands over her eyes; to another, He restores sight by spitting in the dirt and making a bit of mud that He applies to the eyes and then instructs the person to wash off at a nearby pool; another He heals by the mere words He utters; and so on. It is as if Jesus the teacher and healer is so supremely present *in* and *as* Himself, and *in* and *as* relationship with His Heavenly Father, that He instinctively tailors His message and actions to the nature and needs of the specific person with whom He is presently dealing. "How powerful, even to the point of being overbearing," Buber therefore says,

and how legitimate, even to the point of being self-evident, is the saying of *I* by Jesus. For it is the *I* of unconditional relation in which the man calls his *Thou* Father in such a way that he is simply Son, and nothing else but Son. Whenever he says *I*, he can only mean the *I* of the holy primary word that has been raised for him into unconditional being. If separation ever touches him, his solidarity of relation is the greater; he speaks to others only out of this solidarity.[16]

In pedagogies that are founded on dialectic spirituality, the teacher's most important role is to speak to her students out of her solidarity with God. This does not mean using explicitly religious language or even conveying explicitly religious messages, but it does mean speaking with a spiritual authenticity and authority that comes out of her "ultimate concern." Such speech, in turn, awakens students to *their* status as individual beings in relationship with the Eternal Individual.[17] On the other hand, bad teaching occurs whenever we treat our students as merely political, economic, or academic *objects* instead of potentially divine *subjects*. As we have already had many occasions to see, Buber rendered this distinction as the difference between the two primary "words": *I-Thou* and *I-It*.

The primary word *I-It* refers to a pseudo-relationship. In it, the superordinate member of the dyad (the colonizing *I*) has no real interest in exploring or empowering the other, subordinate person (the colonized *It*) as a unique *Thou* with eternal potential. Rather, this *I* sees and treats the other person as an instrument to satisfy its own selfish, sensual desires and goals. This *I*, being one of the terms in a pseudo-word, is itself only a pseudo-self—a momentous truth that Camus captured when he said that *the jailor is bound to the prisoner.* By objectifying its dialogical partner, this *I* strips itself of its own humanity in an act of ethical suicide. This *I* ultimately enslaves itself, then, through its attempt to enslave another. And here is the ultimate punishment for such dialogical enslavement of the other: the person who objectifies another cannot approach God, for we gain access to God only to the degree that we spiritually love others.[18] "For God is love." (1 John 4:8). The horizontal line of *I-Thou* relationship with our fellow beings and the vertical line of *I-Thou* relationship with God issue simultaneously from the same point—and one line cannot radiate without the other.

Seen in these interpersonal terms, curriculum and instruction become a form of prayer, as Palmer has asserted in his call for "a mode of knowing and educating that is prayerful through and through. What do I mean by prayer? I mean the practice of relatedness." Prayerful teaching implies "allowing the power of love to transform the very knowledge we teach, the very methods we use to teach and learn it."[19] Whatever sets itself up against such relationship in education does *moral* violence. It also does *pedagogical* violence because the teacher and student both achieve ever subtler understandings of the subject matter primarily as they explore it *together*. What are some examples of pedagogical violence?

Educational scenarios, such as those of the Reagan administration's *A Nation at Risk* report, which considered "the basic purposes of schooling" to be the reestablishment of America's "once unchallenged preeminence in commerce, industry, science and technological innovation," work against the spirit in education.[20] They (mis)measure the teacher and student in the clinically anonymous terms of standardized, norm-referenced instrumentation. Von Clausewitz said that war is the extension of national policy by other means. In the corporate visions of reform, education is the extension of *economic* policy by *pedagogical* means.

This is not to assert that teaching may not have economically practical purposes. Many parents understandably expect teachers to arm children with pragmatic skills and knowledge that will help them survive in the marketplace. But when such purposes become the centerpiece of a federal agenda—"the basic purpose of education" virtually to the exclusion of anything else—then education is being asked to sell its democratic and spiritual birthright for a mess of corporate fiscal pottage. I am convinced that this is the primary cause of many teachers' disillusionment with and abandonment of American public education. Their sense of calling grows out of the primary word *I-Thou*, out of their need to engage, excite, nurture and shape the burgeoning hearts and minds of their young students. However, corporate reform agendas grow out of the primary word *I-It* in their relentless attempts to maximize profit and dominate markets. As Marx saw, the unspoken but still primary motivation of this mode of (non)relationship is *commodity fetishism*—the objectification of people who are conditioned not only to be *addicted* to commodities but finally to *become* commodities. This is the false god of *I-It* triumphant. It is curricular idolatry.

Cremin has argued in his magisterial study of the history of American education that public schooling is increasingly coming to resemble education at military and commercial sites. President Eisenhower warned about the dangers of the military-industrial complex.[21] With the looming presence of such highly influential federal documents as *A Nation at Risk*, *Goals 2000* and *No Child Left Behind*, it is high time to start worrying about a military-industrial-*educational* complex. Such commodification of self and others is the educational equivalent of the worship of the golden calf. It is a sin. For surely it is not too much to call the dehumanization of children in the schools a sin—and a very grave one at that.

The best antidote to this psychosocial toxicity is the *I-Thou* relationship, and in few environments is this antidote more effective than in the classroom. Where teachers and students find and further ways of learning and growing together within the sacred precinct of *I-Thou*, they are engaged in a spiritual act of political resistance. In this sense, the teacher's mission becomes hortatory, reminding her students (and thus ultimately her people) that "if a man lets it have the mastery, the continuing growing world of *It* overruns him and robs him of the reality of his own *I*, till the incubus over him and the ghost within him whisper to one another the confession of their non-salvation."[22]

Whenever the dialectic spiritual attitude permeates education, then subject matter becomes an occasion for revelation of self, other and God. Such education is religious no matter what the subject matter. Brigham Young once admonished Dr. Karl Maeser, a legendary teacher in early Mormon history, that a teacher should not even teach the multiplication table except by the spirit of God. Huebner has also declared that any curricular content or educational relationship may (and indeed must) be a dwelling place for the divine. For it is the case, said Huebner, that in all the best teaching and learning, whether "sacred" or "secular," the Spirit is inevitably present. "Hovering always is the absolute 'other,' Spirit, that overwhelms us in moments of awe, terror, tragedy, beauty, and peace. Content is the 'other.' Knowing is the process of being in relationship with that 'other.' Knowledge is an abstraction from that process."[23] To define the goal of education in lesser terms is a mistake, for "the journey of the self is short circuited or derailed by those who define the ends of life and education in less than ultimate terms."[24]

In Huebner's call for education in "ultimate terms," one hears echoes of Paul Tillich's definition of religion as "ultimate concern." By watching and internalizing the motions of the Spirit as it discloses the secrets of *any* subject matter and reveals new questions, the individual is brought into relationship with God. Put differently: through her *I-Thou* exploration of the subject matter, the student will hopefully come to an *I-Thou* encounter with that Person who is the eternal truth behind all lesser truths. Huebner notes in similar strains that "the otherness that informs and accompanies education is the absolute Otherness, the transcendent Other, however we name that which goes beyond all appearances and all conditions. Education is the lure of the transcendent—that openness to a future that is beyond all futures."[25]

Curricular content is also encounter with another *person* insofar as what the student is examining—a book, say, or an artifact—embodies the author's or maker's yearning for eternity. This is so because

> content is otherness. The presence of other life in this
> world, life of which I am not yet a part, is the content of my
> future education. That life is the comings and goings of
> other people. In their comings and goings—their journeys
> and pilgrimages—they house themselves, construct tools
> and equipment, negotiate institutions, engage and interact

with flora and fauna. And when they rest and relax from the struggles of life and have time to contemplate and converse, they tell stories of where they have been and where they are going, they sing and dance and paint and build so they will not forget what they have endured and experienced and hoped for.[26]

A spiritually dialectic pedagogy exists primarily, then, to bring students, individually and severally, into living, loving encounter with an "other"—often an "other" who has left this realm of being. They do this so that they may recall, celebrate, and learn from the pain, doubt, wisdom and hope that shaped the departed one's creations, for all of these constitute that person's unique signature on the contract of time. As they ponder that *other's* creations, the teacher and student are also stimulated to ponder their own odysseys, affirming some bearings and shifting others, in furtherance of their own journeys toward eternal identity. It is in this sense, I believe, that Huebner has said that as educators "our primary concern…is the religious formation of ourselves and those we care for."[27]

This does not mean that the teacher must pound a religious doctrine into a student's head. Indeed, not only *should* a teacher not do this; she *must* not do it, for it would be a violation of the student's moral agency—than which nothing could be *less* religious. It does not even mean that curriculum and instruction must always deal in some fashion with explicitly religious themes. Unless the subject matter naturally lends itself to the analysis of religious themes or documents, the introduction of such things is not only pedagogically clumsy and counterproductive; it is illegal in the public school classroom.[28] Furthermore, proselytizing is unacceptable in the multicultural classroom because it forecloses the possibility of an *I-Thou* relationship with one's students. Doctrinaire presentations of particular religious principles will inevitably alienate most students, might make others feel that they must embrace those principles (or pretend to do so) since those principles belong to the person who is giving the grades, and, finally, can too easily create a smug sense of ideological privilege in some students who share the teacher's religion. Doctrinaire religiosity in a classroom prevents the uncoerced dialogue that is necessary for truly spiritual classroom discourse—discourse in which students find the divine *in* and *for* themselves as free individuals through encounter with others as free individuals in particular curricular contexts.

We might think that dialectically spiritual teaching occurs only—or, at least, usually—in such domains as art, history, or philosophy. However, the sciences offer equally abundant and powerful opportunities to commune with our fellows and God. It is only the withering touch of positivism that has led us to believe otherwise—turning the doing of science into the loveless memorization of formulas, not an engagement of the whole person with the pulsing, evolving organism of the universe. No less than the sculptor or novelist, "the scientist awaits the call of the transcendent other."

> The creation of scientific knowledge requires participation in the transcendent and a responsiveness of the other. In one sense, the one who is a scientist is one who lets the object, the phenomenon which is other, love her. She is one who gives up her present ways that she may be formed anew by that strangeness, that otherness before and beyond her. The scientist accepts this incomplete relationship with the world and gives of herself to be drawn out, to be educated or transformed by that which is before her. Scientific knowledge, a symbol system which describes a dance of love with other phenomena, is also a conversation, a dialogue, with human beings. It is a consequence of meeting someone else and of saying, "This is the way I dance with the world. Is it also the way you dance with it? If so, can we dance together?"[29]

Thus, the curriculum is both contingent and crucial. It is *contingent* because it is finally a means of achieving a greater goal: relationship with the divine Other. Whenever curriculum is not in some sense grounded in and pointed toward the teacher's and student's sacred evolution, it ceases to be spiritual. Yet, the curriculum is *crucial* because each curriculum—with its unique assumptions, issues, methods and objectives—forms a unique "grammar" that allows us to converse with each other and the Divine in an existentially particular way that varies not only from subject matter to subject matter but even from class to class. Each subject-matter, each "knowledge," originates in a certain form of encounter with and way of interpreting each other and nature. If all goes well in this process, the result is that teacher and student are finally translated in terms of the specific vocabulary of that subject-matter into a closer communion with the Divine.

We have already seen that, pedagogically, "sin" means treating the student as an object. But now we come to understand as well why

Buber considered it sinful to treat the subject matter as a mere object. "O accumulation of information!" Buber lamented. "It—always it."[30] "Where is the wisdom we have lost in knowledge?/Where is the knowledge we have lost in information?" wondered T.S. Eliot.[31] Approaches to education that obsess on the transmission and regurgitation of facts and figures—threatening teachers and students with dire institutional punishments if they do not march to this compulsive corporate tune— are cruel, despotic, and, as Gandhi said about tyranny, always doomed to decay on the rubbish heap of history in the fullness of time.

History, Magic, and the Curriculum

A defining characteristic of the major monotheistic religions is the conviction that the patterns of human history are neither illusory (as in postmodernism) nor ultimately repetitive (as in Hinduism and Buddhism). History has a purpose: the institution of the Kingdom of God on a transfigured earth. We see this crucial distinction between unitive and dialectic spirituality in their teleological metaphors. While the unitive approach views the cosmos as an illusory game from which we must awaken and detach, dialectic pedagogies see the universe as a divine drama with which we must fully engage and identify. The burden of the dialectic curriculum is to help the student see that "the world is not divine sport, it is divine destiny. There is divine meaning in the life of the world, of man, of human persons, of you and of me."[32]

We are not simply chess pieces on the board of history. We are ourselves potentially divine creatures with moral agency. The dialectical spiritualities all call for the individual to use this agency to *choose the right* and voluntarily join with God in the divine political program of constructing a kingdom based entirely on love, dignity, equity, creativity, and righteousness. Responding to this world-historical call is a crucial step in our own eternal development—the political purpose of our sojourn in this realm of existence.

But because we are so often wayward—both individually and collectively—the God of history must speak to us through the mouths of chosen representatives—prophets—to call us to personal and political repentance, to remind us that we are children of a Heavenly King and must comport ourselves accordingly, creating our communities consistently with our divine lineage. We sense this call to collective righteousness from God in the mouth of the Prophet in the Koran as he cries, "O my people! Enter the holy land which Allah hath assigned unto you, and turn not back ignominiously, for then will ye be overthrown, to your own ruin." (Surah 5, Al Ma'idah 4: 21) In like fashion Micah proclaimed, "What doth the Lord require of thee, but to do justly, and to love mercy, and to walk humbly with thy God? The Lord's voice crieth unto the city...." (Micah 6: 8-9) Amos specifically enjoined the Jewish nation to "hate the evil, and love the good, and establish judgment in the gate." (Amos 5: 15)

Never sentimental, dialectical spirituality and pedagogy are nevertheless politically optimistic. Tillich thus reminds us that

> the content of faith in Providence is this: when death rains from heaven as it does now, when cruelty wields power over nations and individuals as it does now, when hunger and persecution drive millions from place to place, as they do now, and when prisons and slums all over the world throughout history degrade the humanity of the bodies and souls of men as they do now—we can boast in that time, and just in that time, that even all of this cannot separate us from the love of God. In this sense, and in this sense alone, all things work together for good, for the *ultimate* good, the eternal love, and the Kingdom of God. Faith in divine Providence is the faith that nothing can prevent us from fulfilling the ultimate meaning of our existence. Providence does not mean a divine planning by which everything is predetermined as an efficient machine. Rather, Providence means that there is a creative and saving possibility implied in every situation, which cannot be destroyed by any event. Providence means the daemonic and destructive forces within ourselves and our world can never have an unbreakable grasp upon us, and that the bond which connects us with the fulfilling love can never be disrupted.[33]

I have already mentioned the opposing views of history as illusion or circularity. But these pose much less of a threat to the spiritually dialectical view of history than does the vaunting assumption that history *has* a purpose—but one that is entirely in the mind and hands of the human being alone. This is *the idolatry of ideology*—the worship of something that we create with our own hands and to which we then ascribe saving power. The capitalist faith in the marketplace to bring about human fulfillment is an example of such idolatry. Marxism is another. Like all idolatrous political and economic systems (whether on the Right or Left), such ideological idolatry is essentially a form of *magic* because it attempts to manipulate people, events and things by virtue of merely temporal techniques and technologies that are not grounded in the timelessness of Divine Love. What does this mean for education? It means that the curriculum becomes idolatrous and "magical" whenever it serves merely political or economic purposes—whenever, that is, it puts itself at the service of a techno-corporate program that promises social salvation without reference to God. The last century offered gruesome examples of magical pedagogies. For instance, when the Nazis came to power in the 1930s, their educational program had already been prepared with meticulous care and was immediately put in place, for Hitler knew very well the vital role that education would play in training up a generation to serve (completely and unquestioningly) the totalitarian state.[34]

Certainly less vicious but probably not much less idolatrous instances of pedagogical magic exist currently in reform agendas which picture education as existing solely for political or economic goals. Although legitimate as secondary aims of education in certain contexts, such objectives become pernicious when they are the guiding curricular goal. That is education with no moral center. And when the moral center no longer holds pedagogically, then false corporate divinities will rush in to fill the lacuna with their economic "magic."

> What distinguishes sacrifice and prayer from all magic? Magic desires to obtain its effects without entering into relationship and practices its tricks in the void. But sacrifice and prayer are set "before the Face," in the consummation of the holy primary word that means mutual action: they speak the *Thou,* and then they hear.[35]

The dialogical union of teacher and student is thus a form of political resistance. It is a historical affirmation, testimony of the fact that "the world is not divine sport, it is divine destiny."[36] When the curriculum reflects this salvific message, then, in Palmer's words, it is "prayerfully" echoing God's call to us, as His *individual* children, to be His *historical* co-workers. This returns to the student a sense of the *scope* of her identity. The teacher who helps this happen is—no matter her formal religious convictions or lack thereof—a prophetess who will serve no false national or financial gods. The prophetess-teacher announces that God is neither divided nor partial. He is not the special god of a particular tribe, class, race, nation, or corporation, for "the Lord our God is one Lord." (Deuteronomy 6: 4)

Huebner also likened the teacher to the prophet when he wrote, "God educates. We don't. But God can educate only if we hearken to [John the Baptist's] call 'Prepare ye the Way!' We participate in God's educational work by bringing under criticism our self made world, and by proclaiming God's presence.... We are but [His] servants.[37]

Faith, Doubt, Teaching, and Learning

Doubt is often viewed as the opposite of faith, but it is not. If Tillich was right that religion is "ultimate concern" about one's existence, then doubt is itself a form of religious concern, for doubt is an excruciating *surplus* of concern that cries out desperately for a response that does not seem to be forthcoming. Not doubt but *idolatry* is the opposite of faith. The idol worshipper, resting "content" in such temporal half-measures as financial conquest, pet academic theories, expensive toys or adornments, public acclaim, political advancement, or sexual conquest, has forfeited her concern with ultimate matters and eternal possibilities for an evening's revel around some golden calf or other. Doubt is the mortal hunger pang for eternity, but idolatry is a binge on junk food.

What is more, doubt is not only *consistent* with faith; it is the very *precondition* of faith. Without doubt, faith would not be faith—but knowledge. Faith is only necessary where there *is* doubt. This is why Existentialism was, if not a religious phenomenon itself, at least a precursor of it. Indeed, doubt is an inevitable consequence of our paradoxical plight as human beings. "When the eternal truth is related to an existing individual, it becomes a paradox."[38] The courageous response to doubt is the risk of faith. "Without risk there is no faith," averred Kierkegaard, "and the greater the risk, the greater the faith; the more objective security, the less inwardness (for inwardness is precisely subjectivity), and the less objective security, the more profound the possible inwardness." The necessity of risk in knowing God should not be surprising. After all, any relationship that matters deeply risks greatly.

The dialectic spiritual educator, therefore, does not shy away from heart-felt doubt or the riskiness of relationship with students. She openly acknowledges such things, even welcomes them; she adroitly wrestles with their complexity and claims both privately in her meditations and publicly with her students; and she explores their presence and experiences their sway in the texts and subtexts under analysis in the classroom. Above all, she finds ways to harness the resulting energy so as to propel the student into new trajectories of mature commitment to God and others.

What Reinhold Niebuhr said about "an adequate religion" also holds for an adequate pedagogy—namely, that it

> is always an ultimate optimism which has entertained all the facts which lead to pessimism. Its optimism is based upon a faith in a transcendent center of meaning which is never fully expressed in any partial value and is never exhausted in any concrete historical reality. But though it is not exhausted in any such reality, it is incarnated there.[39]

The goal of the dialectic curriculum is nothing less than to help the student—through *what* is studied and *how* it is taught—discover *herself* as an eternal being in dialogue with other eternal beings. When teaching and learning occur in this light, education becomes incarnation.

Topics for Discussion

1. Do you agree or disagree with the idea that the transnational corporate curriculum tends to militate against dialectic-spiritual ideals in education?

2. Given your understanding of the legal constraints and allowances regarding religion in the classroom, what guidelines should the teacher who conceives her role in dialectical terms keep in mind in devising a curriculum and in teaching?

3. Do you find the image of the teacher as a prophet or prophetess useful to you in your professional practice? Why or why not?

Topics for Research

1. Examine the origin and development of Liberation Theology over the last several decades. What are some of the major themes in this literature, and how might these ideas be applicable (or not) to a school where you teach or with which you are familiar.

2. Critically analyze *A Nation at Risk* and *Goals 2000: Educate America*, and *No Child Left Behind*. What are the assumptions that these

documents make about the means and goals of educating children? What potential conflicts exist between these assumptions and those of a spiritually dialectic pedagogy?

3. Read "Curriculum as a Theological Text" from Pinar and his associates' (1995) *Understanding Curriculum*. What are some of the major topics and trends in "theology-centered" approaches to curriculum today?

Notes: Chapter 7

1. T.S. Eliot, *T.S. Eliot: The Complete Poems and Plays: 1909-1950* (New York: Harcourt, Brace and World, Inc., 1971), 119.
2. M. Buber, *I and Thou* (New York: Vintage, 1965), 39.
3. S. Kierkegaard, *A Kierkegaard Anthology,* ed. R. Bretall (Princeton, New Jersey: Princeton University Press, 1969), 211-212.
4. Ibid., 292.
5. Ibid., 351.
6. Buber, 59. Emphasis added.
7. *The Book of Moses* 1: 10-11, (Salt Lake City, Utah: The Church of Jesus Christ of Latter-day Saints, 1981), 121: 39. Emphasis added.
8. Kierkegaard, 348.
9 J. Ferrer, *Revisioning Transpersonal Theory: A Participatory Vision of Human Spirituality* (Albany, New York: State University of New York Press, 2002), 87.
10. Buber, 75.
11. P. Phenix, *Realms of Meaning: A Philosophy of Curriculum for General Education* (New York: McGraw Hill, 1964), 128. Emphasis added.
12. Kierkegaard, 226.
13. M. Buber, *Between Man and Man* (New York: Vintage, 1985), 66.
14. Ibid., 67.
15. Ibid., 117.
16. Ibid., 67.
17. J. Macdonald, "A Transcendental Developmental Ideology of Education," in *Heightened Consciousness, Cultural Revolution, and Curriculum Theory,* ed. W. Pinar. Berkeley, California: McCutchan Publishing (1975), 100.
18. N. Noddings, "Care and Moral Education," in *Critical Conversations in the Philosophy of Education,* ed. W. Kohli, (New York: Routledge, 1995): 137-148.

19. P. Palmer, *To Know as We are Known: A Spirituality of Education* (San Francisco, California: Harper Collins Publishers, 1983), 10.
20. *A Nation at Risk: The Imperative for Educational Reform* (Washington, D.C.: United States Government Printing Office, 1983) 5.
21. L. Cremin, *American Education: The Metropolitan Experience: 1876-1980* (New York: Harper and Row, 1988).
22. M. Buber, *I and Thou.*
23. D. Huebner, *The Lure of the Transcendent: Collected Essays by Dwayne E. Huebner,* ed. V. Hillis (London: Lawrence Erlbaum Associates, 1999), 408.
24. Ibid., 404.
25. Ibid., 360.
26. Ibid., 362.
27. Ibid., 282.
28. Abington Township, Pennsylvania, et al. v. Schempp et al., 374 US 203 (1963).
29. Huebner, 367.
30. M. Buber, *I and Thou*, 5.
31. Eliot, 96.
32. Buber, *I and Thou*, 82.
33. P. Tillich, *The Shaking of the Foundations* (New York: Scribners, 1976), 107.
34. A. Richards, "Education in the Third Reich," A Lecture Delivered in the Department of Educational Leadership and Foundations, Brigham Young University, 2002.
35. M. Buber, *I and Thou*, 127.
36. Ibid., 82.
37. Huebner, 400.
38. Kierkegaard, 219.
39. R. Niebuhr, *The Essential Reinhold Niebuhr: Selected Essays and Addresses,* ed. R. Brown (New Haven, Connecticut: Yale University Press, 1986), 6.

Conclusion

THE CURRICULAR
PANORAMA

The Seven Landscapes

We have covered a good deal of territory in our travels over the seven curricular landscapes. Let us conclude our journey by looking at some "snapshots" of each landscape in order to reflect on where we have been.

The first landscape, the organismic one, is the place where sensori-motor issues predominate. Evident in the work of such early curricularists as Comenius, Pestallozi, and Froebel, organismic concerns were later important in American educational Progressivism, taking on such varied forms as the Kindergarten movement, health-care services in the schools, school lunches, movable chairs in the classroom, sex education, gymnasia for school sports and physical education, and audio-visual aids. During the Progressive period, liberals tended to favor the inclusion of organismic issues in the schools whereas conservatives tended to look askance at such initiatives. At its best, the organismic curriculum sensitively attends to the physical needs and potentials of the child. At its worst, it degenerates into treating the child as merely a physical mechanism to be manipulated by reinforcement schedules—usually in the service of larger corporate agendas.

The transferential landscape is the place where the emotional nurturance of the student is key. Maternal in their orientation, the transferential pedagogies stress the importance of caring for the child. They thus align themselves naturally with the branch of feminism that sees women as more inclined toward care in their interactions than men, whom they see as prone to being guided by rules and regulations. The therapeutic wing of Progressivism was almost entirely transferential in orientation, going so far as to propose that teachers could help students resolve Oedipal and Electra complexes through teacher-student interaction. Transferential curricula are especially powerful in offering alternatives and challenges to the emotional and moral aridity of corporate curricular agendas. The danger of the transferential curriculum lies in its potential for excessive sentimentalism and indulgence regarding the student.

Honoring the student's primary affiliative groups, the concrete-affiliative curricula of the third landscape revolve around the rules and roles that define those groups. In its social constructivist forms, it sees the student's cultural affiliations as the filter through which he learns about the physical world. At its best, the concrete-affiliative curriculum is culturally sensitive, pedagogically powerful, and socially functional. It envisions the classroom itself as a culture of learning, a community of inquiry, where teachers help students formulate questions and construct knowledge in ways that are most psychosocially meaningful to them. It also attempts to explain academic failure (especially that of minority-group students) as a result of the conflict between the epistemic, political and communicative assumptions of the student's primary "reference groups" and the "dominant culture" of the classroom. This wisdom of the concrete-affiliative curriculum lies in its rich responsiveness to cultural diversity; its danger lies in the fact that it can degenerate into ethno-sexual separatism in the combative politics of identity.

On the fourth landscape, we move into the precincts of the interpretive-procedural curriculum. On this landscape, students begin to think about thinking and to imagine alternative worlds. This ability catapults the student beyond local customs and concrete contexts into more universal worldviews. This landscape is the goal of the journey for many conventional developmental theories—Piaget's formal operations and Kohlberg's post-conventional moral reasoning. Called the academic-rationalist curriculum, the intellectual-academic curriculum, the cognitive-processes curriculum, and the formal-reflexive curriculum, this approach includes within its broad scope such diverse phenomena as schema theory, cybernetic models of mind, the structure-of-the-discipline approach, and appeals for a return to the classical European curriculum. At their best, such curricula teach students various canonically "approved" ways of posing questions and finding answers, familiarize them with a socially empowering assortment of prestigious texts, and situate their understanding of current issues in larger historical terms. At their worst, these curricula become a way of privileging culturally relative knowledge as if it were morally and metaphysically absolute—imposing that knowledge on students through the threat of institutional punishment if they do not conform to it.

On the fifth, Existentialist landscape, we enter the outskirts of spirituality. This phenomenological curriculum takes metacognition one step farther by setting consciousness in search of *transrational* metaperspectives. It interprets all perspectives and commitments as ultimately just phenomenological events. It then challenges the student to attain maximum experiential clarity in discovering and living out his unique commitments as validly as possible. This is the realm of Heidegger's *Dasein* and Sartre's "living in good faith." Because art embodies and encourages this process so effectively, and because a piece of art will ideally evoke a similar set of existentially authentic responses in the student, artistic creation and criticism often pervade phenomenological curricula.

On the second curricular landscape we noted a preoccupation with "caring" for the student. We see this also on the fifth landscape with the important difference that the phenomenological form of care does not so much take on the aspect of "emotional nurturance" (which helps the student feel loved) as it does "ontological nurturance" (which helps the student become authentic). Buber's *I-Thou* relationship resides much more comfortably here than on the transferential landscape; for, Buber's view is ontological, not therapeutic. Nevertheless, there *is* a therapeutic dimension to the phenomenological curriculum as is quite evident in its indebtedness to the humanist psychologies of the 1960s with their emphasis on self-actualization—the therapeutic parallel of good faith. For the student to become self-actualized in the classroom requires that the teacher interact with him in ways that are cognitively, socially, and morally empowering. Furthermore, this concern with the student as an existential being has recently extended to a concern with the teacher as an existential being, resulting in a new line of educational research that examines the teacher's "ontological autobiography."

At its best, the phenomenological curriculum provides us with all the benefits that Existentialism in general does: an acute awareness of the moral uniqueness of oneself and the dialogical "other," a heightened sensitivity to how that uniqueness gets expressed in various artistic forms, a mature confrontation with our epistemic limitations in this realm of being, a frank exploration of the inevitable fact that each of us will die, and the almost Buddhistic sense of the "self" as continually emerging. The negatives are equally powerful, however, including hopelessness in the face of both life and death, solipsism, and a paralyzing sense of estrangement from others—all of which Gebser has called "aperspectival madness."

To deal with these and other existential dilemmas, the student may venture onto the first fully spiritual curricular landscape—unitive spirituality. Not usually associated with a specific doctrine—although when it is associated with one, it tends to be Buddhistic or Vedantic—unitive spirituality and the "holistic" curricula it engenders are deeply indebted to the transpersonal approaches to psychology that began in the late 1960s. Unitive spirituality and pedagogy are characterized by belief in a higher cosmic power (often called the "Self"); some type of survival after death; meditative mindfulness leading to a recognition of and disidentification from subpersonalities; intuitive ways of knowing and apophatic ways of teaching; and integration of the physical, intellectual, emotional, and spiritual domains in curriculum and instruction. Unitive spirituality often expresses itself in terms of Green politics. Unitive curricula have been called "transformative," "integral," "integrative," "holarchic," "confluent," and—most commonly—"transpersonal." The teacher is often pictured as a sort of Zen master in the unitive pedagogies, and the best teaching is seen as "teaching as presence."

Educational scholarship has been woefully inadequate in examining and implementing the many insights that unitive spirituality and curricula offer. There is no mention, for instance, of *Encounter: Education for Meaning and Social Justice,* in most guides to scholarly journals in education, although it is the leading journal of the Holistic Education Movement and every issue contains thoughtful, scholarly, and highly creative research from teachers and researchers at major universities in the United States and abroad. The holistic curriculum offers a radical yet commonsensical alternative to many current approaches to educational theory and practice; however, that alternative has gone largely unheeded.

The final curricular landscape—that of dialectic spirituality—focuses on personal encounter with the personal, living God. It celebrates the eternal viability and validity of the unique self. Although not currently the orientation of choice among those who want to interject spiritual terms and concerns into curriculum theory, I attempted to show its pedagogical relevance by teasing out some of the educational implications of the work of such Existentialist theologians as Soren Kierkegaard, Paul Tillich, Reinhold Niebuhr, and Martin Buber. I also examined those few important writers in curriculum theory whose orientation is essentially dialectic, with special reference to Parker Palmer, James McDonald, Philip Phenix, and, above all, that giant of 20th-century curriculum theory, Dwayne Huebner.

Some of the characteristics of the dialectic pedagogy that I tried to imagine and articulate were: the centrality of the *I-Thou* relationship between teacher and student as both the beginning and end of all education; the importance to some teachers of the conviction that they were personally called by a personal God to become teachers; the student's and teacher's ongoing discovery of their relationship to God—and to each other—through an ever richer engagement with their subject matter, which itself becomes a "Thou" with "whom" one enters into a mutually searching dialogue; the insistence on the reality of sin as (in educational terms) the regimentation of teachers, the commodification of students, and the packaging of content as mere fodder for standardized tests.

In dialectic pedagogy, history is seen as neither random, deterministic, nor repetitive, but rather the manifestation and unfolding of the mind of God regarding the collective destiny of His children as they move through this probationary period of earthly experience. The teacher who sees and practices his craft in this light is what I, echoing Bullough, have called the teacher-prophet.[1] Such teaching revolves around the revelation of the Divine in subject matter whether that content is physics, woodwork, or poetry. In such curricula, doubt is not contrary to faith but essential to it. Thus, the dialectically oriented teacher never forecloses classroom explorations by appealing to authority but keeps the discussion open, lively, and always ready to receive God's presence.

The Panoramic Curriculum

Each of the seven curricular approaches generates its own valid educational landscape—along with unique problems and potentials. For instance, the theories and practices of the phenomenological curriculum tell us little if anything about how to help a child whose troubles in school stem from the fact that he was a fetal-alcohol-syndrome baby and is malnourished at home. Ultimately, of course, we want to help the child develop fully enough so that we can address the finer phenomenological points of his life, but first the teacher and school must deal with his tragically unmet organic needs. Conversely, a socio-economically privileged senior in high school who is depressed and possibly even suicidal because he sees no meaning in life may benefit greatly from a curriculum that presents vibrant art, examines new philosophical possibilities, and holds out the promise of psycho-spiritual growth. To try to address the needs of this young person by an exclusive focus on *his* diet would in most cases leave the root of the problem untouched—although, to be sure, his problem might well have dietary components.

When a curriculum theorist or teacher insists upon the validity of one curricular approach to the exclusion of the other approaches, then he is making the "category error" of assuming that a theoretical construct that works best in *one* dimension of human experience works best in *all* dimensions. We do great harm to students and teachers whenever we try to advance our preferred perspective to such an extent that we insist upon framing all educational issues only in our own favorite terms—and no others. When this happens, then the view is advanced that teaching and learning are *only organismic,* as in strict behaviorism; *only psychodynamic,* as in the excessively nurturing view that education is basically another form of esteem-enhancing psychotherapy; *only concrete-affiliative,* as in the Nazi curriculum of Aryan glorification; *only interpretive-procedural,* as in the cybernetic reduction of consciousness to binary algorithms; *only phenomenological,* as in the notion that any artistic product is permissible so long as it is the result of "intense experience"; *only unitive,* as in certain New Age approaches that focus on promoting peak mystical "experiences" for those who have the money to afford them but remain silent about the plight of the socially marginalized; or *only dialectic,* as with the insistence of certain ultra-conservative groups that nothing should be included in the curriculum that is not rigidly consistent with (their particular understanding of) the Judaeo-Christian tradition.

Each curricular landscape *must* be honored in order to nurture the student in all of his physical, psychological, cultural, cognitive, existential, and spiritual complexity and capacity. Without this expansive view of the curriculum, both the theorist and teacher are all too liable to ignore vital components of the student's *total* being. This is dangerous because unattended aspects of the student's total being turn all too easily into wounds that fester and finally poison his entire system. As Philip Phenix reminded us, man is everything the various special inquiries show him to be. He is a complex energy-system; an intelligent, adaptive organism with highly developed neurophysiological mechanisms and the power to perceive, think, and purpose; an organized social animal with demands for good and power that need intelligent allocation; a maker of culture and a user of language; a being who lives in a natural and social environment with which he must cope; a creature of feeling and a creator of interesting forms to objectify them; a unique self; a doer and judge of good and evil; a dweller in time, who remembers, anticipates, and celebrates deeds done; a creature of God partaking of the divine nature through the power of boundless self-transcendence.[2]

Indeed, we are everything that the seven curricular landscapes encompass and celebrate. Being mindful of this integrative reality will make us better guides and companions as, along with our students, we pursue the ever widening paths of eternal progression.

Notes: Conclusion

1. R. Bullough, Jr., R. Patterson, and C. Mayes, (2002). Teaching as Prophecy. *The Journal of Curriculum Inquiry,* 32(3): 310-329.
2. P. Phenix, "Transcendence and the Curriculum," in *Conflicting Conceptions of Curriculum,* eds. E. Eisner and E. Vallance (Berkeley, California: McCutchan Publishing Corporation, 1974), 20.

Bibliography

Abington Township, Pennsylvania, et al. v. Schempp et al., 374 US 203 (1963).

Adler, M. *The Paideia Proposal: An Educational Manifesto*. New York: Mac-Millan, 1982.

Ahlstrom, S. *A Religious History of the American People*. New Haven: Yale University Press, 1972.

Aichhorn, A. "The Transference." In *Essential Papers on Transference*, ed. A. Esman. New York: New York University Press (1990): 94-109.

Almon, J. "From Cognitive Learning to Creative Thinking." In *Education, Information, and Transformation: Essays on Learning and Thinking*, ed. J. Kane. Columbus, Ohio: Merrill (1999): 249-269.

Applebee, A. *Curriculum as Conversation: Transforming Traditions of Teaching and Learning*. Chicago: University of Chicago Press, 1996.

Au, K., and A. Kawakami. "Research Currents: Talk Story and Learning to Read." *Language Arts* 62(4) (1985): 406-411.

Banks, J. *Teaching Strategies for Ethnic Studies*. Boston: Allyn and Bacon, 1997.

Barzun, J. *From Dawn to Decadence: 500 Years of Western Cultural Life*. New York: HarperCollins, 2000.

Beck, A., and M. Weishaar. "Cognitive Psychotherapy." In *Current Psychotherapies*, eds. R. Corsini and D. Wedding. Itasca, Illinois: Peacock Publishers (1995): 229-261.

Beck, J. *Cognitive Therapy: Basics and Beyond*. New York: Guilford Press, 1995.

Belenky, M., B. Clinchy, N. Goldberger, and J. Tarule. (1986). *Women's Way of Knowing*. Cambridge, Mass: Harvard University Press.

Bereiter, C. "Constructivism, Socioculturalism, and Popper's 3rd World." *Educational Researcher* 7(3) (1994): 21-23.

Berger, P. *The Sacred Canopy: Elements of a Sociological Theory of Religion*. New York: Doubleday and Company, 1967.

Berger, P., and T. Luckman. "Sociology of Religion and Sociology of Knowledge." In *The Sociology of Religion*, ed. S. Bruce. Aldershot. U.K.: The International Library of Critical Writings in Sociology 1 (1963): 174-184.

Bernstein, B. *Class, Codes, & Control: Volume 1.* London: Routledge & Kegan Paul, 1971.

Best, S., and D. Kellner, *Postmodern Theory.* New York: The Guilford Press, 1991.

Bestor, A. *Educational Wastelands: The Retreat from Learning in Our Public Schools.* Urbana, Illinois: University of Chicago Press, 1953.

Bissell-Brown, V. "Fear of Feminization: Los Angeles High Schools in the Progressive Era." *Feminist Studies* 16 (1990): 493-518.

Bocock, R., and K. Thompson, eds., *Religion and Ideology.* Manchester University Press, 1985.

Boocock, S. *Sociology of Education: An Introduction* 2nd edition. Boston, Houghton Mifflin, 1980.

Book of Mormon, the. Salt Lake City, Utah: The Church of Jesus Christ of Latter-day Saints, 1981.

Boorstein, S., ed., *Transpersonal Psychotherapy,* Albany, N.Y.: SUNY Press, 1996.

Bourdieu, P. "Cultural Reproduction." In *Power and Ideology in Education,* eds. J. Karabel and A. Halsey. New York: Oxford Press (1977): 487-507.

Bowers, C. "Why Culture Rather Than Data Should Be Understood as the Basis of Intelligence." In *Education, Information, and Transformation,* ed. J. Kane. Columbus, Ohio: Merrill/Prentice Hall (1999): 23-40.

Brandt, R., and R. Tyler. "Goals and Objectives." In *Contemporary Issues in Curriculum,* eds. A. Ornstein and L. Behar-Hornstein. Boston: Allyn and Bacon (1999): 20-29.

Brophy, J. *Motivating Students to Learn.* Boston: McGraw-Hill, 1994.

Broudy, H., and J. Palmer. *Exemplars of Teaching Method.* Chicago: Rand McNally & Company, 1965.

Brown, G., M. Phillips, and S. Shapiro. *Getting It All Together: Confluent Education.* Bloomington, Indiana: Phi Delta Kappa, 1976.

Brown, J., A. Collins, and P. Duguid. "Situated Cognition and the Culture of Learning." *Educational Researcher,* January-February 1989, 32-42.

Brubacher, J., and Rudy, W. *Higher Education in Transition: A History of American Colleges and Universities* 4th Edition. New Brunswick, New Jersey: Transaction Publishers, 1997.

Bruner, J. *The Process of Education.* New York: Vintage, 1960.

Buber, M. *Between Man and Man.* New York: Vintage, 1985.

---. *I and Thou.* New York: Vintage, 1965.

Bullough, R., Jr. *Uncertain Lives: Children of Hope, Teachers of Promise.* New York: Teachers College, Columbia University, 2001.

---. *First-year Teacher: A Case Study.* New York: Teachers College Press, 1989.

Bullough, R., Jr., R. Patterson, and C. Mayes (2002). Teaching as Prophecy. *The Journal of Curriculum Inquiry,* 32(3): 310-329.

Bullough, R., Jr., and A. Gitlin. *Becoming a Student of Teaching: Methodologies for Exploring Self and School Context.* New York: Garland Publishing, Inc., 1995.

Burke, K. *On Symbols and Society.* J. Gusfield, ed., Chicago: University of Chicago Press, 1989.

Byrk, A., V. Lee, and M. Driscoll. *Catholic Schools and the Common Good.* Cambridge: Harvard University Press, 1993.

"Cardinal Principles of Secondary Education." In *The American Curriculum: A Documentary History,* eds. W. Willis, R. Schubert, R., Bullough, Jr., C. Kridel, and J. Holton, eds. London: Praeger (1994).

Chi, M., P. Feltovich, and R. Glaser. "Categorization and Representation of Physics Problems by Experts and Novices." *Cognitive Science* 5 (1981): 121-152.

Chinen, A. *In The Ever After: Fairy Tales and the Second Half of Life.* Wilmette, Illinois: Chiron Publications, 1989.

Chodorow, N. *The Reproduction of Mothering: Psychoanalysis and the Sociology of Gender.* Berkeley: University of California Press, 1978.

Chomsky, N. *Aspects of the Theory of Syntax.* Cambridge, Mass.: MIT Press, 1968.

Clark, E., Jr. "The Search For a New Education Paradigm: The Implications of New Assumptions about Thinking and Learning." In *New Directions in Education: Selections From Holistic Education Review,* ed. R. Miller. Brandon, Vermont: Holistic Education Press (1991): 16-37.

Clift, R., and W. Houston. "The Potential for Research Contributions to Reflective Practice." In *Encouraging Reflective Practice in Education: An Analysis of Issues and Programs,* eds. R. Clift, W. Houston, and M. Pugach. New York: Teachers College Press (1990): 208-222.

Clift, R., R. Houston, and M. Pugach, eds., *Encouraging Reflective Practice in Education: An Analysis of Issues and Programs.* New York: Teachers College Press, 1990.

Cohen, D. "Practice and Policy: Notes on the History of Instruction." In *American Teachers: History of a Profession at Work,* ed. D. Warren. New York: Macmillan, 1989.

Coleman, J. *The Adolescent Society.* New York: Free Press, 1961.

Comer, R. *Abnormal Psychology,* 3rd ed . New York: Freeman Press 1998.

Conger, J., and J. Galambos. *Adolescence and Youth: Psychological Development in a Changing World.* New York: Longman, 1997.

Cortright, B. *Psychotherapy and Spirit: Theory and Practice in Transpersonal Psychotherapy.* Albany, New York: State University of New York Press, 1997.

Cremin, L. *American Education: The Metropolitan Experience: 1876-1980.* New York: Harper and Row, 1988.

---. *The Transformation of the School: Progressivism in American Education, 1876-1957.* New York: Vintage Press, 1964.

Deikman, A. *The Observing Self: Mysticism and Psychotherapy.* Boston, Mass.: Beacon Press, 1982.

Deleuze, G., and F. Guattari. *A Thousand Plateaus.* Minneapolis: University of Minnesota Press, 1987.

Doctrine and Covenants of the Church of Jesus Christ of Latter-day Saints, the. Salt Lake City, Utah: The Church of Jesus Christ of Latter-day Saints, 1981.

Doll, W. "Teaching a Post-Modern Curriculum." In *Teaching and Thinking about Curriculum: Critical Inquiries,* eds. J. Sears and D. Marshall. New York: Teachers College Press (1993): 39-47.

Dryfoos, J. *Full-Service Schools: A Revolution in Health and Social Services for Children, Youth, and Families.* San Francisco: Jossey-Bass, Inc., 1994.

Edinger, E. *Ego and Archetype: Individuation and the Religious Function of the Psyche.* Baltimore: Penguin Press, 1973.

Egan, K., and D. Nadaner. *Education and Imagination.* Stony Stratford, England: Open University Press, 1988.

Eisner, E. *The Educational Imagination: On the Design and Evaluation of School Programs.* New York: Macmillan, 1985.

Eisner, E., and E. Vallance, eds., *Conflicting Conceptions of Curriculum.* Berkeley, California: McCutchan Publishing Corporation, 1974.

Eliot, T.S., *T.S. Eliot: The Complete Poems and Plays: 1909-1950.* New York: Harcourt, Brace and World, Inc., 1971.

Erikson, E. *Childhood and Society.* New York: Norton, 1963.

Fay, B. *Critical Social Science: Liberation and Its Limits.* Ithaca, New York: Cornell University Press, 1987.

Feige, D. "The Legacy of Gregory Bateson: Envisioning Aesthetic Epistemologies and Praxis." In *Education, Information, and Transformation,* ed. J. Kane. Columbus, Ohio: Merrill/Prentice Hall (1999): 77-109.

Ferdman, B. M. "Literacy and Cultural Identity." *Harvard Educational Review* 60(2) (1990): 181-204.

Ferrer, J. *Revisioning Transpersonal Theory: A Participatory Vision of Human Spirituality.* Albany, New York: State University of New York Press, 2002.

Ferrucci, P. *What We May Be: Techniques for Psychological and Spiritual Growth through Psychosynthesis.* Los Angeles, California: Jeremy Tarcher, Inc., 1982.

Foshay, A. *The Curriculum: Purpose, Substance, Practice.* New York: Teachers College Press, 2000.

Foucault, M. *Power and Knowledge: Selected Interviews and Other Writings, 1972-1977.* New York: Pantheon Books, 1980.

Freire, P. *Pedagogy and Freedom: Ethics, Democracy, and Civic Courage.* New York: Rowman and Littlefield, 2001.

Freud, S. "The Dynamics of Transference." In *Essential Papers on Transference,* ed. A. Esman. New York: New York University Press (1990): 28-36.

Gadamer, H. *Dialogue and Dialectic: Eight Hermeneutical Studies on Plato.* New Haven: Yale University Press, 1980.

Gardner, J. "Are There Additional Intelligences? The Case for Naturalist, Spiritual, and Existential Intelligences." In *Education, Information, and Transformation: Essays on Learning and Thinking,* ed. J. Kane. Columbus, Ohio: Merrill (1999): 111-131.

Gebser, J. *The Ever-present Origin.* Athens, Ohio: Ohio University Press, 1985.

Gellert, M. *The Fate of America: An Inquiry into National Character.* Washington, D.C.: Brassey's, Inc, 2001.

Gibson, M. *Accommodation without Assimilation: Sikh Immigrants in an American High School.* Ithaca, New York: Cornell University Press, 1988.

Giddens, A. *The Consequences of Modernity.* Stanford: Stanford University Press, 1990.

---. *Modernity and Self-identity: Self and Society in the Late Modern Age.* Stanford: Stanford University Press, 1991.

Giroux, H. "Theories of Reproduction and Resistance in the New Sociology of Education: A Critical Analysis." *Harvard Educational Review* 53(3) (1983): 257-293.

Gitlin, A. *Teachers' Voices for School Change: An Introduction to Educative Research.* New York: Teachers College Press, 1992.

Greene, M. "Care and Moral Education." In *Critical Conversations in the Philosophy of Education,* ed. W. Kohli. New York: Routledge, 1995.

---. "Curriculum and Consciousness." In *Curriculum Theorizing: The Reconceptualists,* ed. W. Pinar. Berkeley, California: McCutchan Publishing Corporation (1975): 299-317.

---. "Cognition, Consciousness, and Curriculum." In *Heightened Consciousness, Cultural Revolution, and Curriculum Theory,* ed. W. Pinar. Berkeley, California: McCutchan Publishing (1974): 69-83.

Greene, T. "The Function of Criticism." In *The Problems of Aesthetics,* eds. E. Vivas and M. Krieger. New York: Reinhart (1953): 414-418.

Greenson, R. "The Working Alliance and the Transference Neurosis." In *Essential Papers on Transference,* ed. A. Esman. New York: New York University Press (1990): 150-171.

Griffin, D. *Parapsychology, Philosophy, and Spirituality: A Postmodern Exploration.* Albany, New York: State University of New York Press, 1997.

Guenther, H., and L. Kawamura. *Mind in Buddhist Psychology.* Berkeley, California: Dharma Publishing, 1975.

Halliday, M. *Language as Social Semiotic.* London: Edward Arnold, 1978.

---. *Learning How to Mean.* London: Edward Arnold, 1975.

Handy, W. *Kant and the Southern New Critics.* Austin, Texas: University of Texas Press, 1963.

Harris, M. *Teaching and Religious Imagination: An Essay in the Theology of Teaching.* San Francisco: Harper Collins, 1991.

Harris, W.T., "The Theory of Education in the United States of America." In *The American Curriculum: A Documentary History,* eds. W. Willis,

R. Schubert, R., Bullough, Jr., C. Kridel, and J. Holton, eds. London: Praeger (1994).

Heidegger, M. *Being and Time.* New York: Harper and Row, 1964.

Hendricks, G. and J. Fadiman, eds. *Transpersonal Education: A Curriculum for Feeling and Being.* Englewood Cliffs, New Jersey: Prentice-Hall, Inc., 1976.

Herrigel, E. *Zen and the Art of Archery.* New York: Vintage Book, 1971.

Hewson, M. "The Ecological Context of Knowledge: Implications for Learning Science in Developing Countries." *Journal of Curriculum Studies* 20(4) (1988): 317-326.

Hewson, P., and Hewson, M. A'Beckett. "The Role of Conceptual Conflict in Conceptual Change and the Design of Science Instruction." *Instructional Science* 13 (1984): 1-13.

Hofstadter, R. *The American Political Tradition.* New York: Vintage Books, 1958.

Huberman, M., M. Gronauer, and J. Marti. *The Lives of Teachers.* New York: Teachers College Press, 1989.

Huebner, D. *The Lure of the Transcendent: Collected Essays by Dwayne E. Huebner,* ed. V. Hillis. London: Lawrence Erlbaum Associates, 1999.

Huxley, A. "The Perennial Philosophy." In *Paths Beyond Ego: The Transpersonal Vision,* eds. R. Walsh and F. Vaughan. Los Angeles, California: Jeremy P. Tarcher (1996): 212-213.

Johnstone, R. *Religion in Society: A Sociology of Religion.* 5th ed . New Jersey: Prentice-Hall, 1997.

Joseph, P., and G. Burnaford. *Images of Schoolteachers in Twentieth-century America: Paragons, Polarities, Complexities.* New York: St. Martin's Press, 1994.

Jung, C. *The Psychology of the Transference.* Princeton, New Jersey: Princeton University Press, 1992.

---. *Memories, Dreams, Reflections.* New York: Vintage, 1965.

Jung, E., and M. Von Franz. *The Grail Legend.* Boston: Sigo Press, 1960/1986.

Kaestle, C. *Pillars of the Republic: Common Schools and American Society, 1760-1860.* New York: Hill and Wang, 1983.

Kelly, A. *The Curriculum: Theory and Practice* 4th edition. Thousand Oaks, California: Sage Publications, 1999.

Kierkegaard, S. *A Kierkegaard Anthology,* ed. R. Bretall. Princeton, New Jersey: Princeton University Press, 1969.

Kliebard, H. *The Struggle for the American Curriculum: 1893-1958.* New York: Routledge, 1986.

Kohlberg, L. *The Meaning and Measurement of Moral Development.* Clark Lectures: Clark University, 1979.

Kohut, H. *The Search for the Self: Selected Writings of Heinz Kohut, 1950-1978.* Madison, Conn.: International Universities Press, 1978.

Lado, R., and C. Fries. *English Sentence Patterns: Understanding and Producing English Grammatical Structures.* Ann Arbor, Michigan: University of Michigan Press, 1958.

Lickona, T. *Educating for Character: How Our Schools Can Teach Respect and Responsibility.* New York: Bantam, 1991.

Lipman, M. *"From* Philosophy Goes to School." In R. Reed and R. Johnson. *Philosophical Documents in Education,* New York: Longman (1996): 241-272.

Macdonald, J. *Theory as a Prayerful Act: The Collected Essays of James P. Macdonald,* ed. B. Macdonald. New York: Peter Lang, 1995.

---. "A Transcendental Developmental Ideology of Education." In *Heightened Consciousness, Cultural Revolution, and Curriculum Theory,* ed. W. Pinar. Berkeley, California: McCutchan Publishing (1975): 85-116.

Marcuse, H. *Eros and Civilization: A Philosophical Inquiry into Freud.* New York: Vintage, 1962.

Marshak, M. "The Intersubjective Nature of Analysis." In *Contemporary Jungian Analysis: Post-Jungian Perspectives from the Society of Analytic Psychology,* eds. I. Alister and C. Hauke. London: Routledge (1998): 57-72.

Marty, M. *Religion and Republic: The American Circumstance.* Boston: Beacon Press, 1987.

Maslow, A. *Toward a Psychology of Being* 2nd edition. Princeton, New Jersey: D. Van Nostrand, 1968.

May, R., and I. Yalom. "Existential Psychotherapy." In *Current Psychotherapies,* eds. R. Corsini and D. Wedding. Itasca, Illinois: F.E. Peacock Publishers (1995): 262-292.

Mayes, C. "Teaching Mysteries." *Encounter: Education for Meaning and Social Justice,* in press.

---. "The Teacher as a Spiritual Archetype." *Journal of Curriculum Studies,* 34(6), 699-718.

---. "A Transpersonal Model for Teacher Reflectivity." *Journal of Curriculum Studies* 35(2) (2001): 56-70.

---. "Deepening Our Reflectivity." *The Teacher Educator* 36(4) (2001): 248-264.

---. "Reflecting on the Archetypes of Teaching." *Teaching Education* 10(2) (1999): 3-16.

---. "The Use of Contemplative Practices in Teacher Education." *Encounter: Education for Meaning and Social Justice* 11(3) (1998): 17-31.

McCloskey, M. "Naive Theories of Motion." In *Mental Models,* eds. D. Gentner and A. Stevens. Hillsdale, New Jersey: Erlbaum, 1983.

Merrell-Wolff, F. *The Philosophy of Consciousness without an Object: Reflections on the Nature of Transcendental Consciousness.* New York: Julian Press, 1973.

Miller, J. *The Contemplative Practitioner: Meditation in Education and the Professions.* London: Bergin & Garvey, 1994.

---. *The Holistic Curriculum.* Toronto, Ontario: The Ontario Institute for Studies in Education, 1988.

---. *The Educational Spectrum: Orientations to Curriculum.* New York: Longman, 1983.

Miller, J., and W. Seller. *Curriculum: Perspectives and Practice.* New York: Longman, 1985.

Miller, R. *What are Schools For? Holistic Education in American Culture.* Brandon, Vermont: Holistic Education Press, 1990.

Moffett, J. *The Universal Schoolhouse: Spiritual Awakening through Education.* San Francisco, California: Jossey-Bass Publishers, 1994.

Murphy, M. "Education for Transcendence." In *Four Psychologies Applied to Education: Freudian, Behavioral, Humanistic, Transpersonal,* ed. T. Roberts. New York: John Wiley and Sons (1975): 438-447.

Nation at Risk, A: The Imperative for Educational Reform. Washington, D.C.: United States Government Printing Office, 1983.

Nelson, P. "Mystical Experience and Radical Deconstruction: Through the Ontological Looking Glass." In *Transpersonal Knowing: Exploring the Horizon of Consciousness,* eds. T. Hart, P. Nelson, and K. Puhakka. Albany, New York: State University of New York Press (2000): 55-84.

Neumann, E. (1954). *The Origins and History of Consciousness* (vol. 1). New York: Harper & Brothers.

Niebuhr, R. *The Essential Reinhold Niebuhr: Selected Essays and Addresses,* ed. R. Brown. New Haven, Connecticut: Yale University Press, 1986.

Nieto, S. *Affirming Diversity: The Sociopolitical Context of Multicultural Education.* New York: Longman, 2000.

Nikola-Lisa, W. "On the Education of Wonder and Ecstasy." In *New Directions in Education: Selections From Holistic Education Review,* ed. R. Miller. Brandon, Vermont: Holistic Education Press (1991): 256-261.

Noddings, N. "Stories and Conversations in Schools." In *Education, Information, and Transformation: Essays on Learning and Thinking,* ed. J. Kane. Columbus, Ohio: Merrill (1999): 319-336.

---. "Care and Moral Education." In *Critical Conversations in the Philosophy of Education,* ed. W. Kohli. New York: Routledge (1995): 137-148.

---. *The Challenge to Care in Schools: An Alternative Approach to Education.* New York : Teachers College Press, 1992.

Novak, J. "Concept Maps and Vee Diagrams: Two Metacognitive Tools to Facilitate Meaningful Learning," *Instructional Science, 19,* 29-52.

Nussbaum, J. "The Earth as a Cosmic Body." In *Children's Ideas in Science,* eds. R. Driver, E. Guesne, and A. Tiberghein. Philadelphia: Open University Press, 1985.

Ogbu, J. "Variability in Minority School Performance: A Problem in Search of an Explanation." *Anthropology and Education Quarterly* 18 (1987): 312-334.

O'Reilley, M. *Radical Presence: Teaching as a Contemplative Activity.* Portsmouth, New Hampshire: Boynton/Cook Publishers, 1998.

Ornstein, A., and F. Hunkins. *Curriculum: Foundations, Principles, and Issues.* Boston: Allyn and Bacon, 1988.

Orton, R. (1988). *Constructivist and Information Processing Views of Representation in Mathematics Education.* A paper presented at the annual meeting of the American Educational Research Association. New Orleans.

Pajak, E., and J. Blase. "The Impact of Teachers' Personal Lives on Professional Role Enactment: A Qualitative Analysis." *American Educational Research Journal* 26(2) (1989): 283-310.

Palmer, P. *The Courage to Teach: Exploring the Inner Landscape of a Teacher's Life.* San Francisco: Jossey-Bass Publishers, 1998.

---. "'All The Way Down': A Spirituality of Public Life." In *Caring for the Commonweal: Education for Religious and Public Life,* eds., P. Palmer, B. Wheeler, & J. Fowler, eds., Macon, Georgia: Mercer University Press.

---. *To Know as We Are Known: A Spirituality of Education.* San Francisco, California: HarperCollins Publishers, 1983.

Pearl of Great Price, the. Salt Lake City, Utah: The Church of Jesus Christ of Latter-day Saints, 1981.

Phenix, P. "Transcendence and the Curriculum." In *Conflicting Conceptions of Curriculum,* eds. E. Eisner and E. Vallance. Berkeley, California: McCutchan Publishing Corporation, 1974.

---. *Realms of Meaning: A Philosophy of the Curriculum for General Education.* New York: McGraw-Hill, 1964.

Pinar, W., ed ., *Curriculum: Toward New Identities.* New York: Garland, 1998.

---. "Whole, Bright, Deep with Understanding": Issues in Qualitative Research and Autobiographical Method. In P. Taylor ed., *Recent Developments in Curriculum Studies* Philadelphia, Pennsylvania: NFER-NELSON Publishing Co., Ltd, 1988): 16-40.

---. *Curriculum Theorizing: The Reconceptualists.* Berkeley, California: McCutchan Publishing, 1975.

---. "*Currere*: Toward Reconceptualization." In *Curriculum Theorizing: The Reconceptualists,* ed. W. Pinar. Berkeley, California: McCutchan Publishing (1975): 396-414.

Pinar, W., W. Reynolds, P. Slattery, and P. Taubman, eds., *Understanding Curriculum: An Introduction to the Study of Historical and Contemporary Curriculum Discourses.* New York: Peter Lang, 2000.

Pinar, W., and W. Reynolds. *Understanding Curriculum as Phenomenological and Deconstructed Text.* New York: Teachers College Press, 1992.

Polanyi, M. *Towards a Post-Critical Philosophy.* Chicago: University of Chicago Press, 1962.

Popkewitz, T. "The Production of Reason and Power: Curriculum History and Intellectual Traditions." *Journal of Curriculum Studies* 29(2) (1997): 131-164.

Posner, G. *Analyzing the Curriculum.* New York: McGraw Hill, 1992.

Posner, G., K. Strike, P. Hewson, and W. Gertzog. "Accommodation of a Scientific Conception: Toward a Theory of Conceptual Change." *Science Education* 67(4) (1982): 498-509.

Prosser, C. "Vocational Education in the Years Ahead." In *The American*

Curriculum: A Documentary History, eds. W. Willis, R. Schubert, R., Bullough, Jr., C. Kridel, and J. Holton, eds. London: Praeger (1994).

Purpel, D., and S. Shapiro. *Beyond Liberation and Excellence: Reconstructing the Public Discourse on Education.* Westport, Connecticut: Bergin & Garvey, 1995.

Ravitch, D. *Left Back: A Century of Failed School Reforms.* New York: Simon and Schuster, 2000.

---. *The Troubled Crusade: American Education, 1945-1980.* New York: Basic Books, 1983.

Ravitch, D. and M. Vinovskis, eds., *Learning from the Past: What History Teaches Us about School Reform.* Baltimore, Maryland: The Johns Hopkins University Press, 1995.

Reinsmith, W. *Archetypal Forms in Teaching: A Continuum.* New York: Greenwood Press, 1992.

Resnick, L. "The 1987 Presidential Address: Learning in School and Out." *Educational Researcher* 16 (9) (1987): 13-20.

Richards, A. (2002). "Education in the Third Reich." A lecture given in the Department of Educational Leadership and Foundations, McKay School of Education. May 1, 2002. Provo, Utah: Brigham Young University.

Rickover, H. *Education and Freedom.* New York: E.P. Dutton and Co., 1960.

Ridd, K. An unpublished manuscript. Department of Educational Leadership and Foundations, Provo, Utah: Brigham Young University, 2000.

Riordan, C. *Equality and Achievement: An Introduction to the Sociology of Education.* New York: Longman, 1997.

Rivers, W. *A Practical Guide to the Teaching of English as a Second or Foreign Language.* New York: Oxford University Press, 1978.

Roberts, T. "States of Consciousness: A New Intellectual Direction, A New Teacher Education Direction." *Journal of Teacher Education* 36(2) (1985): 55-59.

---. "Expanding Thinking through Consciousness Education." *Educational Leadership* 39(1) (1981): 52-54.

Roberts, T., and F. Clark. *Transpersonal Psychology in Education.* Bloomington, Indiana: The Phi Delta Kappa Educational Foundation, 1975.

Rogoff, B. *Apprenticeship in Thinking: Cognitive Development in Social Context.* New York: Oxford University Press, 1990.

Rugg, H. *Changing Governments and Changing Cultures: The World's March toward Democracy.* New York: Ginn, 1932.

Rummelhart, D. "Schemata: The Building Blocks of Cognition." In *Theoretical Issues in Reading Comprehension,* eds. R. Spiro, B. Bruce, & W. Brewer. Hillside, New Jersey: Lawrence Erlbaum Associates (1980): 125-167.

Samples, B. "Learning as Transformation." In *Education, Information, and Transformation,* ed. J. Kane. Columbus, Ohio: Merrill/Prentice Hall (1999): 185-206.

Sardello, R., and C. Sanders. "Care of the Senses: A Neglected Dimension of Education." In *Education, Information and Transformation: Essays on Learning and Thinking*, ed. J. Kane. Columbus, Ohio: Merrill/Prentice Hall, 1999.

Sartre, J. *Being and Nothingness: An Essay on Phenomenological Ontology.* New York: Philosophical Library, 1956.

Schutz, W. "Education and the Body." In *Transpersonal Education: A Curriculum For Feeling and Being*, eds. G. Hendricks and J. Fadiman. Englewood Cliffs, New Jersey: Prentice-Hall (1976): 104-110.

Scotton, B., A. Chinen and J. Battista, eds. *Textbook of Transpersonal Psychiatry and Psychology.* New York: Basic Books, 1996.

Sedlak, M. "Attitudes, Choices, and Behavior: School Delivery of Health and Social Services." In *Learning from the Past: What History Teaches Us about School Reform*, eds. D. Ravitch, and M. Vinovskis. Baltimore, Maryland: The Johns Hopkins University Press (1995): 57-94.

Selman, R. *The Growth of Interpersonal Understanding: Developmental and Clinical Analyses.* New York: Academic Press, 1980.

Skinner, B. *The Technology of Teaching.* Englewood Cliffs, New Jersey: Prentice Hall, 1968.

Sklar, K. *Catherine Beecher: A Study in American Domesticity.* New Haven: Yale University Press, 1973.

Slattery, P. *Curriculum Development in the Postmodern Era.* New York: Garland Publishing, Inc., 1995.

Smith, M. *And Madly Teach: A Layman Looks at Public Education.* Chicago: H. Regnery Co., 1949.

Spiegelman, J. *Psychotherapy as a Mutual Process.* Tempe, Arizona: New Falcon Publications, 1996.

Spring, J. *The Intersection of Cultures: Multicultural Education in the United States and the Global Economy.* New York: McGraw Hill, 2000.

---. *The Sorting Machine: National Educational Policy since 1945.* New York: David McKay Co., Inc., 1976.

---. *Educating the Worker Citizen.* New York: David McKay Co., Inc. 1972.

Stone, L. "The Transference-countertransference Complex." In *Essential Papers on Counter-transference*, ed. B. Wolstein. New York: New York University Press (1988): 270-281.

Suzuki, D.T. *An Introduction to Zen Buddhism.* New York: Grove Press, Inc., 1964.

Tillich, P. *The Essential Tillich: An Anthology of the Writings of Paul Tillich*, ed. E. Church. New York: Macmillan, 1987.

---. *The Shaking of the Foundations.* New York: Scribners, 1976.

---. *Dynamics of Faith.* New York: Harper and Row, 1957.

Toulmin, S. *Human Understanding: The Collective Use and Evolution of Concepts.* Princeton, N.J.: Princeton University Press, 1972.

Tremmel, R. "Zen and the Art of Reflective Practice in Teacher Education." *Harvard Educational Journal* 63(4) (1993): 434-458.

Trostli, R. "Educating as an Art: The Waldorf Approach." In *New Directions in Education: Selections From Holistic Education Review,* ed. R. Miller. Brandon, Vermont: Holistic Education Press (1991): 338-353.

Tyack, D. *The One Best System: A History of American Urban Education.* Cambridge, Mass.: Harvard University Press, 1974.

Underhill, E. *Mysticism: A Study in the Nature and Development of Man's Spiritual Consciousness.* New York: E.P. Dutton, 1961.

Vallance, E., "Aesthetic Inquiry." In *Forms of Curriculum Inquiry,* ed. E. Short. Albany, New York: State University of New York Press (1991): 155-172.

Valli, L. "Moral Approaches to Reflective Practice." In *Encouraging Reflective Practice in Education: An Analysis of Issues and Programs,* eds. R. Clift, W. Houston and M. Pugach. New York: Teachers College Press (1990): 39-56.

Van Manen, M. "Phenomenological Pedagogy." *Curriculum Inquiry* 12(3) (1982): 283-299.

Vaughan, F. *The Inward Arc: Healing and Wholeness in Psychotherapy and Spirituality.* Boston, Massachusetts: New Science Library, 1985.

Veysey, L. "Toward a New Direction in Educational History: Prospect and Retrospect." *History of Education Quarterly,* Fall (1969): 343-359.

Vygotsky, L. *Mind in Society: The Development of Psychological Functions.* Cambridge, Mass.: Harvard University Press, 1986.

Wacks, V., Jr. "A Case for Self-transcendence as a Purpose of Adult Education." *Adult Education Quarterly* 38(1) (1987): 46-55.

Wade, J. *Changes of Mind: A Holonomic Theory of the Evolution of Consciousness,* 2001.

Walsh, R. "Meditation Research: The State of the Art." In *Paths Beyond Ego: The Transpersonal Vision,* eds. R. Walsh and F. Vaughan. Los Angeles, California: Jeremy P. Tarcher (1993): 60-66.

Walsh, R., and F. Vaughan, eds. *Paths Beyond Ego: The Transpersonal Vision.* Los Angeles, California: Jeremy P. Tarcher, 1980.

---. "Meditation: The Royal Road to the Transpersonal." In *Paths Beyond Ego: The Transpersonal Vision,* eds. R. Walsh and F. Vaughan. Los Angeles, California: Jeremy P. Tarcher (1993): 47-55.

Washburne, M. *Transpersonal Psychology in Psychoanalytic Perspective.* Albany, New York: State University of New York Press, 1994.

Watras, J. *The Foundations of Educational Curriculum and Diversity: 1565 to the Present.* Boston: Allyn and Bacon, 2002.

Wax, M., R. Wax, and R. Dumont, Jr. *Formal Education in an American Indian Community: Peer Society and the Failure of Minority Education.* Prospect Heights, Illinois: Waveland Press, 1964.

Wells, A., and R. Crain. "Consumers and Urban Education." In *The Structure of Schooling: Readings in the Sociology of Education,* eds. R. Arum and I. Beattie. London: Mayfield, 1997.

Wertsch, J. *Vygotsky and the Social Formation of Mind.* Cambridge, Mass.: Harvard University Press, 1985.

Whitehead, A. *The Aims of Education: And Other Essays.* New York: New American Library, 1964.

Whitmore, D. *Psychosynthesis in Education: A Guide to the Joy of Learning.* Rochester, Vermont: Destiny Books, 1986.

Wilber, K. *Integral Psychology: Consciousness, Spirit, Psychology, Therapy.* London: Shambhala, 2000.

---. *A Brief History of Everything.* Boston: Shambhala, 1996.

---. "The Great Chain of Being." *Journal of Humanistic Psychology* 33(3) (1993): 52-65.

---. *A Sociable God: A Brief Introduction to a Transcendental Sociology.* New York: McGraw-Hill Book Company, 1983.

Willis, P. *Learning to Labour.* Aldershot: Gower, 1977.

Willis, G., "Phenomenological Inquiry: Life-World Perceptions." In *Forms of Curriculum Inquiry,* ed. E. Short. Albany, New York: State University of New York Press (1991): 173-186.

Willis, G., W. Schubert, R. Bullough, Jr., C. Kridel, and J. Holton, eds. *The American Curriculum: A Documentary History.* London: Praeger, 1994.

Wilson, G. "Behavior Therapy." In *Current Psychotherapies: Basics and Beyond,* eds. R. Corsini and D. Wedding. Itasca, Illinois: F.E. Peacock (1995): 229-261.

Winn, W. "Some Implications of Cognitive Theory for Instructional Design." *Instructional Science* 19 (1990): 53-69.

Woodman, M. "Transference and Countertransference in Analysis Dealing with Eating Disorders." In *Transference/countertransference,* eds. N. Schwartz-Salant and M. Stein. Wilmette, Illinois: Chiron Publications (1995): 53-66.

Woolstein, B. "The Pluralism of Perspectives on Countertransference." In *Essential Papers on Counter-transference,* ed. B. Wolstein. New York: New York University Press (1988): 339-354.

Zinn, H. *A People's History of the United States.* New York: Harper Perennial, 1990.

Index

About the Author

Clifford Mayes is an associate professor of curriculum history and theory in the Department of Educational Leadership and Foundations at Brigham Young University in Provo, Utah. He received the Ph.D. in the Cultural Foundations of Education at the University of Utah and also holds a doctorate in psychology from Southern California University for Professional Studies. His research revolves around the psycho-spiritual dimensions of the teacher's sense of calling and has appeared in *The Journal of Curriculum Studies, Curriculum Inquiry, The International Journal of Leadership in Education, Religion and Education, Teaching and Teacher Education, The Teacher Education Quarterly, The Teacher Educator, Teaching Education,* and *Encounter.* From 1981 until 1991, Cliff taught British and American Studies at the University of Panama in David, Panama, and Nagoya Gakuin University in Nagoya, Japan. He received a *Teacher of the Year Award* in 1998 from the Brigham Young University Student Alumni Association and is listed in *Who's Who in American Education.* He and his wife, Pam, are members of the Church of Jesus Christ of Latter-day Saints. They have three children, Lizzy, Josh and Dana.